T0365747

FUN

USA EDUCATIONAL ACTIVITIES

with

HERKIMER AND THE STAT PACK

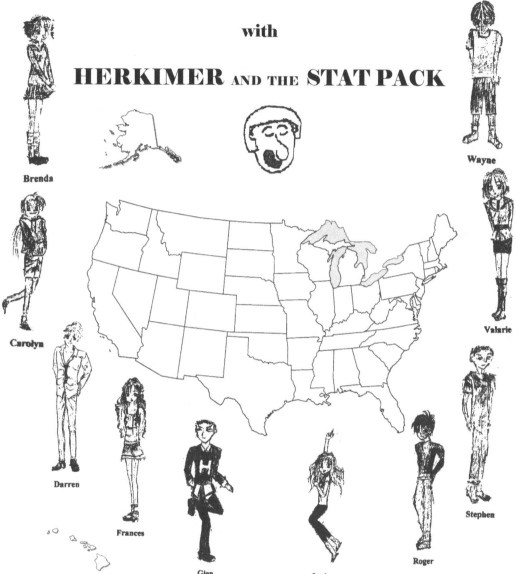

Brenda

Wayne

Carolyn

Valarie

Darren

Frances

Glen

Janice

Roger

Stephen

A series of activities designed to promote appreciation of the great 50 states that make up the United States of America

SANDERSON M. SMITH   STEVEN M. SOLANO

authorHOUSE®

AuthorHouse™
1663 Liberty Drive
Bloomington, IN 47403
www.authorhouse.com
Phone: 1-800-839-8640

First published by AuthorHouse   11/14/2011

ISBN: 978-1-4678-7687-2 (sc)
ISBN: 978-1-4678-7688-9 (ebk)

Library of Congress Control Number: 2011960926

Printed in the United States of America

This book is dedicated to the Solano family:

My lovely wife, Susan Elizabeth,

the love of my life;

to my great kids,

Sarah Elizabeth,

all grown up now and so incredibly talented;

and Michael Andrew,

now ready to take on the world.

Steve

TABLE OF CONTENTS

****

PREFACE.. 11

****

INTRODUCTION... 13

****

U. S. ACTIVITY #1 (Created by Brenda and Wayne).. 15

BEGINNING LETTERS OF STATE NAMES

Among other things find out:

(A) Which letter of the alphabet occurs most at the beginning of a state name?
(B) How many letters of the alphabet do not occur as the beginning letter of a state name?

****

U. S. ACTIVITY #2 (Created by Valarie and Darren).. 17

NUMBER OF LETTERS IN STATE NAMES

Among other things find out:

(A) How many state names contain only 4 letters?
(B) What is the maximum number of letters in a state name?

****

1**

U. S. ACTIVITY #3 (Created by Carolyn and Stephen)... **19**

NUMBER OF STATE NAMES CONTAINING SPECIFIC LETTER

Among other things find out:

(A) How many state names contain the letter A?
(B) Which letter occurs most in a listing of all 50 state names?

****

U. S. ACTIVITY #4 (Created by Glen and Frances).. **21**

NUMBER OF STATE NAMES CONTAINING SPECIFIC LETTER MORE THAN ONCE

Among other things find out:

(A) How many state names contain the letter S more than once?
(B) Which letter appears most frequently as a duplicate letter in the 50 state names?

****

U. S. ACTIVITY #5 (Created by Janice and Roger).. **23**

BEGINNING LETTERS OF STATE CAPITAL CITY NAMES

Among other things find out:

(A) How many state capital city names begin with the letter H?
(B) Which letter occurs most frequently as the first letter of a state capital city?

****

U. S. ACTIVITY #6 (Created by Frances and Wayne).............................. **25**

ATTAINMENT-OF-STATEHOOD YEAR FOR EACH OF THE 50 STATES

Among other things find out:

(A) How many states entered the union after 1900?
(B) How many states entered the union before 1800?

****

U. S. ACTIVITY #7 (Created by Glen and Janice).................................... **27**

UNSCRAMBLE LETTERS TO YIELD STATE AND CAPITAL CITY

Find out how quickly you can recognize a state name and the name of its capital
city if the letters are scrambled.

****

U. S. ACTIVITY #8 (Created by Brenda and Carolyn).. **29**

CREATE WORDS FROM LETTERS IN A STATE NAME

Test your ability to create words from
the letters that make of the name of each of the
50 states.

****

****

U. S. ACTIVITY #9 (Created by Darren and Roger).. 35

ANOTHER ACTIVITY CREATING WORDS FROM LETTERS IN A STATE NAME

Given the name of a state find out how many words you can create from the first three letters of the state name; the first four letters; the first five letters; the first six letters.

****

U. S. ACTIVITY #10 (Created by Valarie and Stephen)... 41

ORDER THE STATES BY POPULATION RANK

Among other things find out:

(A) Which is the most populous state in the U.S.?
(B) Which is the least populous state in the U.S.?

****

U. S. ACTIVITY #11 (Created by Brenda, Carolyn and Wayne)........................... 43

ORDER CAPITAL CITIES BY POPULATION RANK

Among other things find out:

(A) Which is the most populous state capital city in the U.S.?
(B) Which is the least populous state capital city in the U.S.?

****

```
**************************************
```

U. S. ACTIVITY #12 (Created by Darren and Frances).. **45**

ORDER OF STATEHOOD FOR THE 50 STATES

Among other things find out:

(A) Which state was the first to join the union?
(B) Which state was the 50th to join the union?

```
**************************************
```

U. S. ACTIVITY #13 (Created by Valarie and Glen).. **47**

ORDER OF STATES BY SIZE (SQ. MILES)

Among other things find out:

(A) In terms of area, which are the smallest and largest states?
(B) How many times larger is the largest state than the smallest state?

```
**************************************
```

U. S. ACTIVITY #14 (Created by Stephen and Janice).. **49**

ORDER OF STATES BY PEOPLE PER SQUARE MILE

Among other things find out:

(A) Which state has the largest number of people per square mile?
(B) How many states have less than 10 people per square mile?

```
**************************************
```

****

U. S. ACTIVITY #15 (Created by Herkimer and the Stat Pack)............................ 51

THE SEPARATOR STATE CHALLENGES

This extensive set of 48 state maps offers what we believe is a unique set of challenges relating to travel by land from one state to another. You can really have some fun with this activity while creating some surprising travel routes from one state to another.

****

U. S. ACTIVITY #16 (Created by Herkimer and the Stat Pack)............................ 157

STATE IDENTIFICATION CHALLENGE FROM SEPARATOR STATE HISTOGRAMS

Can you identify a state by looking at a chart displaying the number of its bordering states, the number of states that are 1 separator state away, etc.?

****

****

U. S. ACTIVITY #17 (Created by Herkimer and the Stat Pack)............................ **181**

STATE TRIVIA QUIZ

This is a series of trivia questions relating to the United States.
Sample questions:
(1) Which state name contains only 3 letters of the alphabet?
(2) How many states share a border with Canada?
(3) Which state has 75% of its land area covered by forests?

****

ACTIVITY SOLUTIONS... **187**

DISPLAY SECTION... **273**

    Display #1:
    LETTER DISTRIBUTION IN STATE NAMES............................ **273**

    Display #2:
    STATE INFORMATION TABLE.. **277**

    Display #3:
    SEPARATOR STATE SUMMARY.. **289**

    Display #4:
    SEPARATOR STATE TABLE.. **293**

SUPPLEMENTAL MATERIALS.. **297**

Lines from
AMERICA, THE BEAUTIFUL

O beautiful for spacious skies,
For amber waves of grain,
For purple mountain majesties
Above the fruited plain.

PREFACE

This is the third in a series of books involving Herkimer and a group of ten students who call themselves the Stat Pack. Their first educational adventures occurred in the AuthorHouse book

THE STATISTICAL ODDYSSEY OF HERKIMER AND THE STAT PACK.

The fantasy character Herkimer provided activities and guidance for the students as they worked their way through an introductory statistics course. It was here the students adopted the name Stat Pack.

Following their satisfying statistical journey the Stat Pack asked Herkimer to guide them through an educational series of activities that would help them learn how money works in a capitalistic society. Given the lack of financial literacy that contributed to the financial crisis that began in 2008 Herkimer was delighted to take on this assignment. The story of their adventures is told in the AuthorHouse publication,

HERKIMER AND THE STAT PACK VENTRUE INTO MONEY MATHEMATICS

In this book Herkimer and the Stat Pack have combined their talents and efforts to produce a series of activities to help people of all ages gain an understanding and an appreciation of their wonderful homeland, the United States of America. They hope that you, the reader, will find enjoyment and educational excitement by accepting the fun challenges they have created.

Herkimer expresses his thanks and gratitude to Barbara and Susan, wives of the authors, for their contributions and patience during the creation of this book. Appreciation is also extended to multiple web sources offering free patriotic clip art that has been used on many pages. A listing of these sources appears on page 320.

> *If your actions inspire others to dream more, learn more,*
> *do more and become more,*
> *you are a leader.*
>
> (John Quincy Adams)

Lines from
AMERICA ("My country, 'tis of Thee")

My country, 'tis of Thee, Sweet Land of Liberty
Of thee I sing; Land where my fathers died,
Land of the pilgrims' pride, From every mountain side
Let Freedom Ring.

INTRODUCTION

While previously working with the Stat Pack in statistical educational activities, Herkimer presented many exercises that enhanced the group's knowledge about the geography and history of the great country known as the United States of America. Upon reflection on their statistical studies, Pack members realized how little they knew about the U.S. before Herkimer appeared to them, and then how much they knew when they had completed the activities and exercises he had created for them.

It was after the Pack completed working with Herkimer on financial
literacy that they came up with the idea to create a series of fun activities
that would help people of all ages increase their knowledge of each of
the 50 states that make up the United States of America. Herkimer agreed to help them out with thoughts and ideas but he told the students they were smart enough to create educational activities with very little guidance from him. This was fine with the Pack. They met as a group and started to make plans to create a collection of challenges and activities that they hoped would be fun for all who encountered them. Herkimer knew the Pack
was an enthusiastic group of young people. He knew they would come up
with some very interesting projects.

After a few days of deliberations the Pack came up with a collection of 17 activity ideas. They divided themselves into groups of teams to create these activities. They had gained considerable experience working with spreadsheets from their statistical and financial adventures with Herkimer and they put these skills to good use while constructing the activities.

Putting together the activities took a considerable amount of time. Among other things, a team would take time to test their activity on other Pack members and Herkimer. The Separator State Activity (#15) was very time consuming but the Pack enjoyed the work involved and think it may be unique; that is, they could find no activity like this in the research they did.

This book contains their finished products. The Stat Pack hopes you have as much fun working on the activities as they did putting them together.

Now, enjoy your journey across America in the pages that follow!

U.S. ACTIVITY #1
Created by Brenda and Wayne

BEGINNING LETTERS OF STATE NAMES

From previous learning experiences with Herkimer, Brenda and Wayne developed proficiency with spreadsheet construction. On the following page they created a bar chart displaying the number of times each letter represented the first letter of a state name. If you turn the page you will see this chart and your challenge is to identify the state names beginning with each of the 26 alphabetic letters.

When you turn to the next page you will know HOW MANY states have names beginning with each of the 26 letters. Prior to turning the page you might wish to accept the challenge of finding out HOW MANY states have names beginning with each of the 26 letters. If you accept this challenge indicate the number of states beginning with each letter in the table below.

Letter	A	B	C	D	E	F	G
# state names beginning with letter							

Letter	H	I	J	K	L	M	N
# state names beginning with letter							

Letter	O	P	Q	R	S	T	U
# state names beginning with letter							

Letter	V	W	X	Y	Z
# state names beginning with letter					

Brenda and Wayne now invite you to turn the page for more fun relating to the first letter in each of the 50 U.S. state names.

U.S. ACTIVITY #1
NUMBER OF STATE NAMES BEGINNING WITH LETTER
Spreadsheet by Brenda and Wayne

A	4
B	0
C	3
D	1
E	0
F	1
G	1
H	1
I	4
J	0
K	2
L	1
M	8
N	8
O	3
P	1
Q	0
R	1
S	2
T	2
U	1
V	2
W	4
X	0
Y	0
Z	0

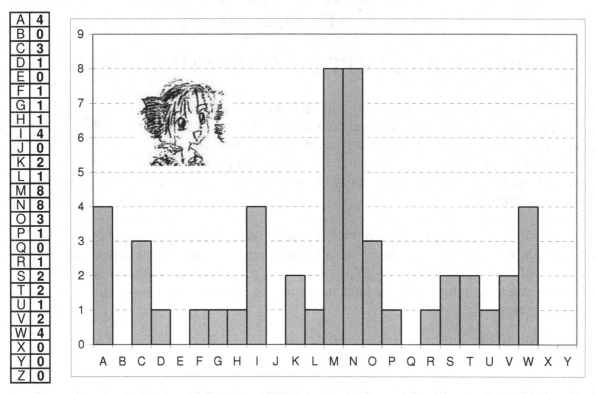

FILL IN STATE NAMES IN THE APPROPRIATE BOXES BELOW.

A	4
B	0
C	3
D	1
E	0
F	1
G	1
H	1
I	4
J	0
K	2
L	1
M	8
N	8
O	3
P	1
Q	0
R	1
S	2
T	2
U	1
V	2
W	4
X	0
Y	0
Z	0

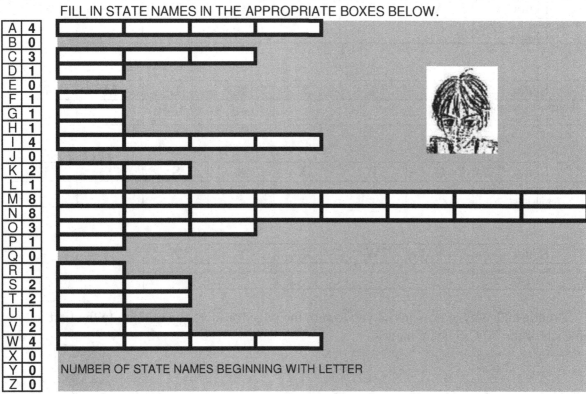

NUMBER OF STATE NAMES BEGINNING WITH LETTER

16

U.S. ACTIVITY #2
Created by Valarie and Darren

NUMBER OF LETTERS IN STATE NAMES

Valarie and Darren took on this project. The basic challenge is to organize states by the number of letters making up the name of each state. On the next page they developed a spreadsheet histogram displaying the number of states having 3-letter names, 4-letter names, etc. and your job will be to identify those states.

Prior to turning the page a first challenge, should you choose to accept it, is to determine HOW MANY states have 3-letter names, 4-letter names, etc. If you choose to accept this challenge, fill in the table below BEFORE turning to the next page.

Number of letters in state name	3	4	5	6	7	8	9
Number of states name containing indicated number of letters							

Number of letters in state name	10	11	12	13	14	15	16
Number of states name containing indicated number of letters							

From previous experience with Herkimer the Stat Pack learned many mathematical realities. In this situation, if you took the time to fill in the table above Valarie suggests that you total the numbers you produced. Darren correctly notes that if the numbers don't total to 50 then you have definitely made a mistake in the computation process. Of course if they do total to 50 it doesn't mean that your numbers are correct but if you were careful during the computation process you have a good chance of being correct.

Now turn the page for more fun with this activity.

U.S. ACTIVITY #2
NUMBER OF LETTERS IN STATE NAME
Spreadsheet by Valarie and Darren

In the frequency histogram below fill the 50 rectangles with the 50 states names so they are correctly caterogrized by the number of letters in the name.

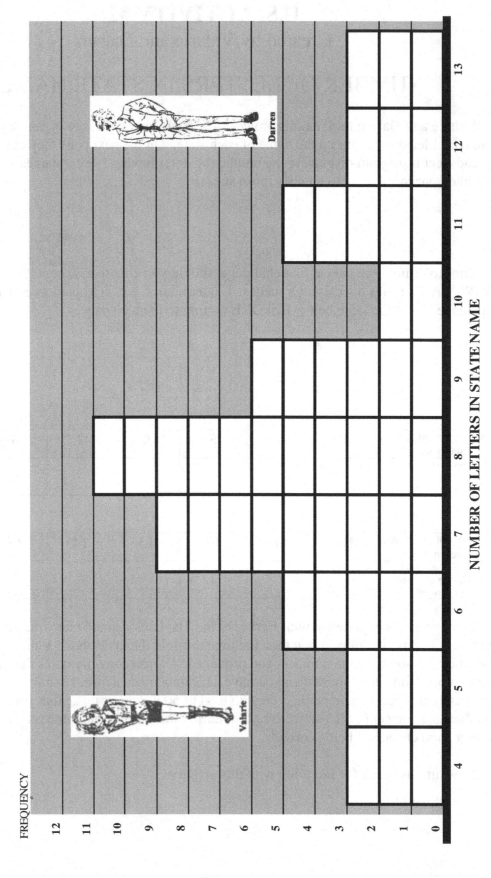

U.S. ACTIVITY #3
Created by Carolyn and Stephen

NUMBER OF STATE NAMES
CONTAINING SPECIFIC LETTER

In a list of the names of the 50 United States, which letters appear in more than half of the names? Are there any letters that don't appear at all? The answers to these questions might surprise you.

This activity and the related spreadsheets were created by Carolyn and Stephen. If you want another challenge relating to the U.S. then prior to turning to the next page complete the table below by listing the NUMBER OF STATE NAMES that contain each letter at least once. On a separate piece of paper list the state names that contain the letter A, the letter B, etc.

Letter	A	B	C	D	E	F	G
# state names containing letter							

Letter	H	I	J	K	L	M	N
# state names containing letter							

Letter	O	P	Q	R	S	T	U
# state names containing letter							

Letter	V	W	X	Y	Z
# state names containing letter					

Turn the page to see if your numbers agree with those displayed in the charts produced by Carolyn and Stephen.

U. S. ACTIVITY #3
NUMBER OF STATE NAMES CONTAINING SPECIFIC LETTER
Spreadsheet be Carolyn and Stephen

A	36
B	2
C	10
D	10
E	20
F	2
G	7
H	14
I	28
J	1
K	9
L	14
M	14
N	33
O	27
P	3
Q	0
R	21
S	21
T	15
U	8
V	5
W	11
X	2
Y	6
Z	1

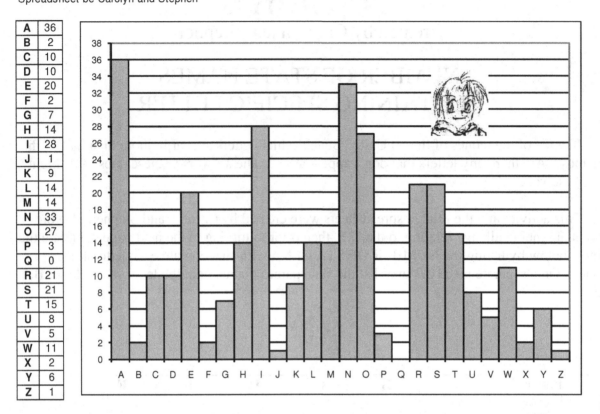

A	36
N	33
I	28
O	27
R	21
S	21
E	20
T	15
H	14
L	14
M	14
W	11
C	10
D	10
K	9
U	8
G	7
Y	6
V	5
P	3
B	2
F	2
X	2
J	1
Z	1
Q	0

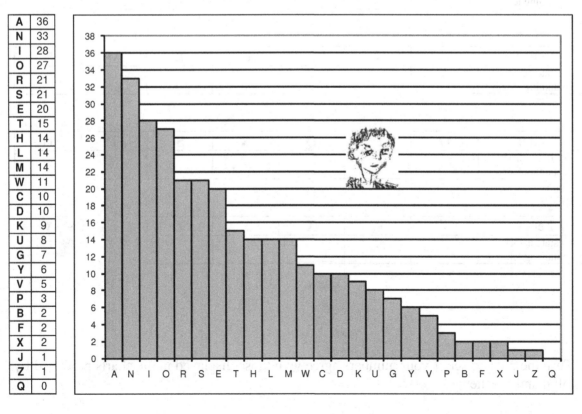

U.S. ACTIVITY #4
Created by Glen and Frances

NUMBER OF STATE NAMES
CONTAINING SPECIFIC LETTER MORE THAN ONCE

How many state names contain the letter E more than once? How about the letter M? The letter S? Which letter appears more than any other as a multiple letter in a state name? Glen and Frances constructed this activity to address questions like these.

If you accept the challenge offered by Glen and Frances then prior to turning the page complete the table below. When you turn the page you will find a display created by the two students that will allow you to determine if your numbers are correct. You will also find a convenient chart in which you can list the states with specific multiple letters.

Letter	A	B	C	D	E	F	G
# state names containing letter more than once							

Letter	H	I	J	K	L	M	N
# state names containing letter more than once							

Letter	O	P	Q	R	S	T	U
# state names containing letter more than once							

Letter	V	W	X	Y	Z
# state names containing letter more than once					

U.S. ACTIVITY #4
NUMBER OF STATE NAMES CONTAINING LETTER MORE THAN ONCE
Spreadsheet by Glen and Frances

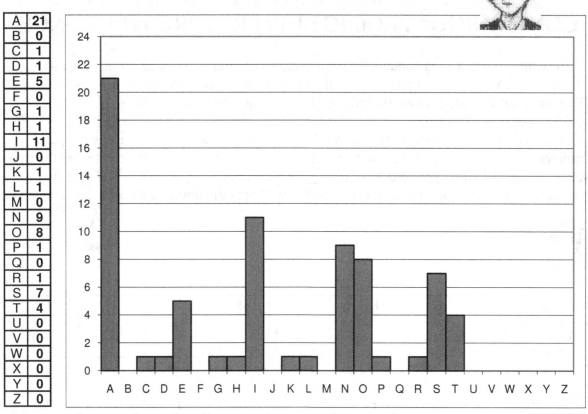

A	21
B	0
C	1
D	1
E	5
F	0
G	1
H	1
I	11
J	0
K	1
L	1
M	0
N	9
O	8
P	1
Q	0
R	1
S	7
T	4
U	0
V	0
W	0
X	0
Y	0
Z	0

STATES CONTAINING LETTER MORE THAN ONCE.

A	21
B	1
C	1
D	1
E	5
G	1
H	1
I	11
K	1
L	1
N	9
O	8
P	1
R	1
S	7
T	4

22

U.S. ACTIVITY #5
Created by Janice and Roger

BEGINNING LETTERS OF
STATE CAPITAL CITY NAMES

Janice and Roger took on the project of creating this activity relating to the capital cities of states. If you choose to participate use the table below to indicate the number of capital cities that begin with each of the 26 letters. When you have completed the table you can turn the page to see if you agree with the totals displayed by Janice and Roger in spreadsheet charts they constructed.

The following page also provides an opportunity to list the capital cities that begin with each letter of the alphabet.

Letter	A	B	C	D	E	F	G
# state capital city names beginning with letter							

Letter	H	I	J	K	L	M	N
# state capital city names beginning with letter							

Letter	O	P	Q	R	S	T	U
# state capital city names beginning with letter							

Letter	V	W	X	Y	Z
# state capital city names beginning with letter with letter					

23

U.S. ACTIVITY #5
NUMBER OF NAMES OF STATE CAPITALS BEGINNING WITH LETTER
Spreadsheet by Janice and Roger

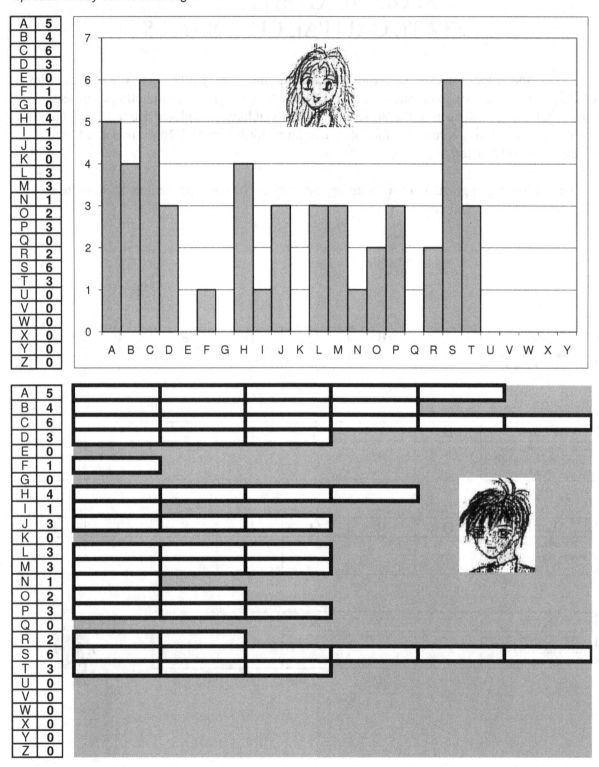

A	5
B	4
C	6
D	3
E	0
F	1
G	0
H	4
I	1
J	3
K	0
L	3
M	3
N	1
O	2
P	3
Q	0
R	2
S	6
T	3
U	0
V	0
W	0
X	0
Y	0
Z	0

U.S. ACTIVITY #6
Created by Frances and Wayne

ATTAINMENT-OF-STATEHOOD YEAR
FOR EACH OF THE 50 STATES

If a reader is less then 50 years old then the United States has always consisted of 50 states during his or her lifetime. However, the "birth" of the oldest state occurred in 1787 and the "birth" of the newest state took place in 1959, a difference of 172 years. Frances and Wayne teamed up to create this activity.

Before turning to the page complete the table below indicating the number of states that achieved statehood during the indicated ten-year time intervals.

10-year interval	1770-1779	1780-1789	1790-1799	1800-1809	1810-1819
# states achieving statehood during the time interval					

10-year interval	1820-1829	1830-1839	1840-1849	1850-1859	1860-1869
# states achieving statehood during the time interval					

10-year interval	1870-1879	1880-1889	1890-1899	1900-1909	1910-1919
# states achieving statehood during the time interval					

10-year interval	1920-1929	1930-1939	1940-1949	1950-1959	1960-1969
# states achieving statehood during the time interval					

Now turn the page to check your numbers and complete the spreadsheet histogram put together by Frances and Wayne.

U.S. ACTIVITY #6
COMPLETE THE STATEHOOD CHART (10 YEAR INTERVALS)
Spreadsheet by Frances and Wayne

Put state names in the appropriate 10-year time interval during which statehood was attained.
As an extra challenge, put names in the order in which statehood was attained.

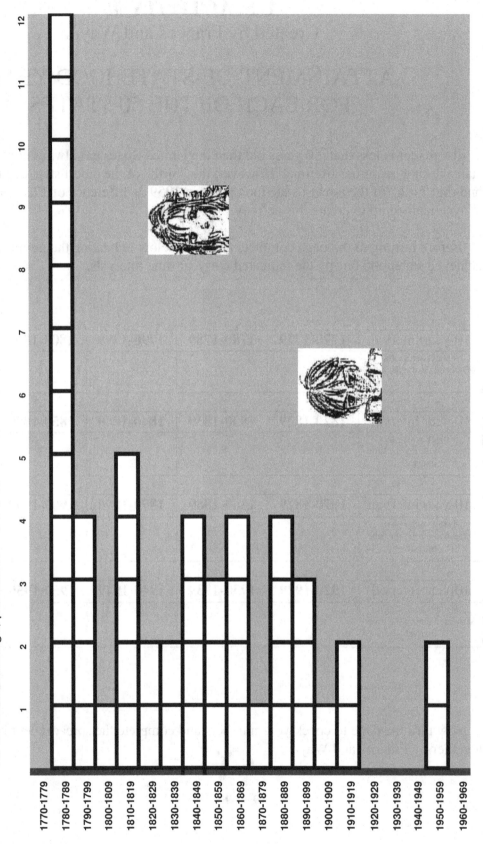

U.S. ACTIVITY #7
Created by Glen and Janice

UNSCRAMBLE LETTERS TO YIELD
STATE AND CAPITAL CITY

Glen and Janice came up with the idea taking the name of a state and its capital city, scrambling the letters by a random process, and then presenting the scrambled letters to a reader to see if he or she could unscramble them to identify the state and city. Using our good neighbor Canada to illustrate the challenge, can you unscramble these letters to produce a capital city and the corresponding province in Canada? (Don't look beyond the pictures of Herkimer, Glen, and Janice if you want to accept the challenge before seeing the solution which will be written in very small letters so it won't stand out before you really want to read it.)

OROOTATNOINROT

Were you able to come up with Toronto, Ontario? In any case, you get the idea. On the following page produced by Glen and Janet you will be presented with 50 sets of scrambled letters that you can attempt to unscramble to yield a state of the good ole USA and its capital city.

U.S. ACTIVITY #7

UNSCRAMPLE THE LETTERS TO PRODUCE A STATE AND ITS CAPITAL CITY

Spreadsheet by Glen and Janice

	Scrambled State and Capital City		Unscrambled
1	GTAGAENAORILAT	1	
2	EFKTFOKURKNYANCTR	2	
3	NNASOESUTLIAMPT	3	
4	GNHNIACIMALSNGI	4	
5	NNLMEOHAANAET	5	
6	AMRSIRKDAOTBTHANKO	6	
7	ANXMCSINEETOFEWA	7	
8	WROEEOHNRCAINDHCMPS	8	
9	AADPONRIANMNLYASL	9	
10	RIHINAIVDMNGCOIR	10	
11	DAVERLCRODEONO	11	
12	TRWNCRSELGIASIEANTOHIV	12	
13	NGSIAAEAUMTU	13	
14	KYAKOHAMLLATOHCMIOAO	14	
15	WLAOILHOHNAUUI	15	
16	TTDIFNURNORACTHOCEC	16	
17	SIMNOOIWDEEAS	17	
18	KYYAALERBNOWN	18	
19	UIOAMIOTSCHARUONLCLBA	19	
20	TLOAILLSAEFSHRDAAE	20	
21	KURIOHEATRDTAPSEO	21	
22	ENOEWRNNSERETTYJ	22	
23	SANSSEHBCOTUMOTTSSA	23	
24	KSUEAJLNAAUA	24	
25	DLPGIFLRNIOIISNLIES	25	
26	SAXTEUITSAN	26	
27	IUSOFRECRSTSOYENFMIJI	27	
28	NAHEOXIIONZARP	28	
29	ESNKOASAPTKA	29	
30	SDHIBAOOIE	30	
31	WOPMLHONATIYSANGI	31	
32	NKSTRATEAICSKRLOLA	32	
33	SOSCISWMNDOINAIN	33	
34	AAOERINRIOHLNHCLTRAG	34	
35	NDNCAYCVITESRAOA	35	
36	AITLNORUSOUIGAOAEBN	36	
37	GOLSAENREMO	37	
38	ARRGBRNVINHLEPNUSIASYA	38	
39	RAOOMAAYMLGNTAMEB	39	
40	EVIELSTSNENESALNEH	40	
41	TROMAONLNIAAESICRCFA	41	
42	AEVODEWDRRLAE	42	
43	PKIASMSJSPSISIOINC	43	
44	OENNEMIYNEYWHGC	44	
45	AONNSIAENKRLBLC	45	
46	INLVRHIENRDEPOCEDOADS	46	
47	ATTTHLSUYELCAAKI	47	
48	ANALNAIISOIDDPAINNI	48	
49	ETMRMIROVELTONNPE	49	
50	HUCIBLOUSOMO	50	

U.S. ACTIVITY #8
Created by Brenda and Carolyn

CREATE WORDS FROM LETTERS IN A STATE NAME

Brenda and Carolyn combined their talents to produce a clever word game that consisted of creating words from the letters that make up the name of a state. They used the Canadian provinces of ALBERTA and SASKATCHEWAN to demonstrate the activity. They gave themselves 5 minutes to fill in the following table with as many words as they could create from the province names.

	3 points per word	4 points per word	5 points per word	8 points per word	
Province	3-letter words	4 letter words	5-letter words	6-or-more letter words	Score
ALBERTA					
SASKATCHEWAN					

Here is what Brenda and Carolyn were able to accomplish in 5 minutes.

	3 points per word	4 points per word	5 points per word	8 points per word	
Province	3-letter words	4 letter words	5-letter words	6-or-more letter words	Score
ALBERTA	bat, tab, rat, tea, art, eat, ear, lab, are	beat, rate, bear, late, able, real, tear	alert, alter		69
SASKATCHEWAN	ask, sat, awe, net, ten, eat, saw, was, has, wet	asks, chat, swan, want, swat, neat, nets, saws, seat, sake, wean, when, what, nest, wets, take	watch, cheat, teach, tasks, chats, swans, wants, swats, seats, nests, takes, taken, skate, ketch	casket, caskets, watches, teaches, cheats, skates	212

The calculation of scores for the two provinces is as follows:

ALBERTA: 3(9) + 4(8) + 5(2) = 69
SASKATCHEWAN: 3(10) + 4(16) + 5(14) + 8(6) = 212

If you choose to accept the challenge with the 50 state names offered by Brenda and Carolyn, turn the page and have some fun.

ACTIVITY #8a

	State	3 points per word 3-letter words	4 points per word 4-letter words	5 points per word 5-letter words	8 points per word 6-or-more-letter words	Score
1	ALABAMA					
2	ALASKA					
3	ARIZONA					
4	ARKANSAS					
5	CALIFORNIA					
6	COLORADO					
7	CONNECTICUT					
8	DELAWARE					
9	FLORIDA					
10	GEORGIA					
11	HAWAII					
12	IDAHO					
13	ILLINOIS					
14	INDIANA					
15	IOWA					

ACTIVITY #8b

	State	3 points per word 3-letter words	4 points per word 4-letter words	5 points per word 5-letter words	8 points per word 6-or-more-letter words	Score
16	KANSAS					
17	KENTUCKY					
18	LOUISIANA					
19	MAINE					
20	MARYLAND					
21	MASSACHUSETTS					
22	MICHIGAN					
23	MINNESOTA					
24	MISSISSIPPI					
25	MISSOURI					
26	MONTANA					
27	NEBRASKA					
28	NEVADA					
29	NEW HAMPSHIRE					
30	NEW JERSEY					

ACTIVITY #8c

	State	3 points per word 3-letter words	4 points per word 4-letter words	5 points per word 5-letter words	8 points per word 6-or-more-letter words	Score
31	NEW MEXICO					
32	NEW YORK					
33	NORTH CAROLINA					
34	NORTH DAKOTA					
35	OHIO					
36	OKLAHOMA					
37	OREGON					
38	PENNSYLVANIA					
39	RHODE ISLAND					
40	SOUTH CAROLINA					
41	SOUTH DAKOTA					
42	TENNESSEE					
43	TEXAS					
44	UTAH					
45	VERMONT					

ACTIVITY #8d

	State	3 points per word	4 points per word	5 points per word	8 points per word	
		3-letter words	4-letter words	5-letter words	6-or-more-letter words	Score
46	VIRGINIA					
47	WASHINGTON					
48	WEST VIRGINIA					
49	WISCONSIN					
50	WYOMING					

Lines from that wonderful patriotic song
GOD BLESS AMERICA

God Bless America,
Land that I love,
Stand beside her and guide her
Thru the night with a light from above.

U.S. ACTIVITY #9

Created by Darren and Roger

ANOTHER ACTIVITY CREATING WORDS FROM LETTERS IN A STATE NAME

Word creation can be fun and educational. While Brenda and Carolyn were working on their word creation activity using state names, Darren and Roger were producing one also. Their activity involved creating words using just the first 3 letters of a state name, then using the first 4 letters, then the first 5 letters, etc. Darren and Roger illustrated their game using two Canadian provinces, MANITOBA and NOVA SCOTIA. An individual accepting the challenge should create as many words as possible in the appropriate box in the table below. Two basic rules: A word must **contain at least two letters** and a word **cannot be repeated**.

	4 points per word	3 points per word	2 points per word	1 point per word	
Province	**Words using first 3 letters**	**Words using first 4 letters**	**Words using first 5 letters**	**Words using first 6 letters**	**Score**
MANITOBA					
NOVA SCOTIA					

 The two friends gave themselves two minutes per province name and came up with the indicated words.

	4 points per word	3 points per word	2 points per word	1 point per word	
Province	**Words using first 3 letters**	**Words using first 4 letters**	**Words using first 5 letters**	**Words using first 6 letters**	**Score**
MANITOBA	an, am, ma, man	main, aim, in	it, tin, mat	To, ton, no, on, anti, into	
NOVA SCOTIA	no, on	an, van, nova	as, so, son, vans, novas	con, cons, can, cans	

The calculation of scores for the produced words is shown below:

MANITOBA: 4(4) + 3(3) + 2(3) + 1(6) = 37
NOVA SCOTIA: 4(2) + 3(3) + 2(5) + 1(4) = 31
The challenge using the 50 state names follows. For each state of the U.S., challenge yourself to produce as many words as you can, or create teams to compete against each other. In any case, enjoy yourself!

U.S. ACTIVITY #9a

EACH WORD MUST CONTAIN AT LEAST TWO LETTERS

NO REPEAT WORDS ALLOWED

	State	4 points per word Words using first 3 letters	3 points per word Words using first 4 letters	2 points per word Words using first 5 letters	1 point per word Words using first 6 letters	Score
1	ALABAMA					
2	ALASKA					
3	ARIZONA					
4	ARKANSAS					
5	CALIFORNIA					
6	COLORADO					
7	CONNECTICUT					
8	DELAWARE					
9	FLORIDA					
10	GEORGIA					
11	HAWAII					
12	IDAHO					
13	ILLINOIS					
14	INDIANA					

U.S. ACTIVITY 9b

	State	4 points per word **Words using first 3 letters**	3 points per word **Words using first 4 letters**	2 points per word **Words using first 5 letters**	1 point per word **Words using first 6 letters**	Score
15	**IOWA**					
16	**KANSAS**					
17	**KENTUCKY**					
18	**LOUISIANA**					
19	**MAINE**					
20	**MARYLAND**					
21	**MASSACHUSETTS**					
22	**MICHIGAN**					
23	**MINNESOTA**					
24	**MISSISSIPPI**					
25	**MISSOURI**					
26	**MONTANA**					
27	**NEBRASKA**					
28	**NEVADA**					
29	**NEW HAMPSHIRE**					

U.S. ACTIVITY 9c

	State	4 points per word Words using first 3 letters	3 points per word Words using first 4 letters	2 points per word Words using first 5 letters	1 point per word Words using first 6 letters	Score
30	NEW JERSEY					
31	NEW MEXICO					
32	NEW YORK					
33	NORTH CAROLINA					
34	NORTH DAKOTA					
35	OHIO					
36	OKLAHOMA					
37	OREGON					
38	PENNSYLVANIA					
39	RHODE ISLAND					
40	SOUTH CAROLINA					
41	SOUTH DAKOTA					
42	TENNESSEE					
43	TEXAS					
44	UTAH					

U.S. ACTIVITY 9d

	State	4 points per word Words using first 3 letters	3 points per word Words using first 4 letters	2 points per word Words using first 5 letters	1 point per word Words using first 6 letters	Score
45	**VERMONT**					
46	**VIRGINIA**					
47	**WASHINGTON**					
48	**WEST VIRGINIA**					
49	**WISCONSIN**					
50	**WYOMING**					

Lines from
BATTLE HYMN OF THE REPUBLIC

Mine eyes have seen the glory of
the coming of the Lord.
He is trampling out the vintage where the
grapes of wrath are stored.
He had loosed the fateful lightning
of His terrible swift sword.
His truth is marching on.

U.S. ACTIVITY #10

Created by Stephen and Valarie

ORDER THE STATES BY POPULATION RANK

Stephen and Valarie took the lead roles in creating a series of activities where states can be ranked 1 through 50 according to specific categories. They took 2008 state population figures and created the activity on the following page. They rounded state populations to thousands for this educational endeavor.

They arranged the state names in blocks of 5 states. For instance, the first block is

CALIFORNIA
FLORIDA
ILLINOIS
NEW YORK
TEXAS

These are the five most populous states. They are listed alphabetically, but NOT in order of population rank. If you accept the challenge offered by this activity you would arrange the names in order of population rank and place them in the provided table displaying state populations in order of decreasing magnitude. You would do the same with the second set of listed state names representing rankings 6 - 10, the third set representing rankings 11 - 15, etc.

As years go by the population rankings may shift somewhat as state populations increase or decrease. One can adjust the state population and still have lots of fun with this activity.

ACTIVITY #10

Each block of 5 states is listed alphabetically.
Put each state in the appropriate position in
the table listing ranking by population.

STATES SORTED BY POPULATION RANK

State			population
CALIFORNIA		1	36,962,000
FLORIDA		2	24,783,000
ILLINOIS	*RANKINGS 1 - 5*	3	19,542,000
NEW YORK		4	18,538,000
TEXAS		5	12,911,000
	GEORGIA	6	12,605,000
	MICHIGAN	7	11,543,000
RANKINGS 6 - 10	NORTH CAROLINA	8	9,970,000
	OHIO	9	9,830,000
	PENNSYLVANIA	10	9,381,000
ARIZONA		11	8,708,000
MASSACHUSETTS		12	7,883,000
NEW JERSEY	*RANKINGS 11 - 15*	13	6,665,000
VIRGINIA		14	6,596,000
WASHINGTON		15	6,594,000
	INDIANA	16	6,424,000
	MARYLAND	17	6,297,000
RANKINGS 16 - 20	MISSOURI	18	5,988,000
	TENNESSEE	19	5,700,000
	WISCONSIN	20	5,655,000
ALABAMA		21	5,267,000
COLORADO		22	5,025,000
LOUISIANA	*RANKINGS 21 - 25*	23	4,710,000
MINNESOTA		24	4,562,000
SOUTH CAROLINA		25	4,493,000
	CONNECTICUT	26	4,315,000
	IOWA	27	3,826,000
RANKINGS 26 - 30	KENTUCKY	28	3,688,000
	OKLAHOMA	29	3,519,000
	OREGON	30	3,008,000
ARKANSAS		31	2,952,000
KANSAS		32	2,890,000
MISSISSIPPI	*RANKINGS 31 - 35*	33	2,819,000
NEVADA		34	2,785,000
UTAH		35	2,644,000
	IDAHO	36	2,010,000
	NEBRASKA	37	1,820,000
RANKINGS 36 - 40	NEW HAMPSHIRE	38	1,797,000
	NEW MEXICO	39	1,546,000
	WEST VIRGINIA	40	1,325,000
DELAWARE		41	1,319,000
HAWAII		42	1,296,000
MAINE	*RANKINGS 41 - 45*	43	1,054,000
MONTANA		44	975,000
RHODE ISLAND		45	885,122
	ALASKA	46	812,400
	NORTH DAKOTA	47	699,000
RANKINGS 46 - 50	SOUTH DAKOTA	48	647,000
	VERMONT	49	622,000
	WYOMING	50	545,000

42

U.S. ACTIVITY #11
Created by Brenda, Carolyn and Wayne

ORDER CAPITAL CITIES BY POPULATION RANK

A team of three Pack members took on the challenge of finding the populations of the 50 state capital cities. Brenda, Carolyn and Wayne then created a challenge somewhat similar to the one relating to the state populations.

They arranged the state capital names and the corresponding states in blocks of 5 city names. For instance, the first block looks like this:

ARIZONA	**Austin**
INDIANA	**Columbus**
OHIO	**Indianapolis**
TENNESSEE	**Nashville**
TEXAS	**Phoenix**

The cities listed are the five state capitals with the greatest population. They are listed alphabetically, but NOT in order of population rank. The states are also listed alphabetically and do not necessarily correspond with the indicated capital city. If you accept the challenge offered by this activity you would arrange the capital city names in order of population rank and place them in the provided table displaying city populations in order of decreasing magnitude. You would also match each of the five states with the appropriate capital city. Then you would move to the second block of five cities (representing population rankings 6-10) and do a similar reordering. You would do the same with the each of the ten blocks of alphabetized names for state capital cities.

Perhaps you have thought that capital cities would always be large cities. If so, the population size of some U. S. capital cities might surprise you.

43

U.S. ACTIVITY #11

Each block of five capital cities is listed alphabetically **STATES SORTED BY POPULATION OF CAPITAL CITY**

Each block of five states corresponding to the capital cities is listed alphabetically

Put each capital city in the appropriate position in the Capital City column according to population ranking.

Put each state corresponding to the capital city in the State column.

State	Capital	Block
ARIZONA	**Austin**	*RANKINGS 1 - 5*
INDIANA	**Columbus**	
OHIO	**Indianapolis**	
TENNESSEE	**Nashville**	
TEXAS	**Phoenix**	

Block	State	Capital
RANKINGS 6 - 10	CALIFORNIA	**Atlanta**
	COLORADO	**Boston**
	GEORGIA	**Denver**
	MASSACHUSETTS	**Oklahoma City**
	OKLAHOMA	**Sacramento**

State	Capital	Block
HAWAII	**Baton Rouge**	*RANKINGS 11 - 15*
LOUISIANA	**Honolulu**	
MINNESOTA	**Lincoln**	
NEBRASKA	**Raleigh**	
NORTH CAROLINA	**St. Paul**	

Block	State	Capital
RANKINGS 16-20	ALABAMA	**Boise**
	ARKANSAS	**Des Moines**
	IDAHO	**Little Rock**
	IOWA	**Madison**
	WISCONSIN	**Montgomery**

State	Capital	Block
FLORIDA	**Jackson**	*RANKINGS 21 - 25*
MISSISSIPPI	**Providence**	
RHODE ISLAND	**Richmond**	
UTAH	**Salt Lake City**	
VIRGINIA	**Tallahassee**	

Block	State	Capital
RANKINGS 26 - 30	CONNECTICUT	**Columbia**
	KANSAS	**Hartford**
	MICHIGAN	**Lansing**
	OREGON	**Salem**
	SOUTH CAROLINA	**Topeka**

State	Capital	Block
ILLINOIS	**Albany**	*RANKINGS 31 - 35*
NEVADA	**Carson City**	
NEW JERSEY	**Santa Fe**	
NEW MEXICO	**Springfield**	
NEW YORK	**Trenton**	

Block	State	Capital
RANKINGS 36 - 40	NORTH DAKOTA	**Bismark**
	PENNSYLVANIA	**Charleston**
	WASHINGTON	**Cheyenne**
	WEST VIRGINIA	**Harrisburg**
	WYOMING	**Olympia**

State	Capital	Block
ALASKA	**Annapolis**	*RANKINGS 41 - 45*
DELAWARE	**Concord**	
MARYLAND	**Dover**	
MISSOURI	**Jefferson City**	
NEW HAMPSHIRE	**Juneau**	

Block	State	Capital
RANKINGS 45 - 60	KENTUCKY	**Augusta**
	MAINE	**Frankfort**
	MONTANA	**Helena**
	SOUTH DAKOTA	**Montpelier**
	VERMONT	**Pierre**

#	Capital city	Capital city population	State of capital city
1		1,512,990	
2		791,930	
3		733,210	
4		709,900	
5		607,420	
6		590,770	
7		566,980	
8		541,510	
9		486,420	
10		467,350	
11		380,180	
12		377,360	
13		287,160	
14		225,590	
15		224,100	
16		221,560	
17		209,130	
18		204,380	
19		201,290	
20		200,130	
21		195,260	
22		184,260	
23		181,750	
24		176,870	
25		168,980	
26		149,310	
27		124,400	
28		122,820	
29		122,330	
30		119,130	
31		116,490	
32		96,000	
33		84,640	
34		70,631	
35		57,710	
36		55,540	
37		55,370	
38		52,710	
39		48,960	
40		42,520	
41		42,230	
42		39,640	
43		36,220	
44		32,140	
45		30,990	
46		27,750	
47		25,790	
48		18,570	
49		13,880	
50		8,040	

U.S. ACTIVITY #12

Created by Darren and Frances

ORDER OF STATEHOOD FOR THE 50 STATES

As indicated in an earlier activity the last state admitted to the union gained statehood 172 years after the first state was created. Darren and Frances produced this activity that should be of interest to history buffs.

Following the pattern established by classmates in other activities, they arranged the state names in 10 blocks of 5 names each. The first block looks like this:

CONNECTICUT
DELAWARE
GEORGIA
NEW JERSEY
PENNSYLVANIA

These are the first 5 states to enter the union. The names are listed alphabetically, but NOT in the order of admission. Your challenge on the following page is to arrange the states in order of admission in the provided table. This block is followed by another alphabetized list of 5 state names representing the 6th through 10th states to enter the union. You should arrange them in the proper order of admission. Continue this process for all ten blocks of state names.

Darren and Frances hope you enjoy this activity and that it will help you realize how young the United States of America really is compared to other countries of the world. And, think how much has been accomplished during its young life.

U.S. ACTIVITY #12

Each block of 5 states is ordered alphabetically.

Put each state in the appropriate position in the
table listing order in which it entered the union.

STATES SORTED BY ADMISSION TO THE UNION

		Order of entrance into union	State
CONNECTICUT		1	
DELAWARE		2	
GEORGIA	*Rankings 1 - 5*	3	
NEW JERSEY		4	
PENNSYLVANIA		5	
	MARYLAND	6	
	MASSACHUSETTS	7	
Rankings 6 - 10	NEW HAMPSHIRE	8	
	SOUTH CAROLINA	9	
	VIRGINIA	10	
KENTUCKY		11	
NEW YORK		12	
NORTH CAROLINA	*Rankings 11 - 15*	13	
RHODE ISLAND		14	
VERMONT		15	
	INDIANA	16	
	LOUISIANA	17	
Rankings 16 - 20	MISSISSIPPI	18	
	OHIO	19	
	TENNESSEE	20	
ALABAMA		21	
ARKANSAS		22	
ILLINOIS	*Rankings 21 - 25*	23	
MAINE		24	
MISSOURI		25	
	FLORIDA	26	
	IOWA	27	
Rankings 26 - 30	MICHIGAN	28	
	TEXAS	29	
	WISCONSIN	30	
CALIFORNIA		31	
KANSAS		32	
MINNESOTA	*Rankings 31 - 35*	33	
OREGON		34	
WEST VIRGINIA		35	
	COLORADO	36	
	NEBRASKA	37	
Rankings 36 - 40	NEVADA	38	
	NORTH DAKOTA	39	
	SOUTH DAKOTA	40	
IDAHO		41	
MONTANA		42	
UTAH	*Rankings 41 - 45*	43	
WASHINGTON		44	
WYOMING		45	
	ALASKA	46	
	ARIZONA	47	
Rankings 46 - 50	HAWAII	48	
	NEW MEXICO	49	
	OKLAHOMA	50	

46

U.S. ACTIVITY #13
Created by Valarie and Glen

ORDER OF STATES BY SIZE (SQ. MILES)

Valarie and Glen took charge of creating this activity. It was an easy task since, unlike population, the area of a state remains constant. It really wasn't difficult for them to find a listing of the size of each state in terms of square mile.

However, some discoveries surprised them. They were aware that the states differed considerably in size but being good math students they discovered some amazing facts, including:

(1) The land area of our largest state is 545 times the land area of our smallest state.

(2) The total land area of our 21 smallest states is less than the land area of our largest state.

Valarie and Glen followed the pattern established by some of their Stat Pack classmates who produced other activities. They created 10 blocks of 5 states each. The first block included our five largest states (by size) listed in alphabetical order:

ALASKA
CALIFORNIA
MONTANA
NEW MEXICO
TEXAS

If you accept this challenge then your project involves putting each block of 5 states in order of size in the table provided on the following page. Basically, can you produce the correct listing of our states in order by size? Valarie and Glen invite you to accept this challenge.

U. S. ACTIVITY #13

Each block of 5 states is ordered alphabetically.
Put each state in the appropriate position in the table listing order in terms of size (square miles).

STATES SORTED BY AREA

	State	Area (sq. miles)
ALASKA	1	570,374
CALIFORNIA	2	261,914
MONTANA *Rankings 1 - 5*	3	155,973
NEW MEXICO	4	145,556
TEXAS	5	121,365
ARIZONA	6	113,641
COLORADO	7	109,806
Rankings 6 - 19 NEVADA	8	103,730
OREGON	9	97,105
WYOMING	10	93,003
IDAHO	11	82,751
KANSAS	12	82,168
MINNESOTA *Rankings 11 - 15*	13	81,823
NEBRASKA	14	79,617
UTAH	15	76,878
MISSOURI	16	75,898
NORTH DAKOTA	17	70,704
Rankings 16 - 20 OKLAHOMA	18	68,898
SOUTH DAKOTA	19	68,679
WASHINGTON	20	66,582
GEORGIA	21	57,919
ILLINOIS	22	56,809
IOWA *Rankings 21 - 25*	23	55,875
MICHIGAN	24	55,053
WISCONSIN	25	54,314
ALABAMA	26	54,153
ARKANSAS	27	50,750
Rankings 26 - 30 FLORIDA	28	50,075
NEW YORK	29	48,718
NORTH CAROLINA	30	47,224
LOUISIANA	31	46,914
MISSISSIPPI	32	44,820
OHIO *Rankings 31 - 35*	33	43,566
PENNSYLVANIA	34	41,220
TENNESSEE	35	40,953
INDIANA	36	39,732
KENTUCKY	37	39,598
Rankings 36 - 40 MAINE	38	35,870
SOUTH CAROLINA	39	30,865
VIRGINIA	40	30,111
MARYLAND	41	24,087
MASSACHUSETTS	42	9,775
NEW HAMPSHIRE *Rankings 41 - 45*	43	9,249
VERMONT	44	8,969
WEST VIRGINIA	45	7,838
CONNECTICUT	46	7,419
DELAWARE	47	6,423
Rankings 46 - 50 HAWAII	48	4,845
NEW JERSEY	49	1,955
RHODE ISLAND	50	1,045

48

U.S. ACTIVITY #14

Created by Janice, Roger and Stephen

ORDER OF STATES BY PEOPLE PER SQUARE MILE

The trio of Janice, Roger and Stephen had to do some calculator work to set up this activity. They wanted a ranking of states by population density; that is, but number of people per square mile. There were some surprising revelations during the creation of this activity including the fact that the highest population density state has about 977 TIMES more people per square mile than the lowest population density state. Also, the highest density state had 1,172 MORE people per square mile than the lowest density state. The students also found that there was an interesting "relationship" between the population density of states and their size (in terms of square miles).

This Stat Pack trio followed the pattern established by classmates in similar activities. They created 10 blocks of 5 states each. The first block included our five highest population density states in alphabetical order:

CONNECTICUT
MARYLAND
MASSACHUSETTS
NEW JERSEY
RHODE ISLAND

Accepting the challenge involves putting each block of 5 states in order of population density per square mile in the table provided on the following page. Basically, how close can you come to producing a correct listing of the states in order by population density?

If you complete this activity you should have some idea as to where you might want to live if you want to have a lot of space to yourself OR if you want to be around a lot of people.

U. S. ACTIVITY #14

Each block of 5 states is ordered alphabetically.
Put each state in the appropriate position in the
table listing order in terms of people per square mile.

STATES SORTED BY # PEOPLE PER SQUARE MILE

			State	# people per square mile
CONNECTICUT		1		1,173.7
MARYLAND		2		1,008.6
MASSACHUSETTS	*Rankings 1 - 5*	3		841.3
NEW JERSEY		4		726.3
RHODE ISLAND		5		583.1
	DELAWARE	6		452.7
	FLORIDA	7		413.8
Rankings 6 - 10	NEW YORK	8		342.3
	OHIO	9		281.9
	PENNSYLVANIA	10		281.2
CALIFORNIA		11		237.0
HAWAII		12		234.5
ILLINOIS	*Rankings 11 - 15*	13		201.8
NORTH CAROLINA		14		199.1
VIRGINIA		15		192.6
	GEORGIA	16		179.1
	INDIANA	17		175.5
Rankings 16 - 20	MICHIGAN	18		169.7
	SOUTH CAROLINA	19		152.8
	TENNESSEE	20		151.5
KENTUCKY		21		147.7
LOUISIANA		22		108.6
NEW HAMPSHIRE	*Rankings 21 - 25*	23		104.1
WASHINGTON		24		103.1
WISCONSIN		25		100.1
	ALABAMA	26		94.6
	MISSOURI	27		92.8
Rankings 26 - 30	TEXAS	28		86.9
	VERMONT	29		75.6
	WEST VIRGINIA	30		67.3
ARIZONA		31		66.2
ARKANSAS		32		62.9
IOWA	*Rankings 31 - 35*	33		58.0
MINNESOTA		34		57.7
MISSISSIPPI		35		53.8
	COLORADO	36		53.7
	KANSAS	37		48.4
Rankings 36 - 40	MAINE	38		42.7
	OKLAHOMA	39		41.1
	OREGON	40		34.5
IDAHO		41		33.9
NEBRASKA		42		24.1
NEVADA	*Rankings 41 - 45*	43		23.4
NEW MEXICO		44		18.7
UTAH		45		16.6
	ALASKA	46		10.7
	MONTANA	47		9.2
Rankings 46 - 50	NORTH DAKOTA	48		6.7
	SOUTH DAKOTA	49		5.6
	WYOMING	50		1.2

U. S. ACTIVITY #15
Created by Herkimer and the Stat Pack

THE SEPARATOR STATE CHALLENGES

All members of the Stat Pack worked with Herkimer to create this set of 48 activities designed to help readers identify each state and its capital city on a United States map along with finding a somewhat unusual travel route between two specific states. In creating the challenge set they made some very interesting discoveries about land travel features in the amazing country we call the United States of America.

Excluding Alaska and Hawaii the remaining 48 states form a land mass on which it is possible to travel from a state to any other state by

> (1) staying entirely on land, and
> (2) never leaving the country.

The geography of these 48 states prompts the following question:

> Given two distinct states, what is the minimum number of states, excluding the two states, that one must travel through to get from one state to the other while satisfying conditions (1) and (2) stated above?

The Pack provided the following stipulations to remove possible travel confusion in the activities:

(a) The travel does not have to be on existing roads. For simplicity, think in terms of traveling on foot.

(b) When considering the **point border** shared by Arizona and Colorado, and the same **point border** shared by Utah and New Mexico, it is assumed that one can Travel from Arizona to Colorado without passing through any other state. For the purist, think of taking a running start in Arizona and jumping over the **point border** to land in Colorado. The jumper never sets foot in Utah or New Mexico. A similar assumption is made for the **point border** between Utah and New Mexico.

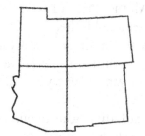

(c) The two peninsulas of Michigan are considered to be one continuous state. In reality one can get from one peninsula to the other by driving or walking over the Mackinac Bridge connecting the two land masses.

Janice took charge of creating an example to illustrate the concept of separator states. She created a fictional country called EXAMPLELAND that contains 19 states designated by the letters

A, B, C, D, E, F, G, H, I, J, K, L, M, N, O, P, Q, R and **S**.

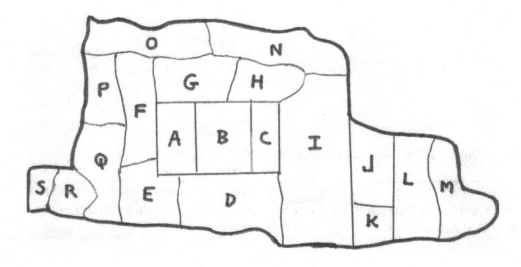

52

The separator state challenges involve determining the minimum number of states through which Herkimer must travel to get from the state he is in (**A**) to each of the states containing a Pack member. In the example below, Roger is in **R**, Valarie is in **F**, Frances is in **N**, and Brenda is in **M**.

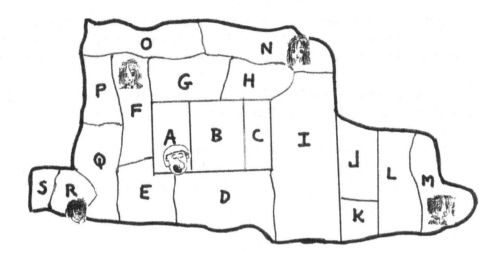

In the following illustration Janice has displayed possible journeys. A state bordering state **A** contains a 0 since Herkimer would not have to travel through any other state to get from **A** into a bordering state.

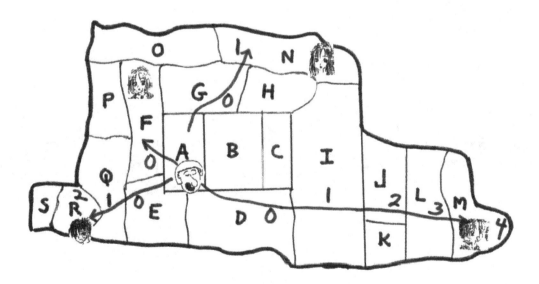

The diagram indicates that

> **Herkimer can visit Valarie in state F by going without traveling through any other state. F is a border state for A. Any border state for A has 0 states separating it from A.**

Herkimer can travel to visit Frances in state N by going through one other state. In the illustration he goes through G before entering N. In this situation G is a separator state. The 1 in N indicates that Herkimer must travel through 1 separator state to get from A to N.

In a similar manner, Herkimer can get to Roger in state R by traveling through 2 separator states. The route displayed takes Herkimer through E and Q before entering R. The displayed route is not the only one with 2 separator states.

Finally, Herkimer can visit Brenda in state M by traveling through 4 separator states as indicated on the map of Exampleland.

Janice also constructed a detailed map below indicating the number of separator states from A for each other state in Exampleland. She also produced a frequency histogram displaying the distribution of separator state number for A. Her display follows the map and will be referenced in U.S. Activity #16.

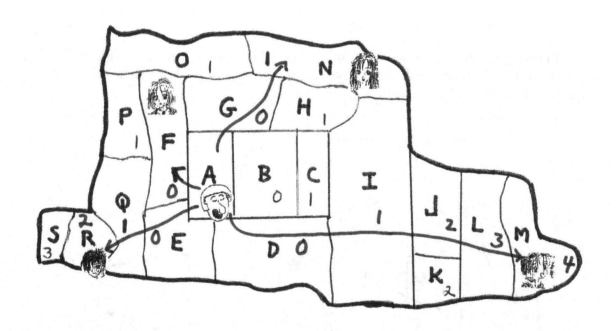

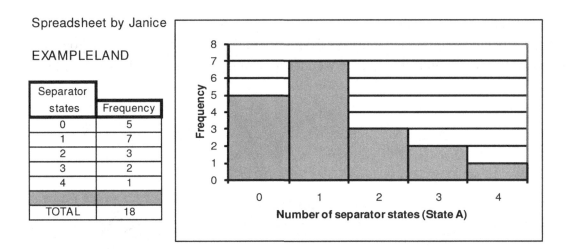

Spreadsheet by Janice

EXAMPLELAND

Separator states	Frequency
0	5
1	7
2	3
3	2
4	1
TOTAL	18

Janice made a point to stress that it is important to note that the separator state challenges do not seek the shortest (straight line) distance between two states but rather a route that requires a traveler to go through a minimum number of other states in getting from one state to the other. In seeking such a route between two states in the United States one will discover some very interesting travel features on a map of the States.

.

Herkimer and the Stat Pack students hope that those who accept the separator state challenges will enjoy your many journeys from state to state. They are sure that you will find many interesting routes through the wonderful country we know as the United States of America

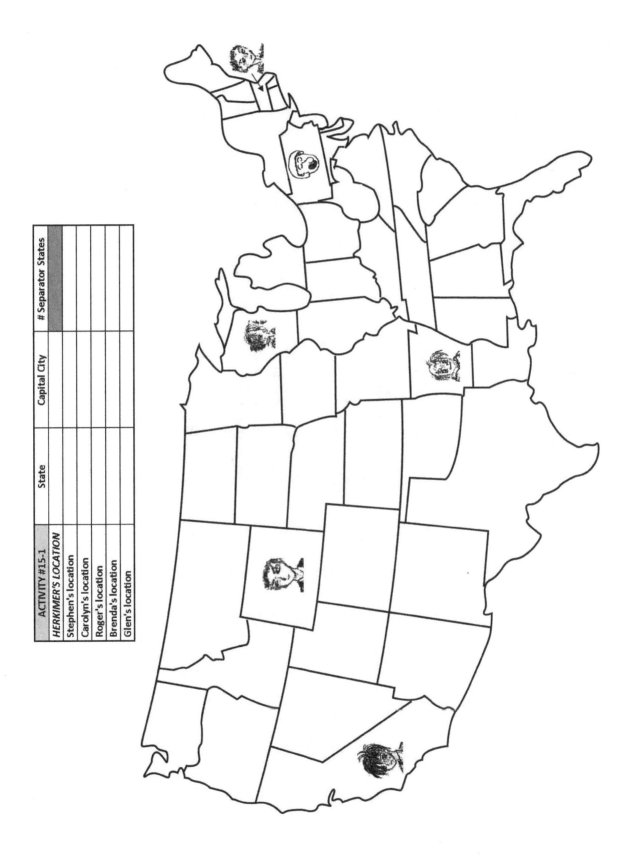

ACTIVITY #15-1	State	Capital City	# Separator States
HERKIMER'S LOCATION			
Stephen's location			
Carolyn's location			
Roger's location			
Brenda's location			
Glen's location			

On the previous page Herkimer
began his U.S. journeys in the state of
PENNSYLVANIA

Lines from the PENNSYLVANIA state song

Pennsylvania, Pennsylvania,
May your future be,
Filled with honor everlasting
As your history. ☆

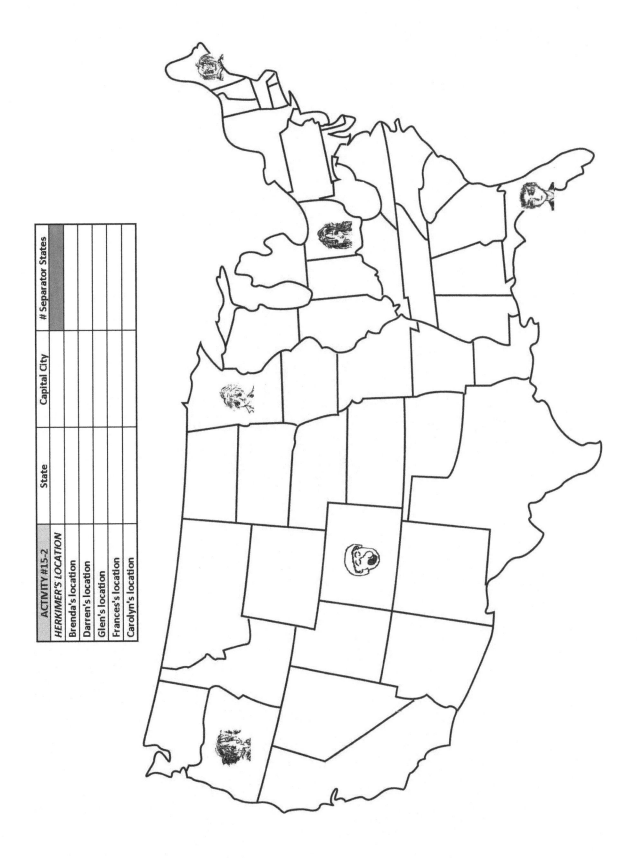

ACTIVITY #15-2	State	Capital City	# Separator States
HERKIMER'S LOCATION			
Brenda's location			
Darren's location			
Glen's location			
Frances's location			
Carolyn's location			

On the previous page Herkimer
began his U.S. journeys in the state of
COLORADO

Lines from the COLORADO state song

'Tis the land where the columbines grow,
Overlooking the plains far below,
While the cool summer breeze in the evergreen trees
Softly sings where the columbines grow.

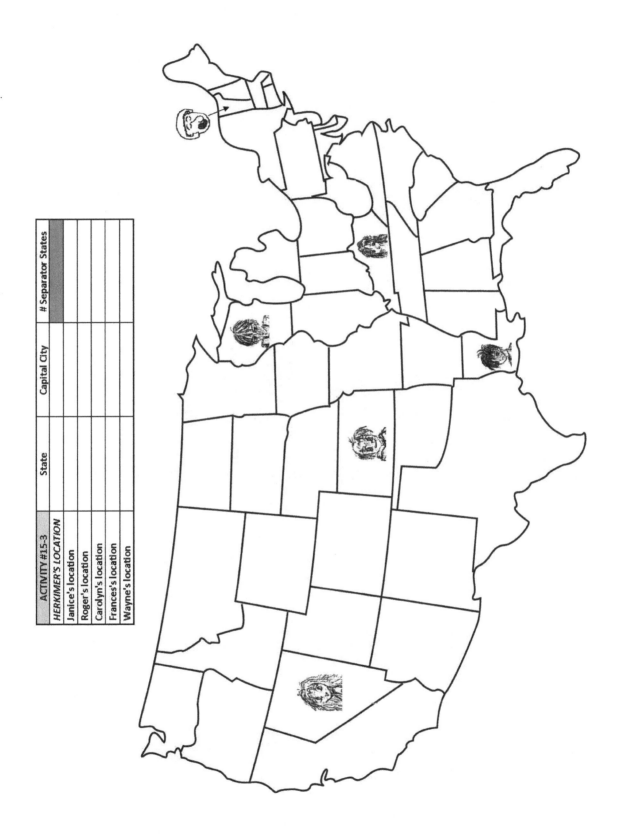

ACTIVITY #15-3	State	Capital City	# Separator States
HERKIMER'S LOCATION			
Janice's location			
Roger's location			
Carolyn's location			
Frances's location			
Wayne's location			

On the previous page Herkimer
began his U.S. journeys in the state of
VERMONT

Lines from the VERMONT state song

Hail to Vermont! Lovely Vermont!
Hail to Vermont so fearless!
Sing we a song! Sing loud and long!
To our little state so peerless!

ACTIVITY #15-4	State	Capital City	# Separator States
HERKIMER'S LOCATION			
Wayne's location			
Janice's location			
Carolyn's location			
Darren's location			
Frances's location			

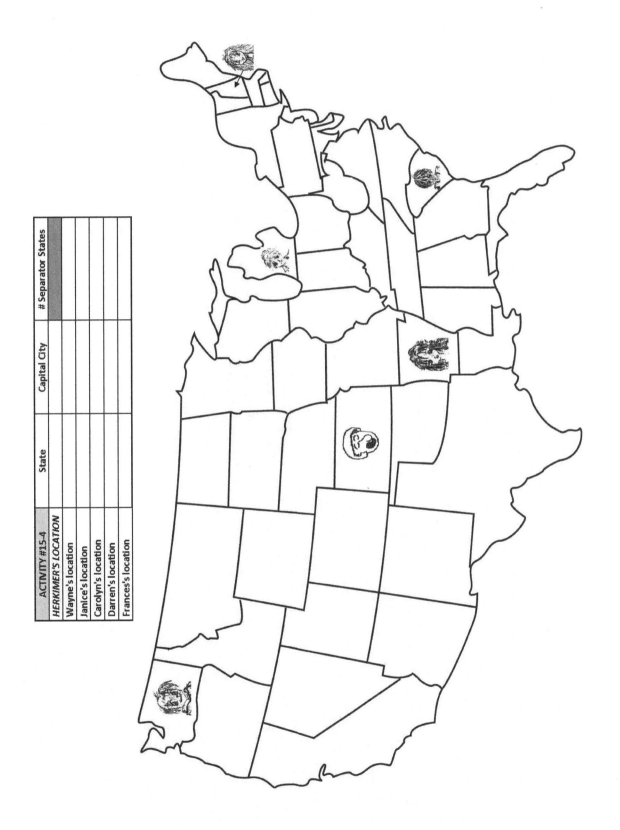

63

On the previous page Herkimer
began his U.S. journeys in the state of
KANSAS

Lines from the KANSAS state song

Home, home on the range,
Where the deer and the antelope play
Where seldom is heard a discouraging word,
And the skies are not cloudy all day.

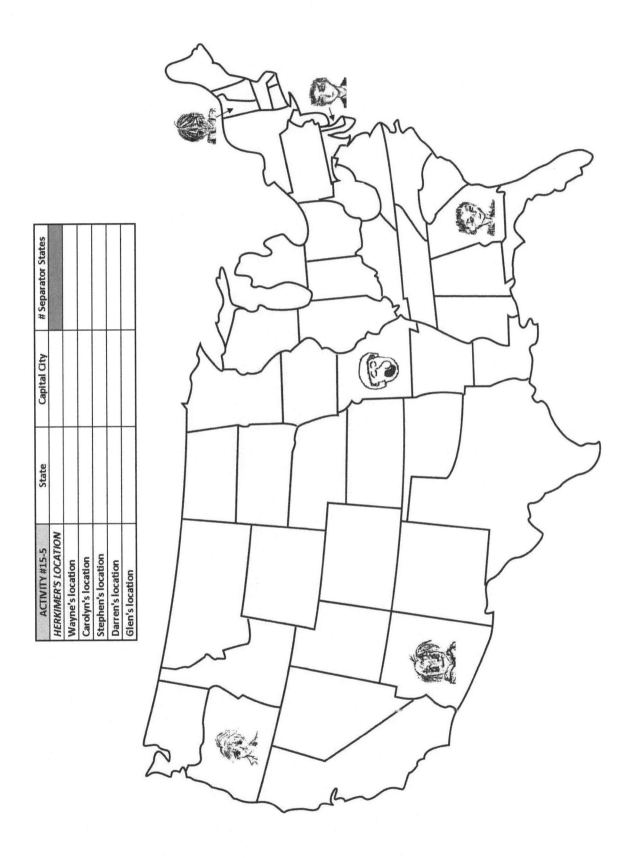

ACTIVITY #15-5	State	Capital City	# Separator States
HERKIMER'S LOCATION			
Wayne's location			
Carolyn's location			
Stephen's location			
Darren's location			
Glen's location			

On the previous page Herkimer
began his U.S. journeys in the state of
MISSOURI

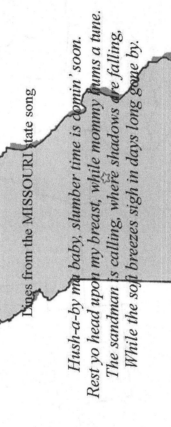

Lines from the MISSOURI state song

Hush-a-by ma baby, slumber time is comin' soon.
Rest yo head upon my breast, while mommy hums a tune.
The sandman is calling, where shadows are falling,
While the soft breezes sigh in days long gone by.

ACTIVITY #15-6	State	Capital City	# Separator States
HERKIMER'S LOCATION			
Valarie's location			
Stephen's location			
Roger's location			
Glen's location			
Brenda's location			

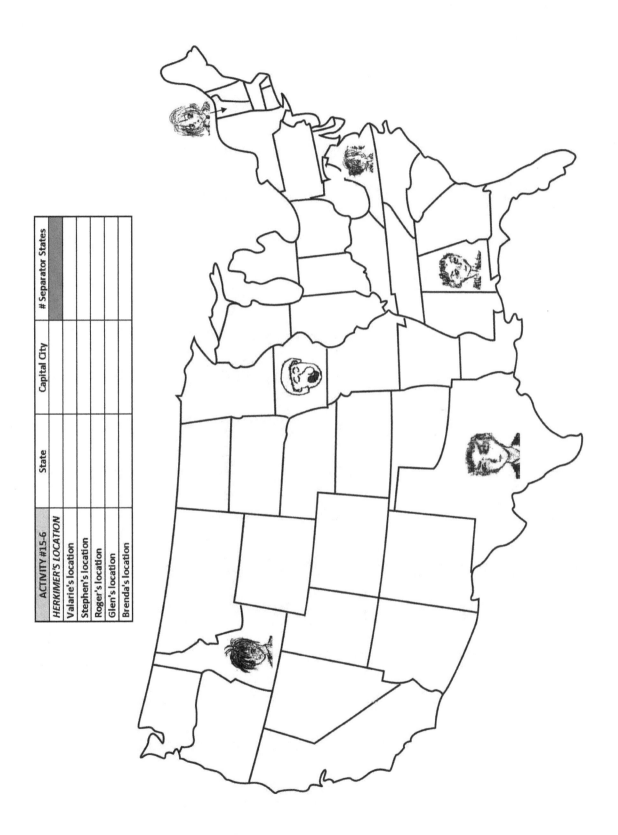

On the previous page Herkimer
began his U.S. journeys in the state of
IOWA

Lines from the IOWA state song

You ask what land I love the best, Iowa, 'tis Iowa,
The fairest state of all the west, Iowa, O! Iowa,
From yonder Mississippi's stream
To where Missouri's waters gleam
O! fair it is as poet's dream, Iowa, in Iowa

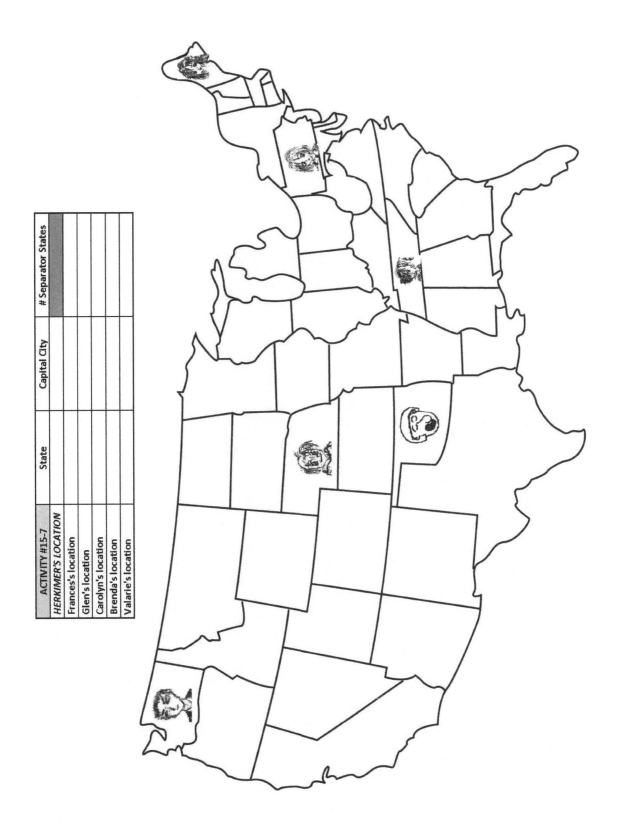

ACTIVITY #15-7	State	Capital City	# Separator States
HERKIMER'S LOCATION			
Frances's location			
Glen's location			
Carolyn's location			
Brenda's location			
Valarie's location			

69

On the previous page Herkimer
began his U.S. journeys in the state of
OKLAHOMA

Lines from the OKLAHOMA state song

We know we belong to the land
And the land we belong to is grand!
And when we say – Yeeow! A-yip-i-o-ee ay!
We're only sayin' you're doin' fine, Oklahoma!
Oklahoma – OK!

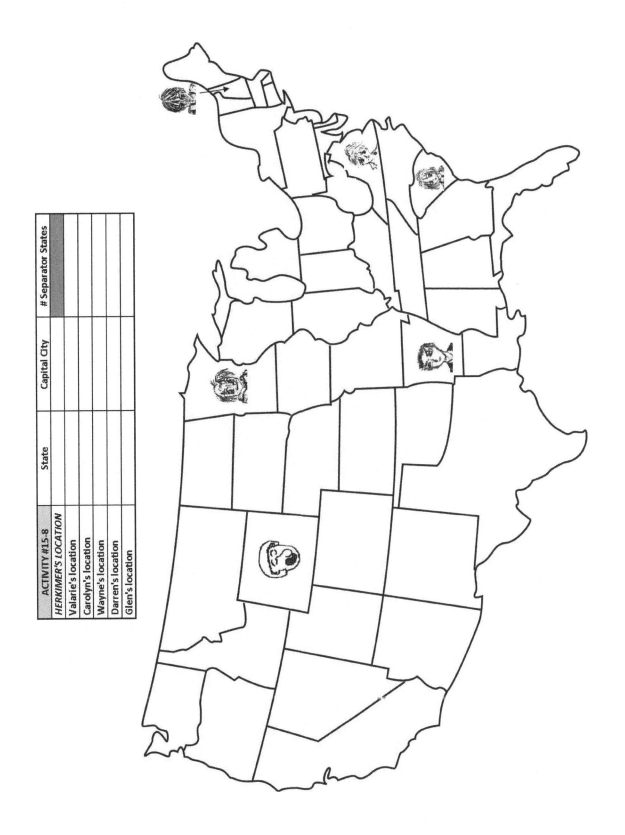

ACTIVITY #15-8	State	Capital City	# Separator States
HERKIMER'S LOCATION			
Valarie's location			
Carolyn's location			
Wayne's location			
Darren's location			
Glen's location			

On the previous page Herkimer
began his U.S. journeys in the state of
WYOMING

Lines from the WYOMING state song

Wyoming, Wyoming! Land of the sunlight clear!
Wyoming, Wyoming! Land that we hold so dear!
Wyoming, Wyoming! Precious art thou and thine!
Wyoming, Wyoming! Beloved state of mine!

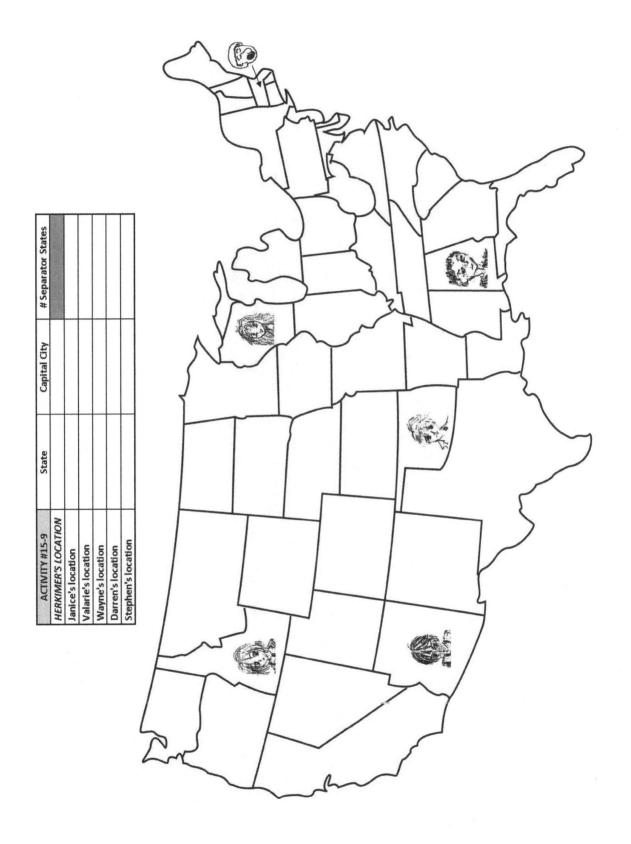

ACTIVITY #15-9	State	Capital City	# Separator States
HERKIMER'S LOCATION			
Janice's location			
Valarie's location			
Wayne's location			
Darren's location			
Stephen's location			

On the previous page Herkimer
began his U.S. journeys in the state of
MASSACHUSETTS

Lines from the MASSACHUSETTS state song

All hail to Massachusetts, renowned in the Hall of Fame!
How proudly wave her banners emblazoned with her name!
In unity and brotherhood, sons and daughters go in hand;
All hail to Massachusetts, there is no other land.

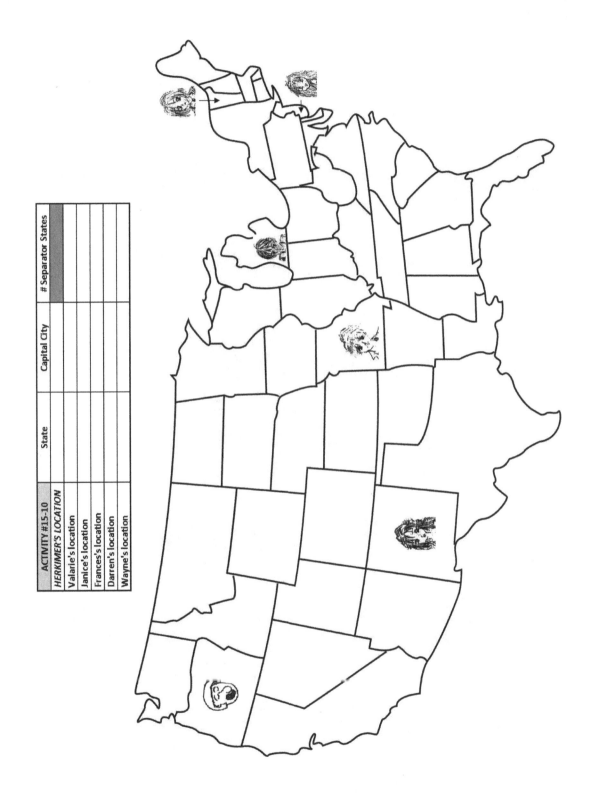

ACTIVITY #15-10	State	Capital City	# Separator States
HERKIMER'S LOCATION			
Valarie's location			
Janice's location			
Frances's location			
Darren's location			
Wayne's location			

On the previous page Herkimer
began his U.S. journeys in the state of
OREGON

Lines from the OREGON state song

☆

Land of the Empire Builders, Land of the Golden West;
Conquered and held by free men, Fairest and the best.
Onward and upward ever, Forward and on, and on;
Hail to thee, Land of the Heroes, My Oregon.

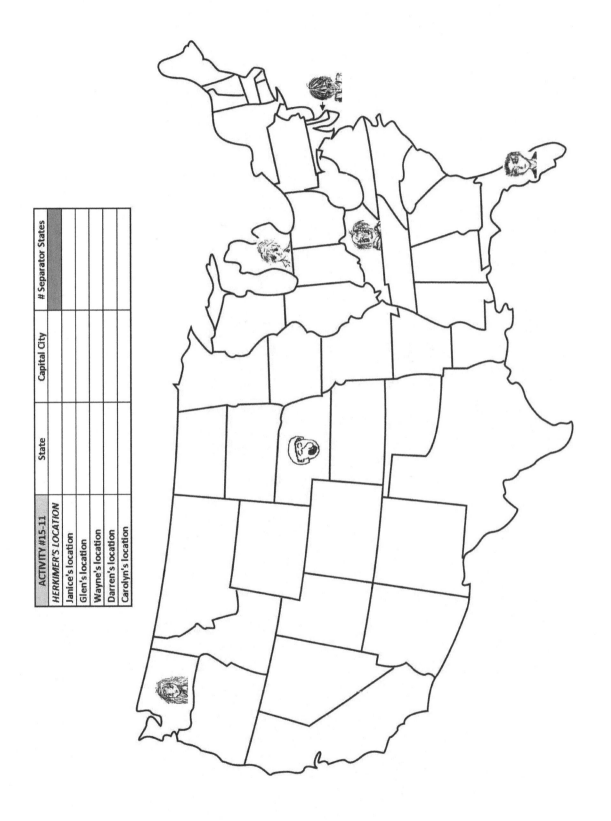

ACTIVITY #15-11	State	Capital City	# Separator States
HERKIMER'S LOCATION			
Janice's location			
Glen's location			
Wayne's location			
Darren's location			
Carolyn's location			

On the previous page Herkimer
began his U.S. journeys in the state of
NEBRASKA

Lines from the NEBRASKA state song

Beautiful Nebraska, as you look around,
You will find a rainbow reaching to the ground,
All these wonders by the Master's hand, ☆
Beautiful Nebraskaland

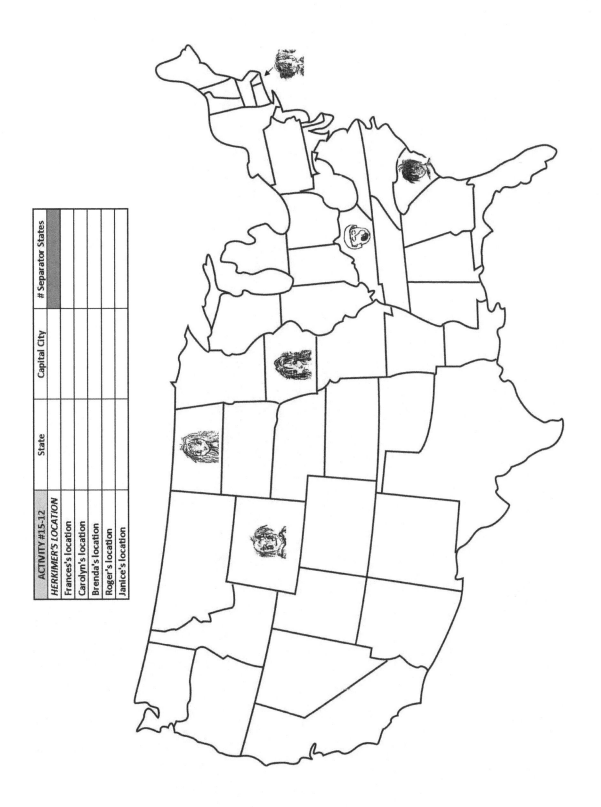

ACTIVITY #15-12	State	Capital City	# Separator States
HERKIMER'S LOCATION			
Frances's location			
Carolyn's location			
Brenda's location			
Roger's location			
Janice's location			

On the previous page Herkimer
began his U.S. journeys in the state of
KENTUCKY

Lines from the KENTUCKY state song

Weep no more, my lady,
Oh weep no more today!
We will sing one song for the old Kentucky home,
For the old Kentucky home far away.

80

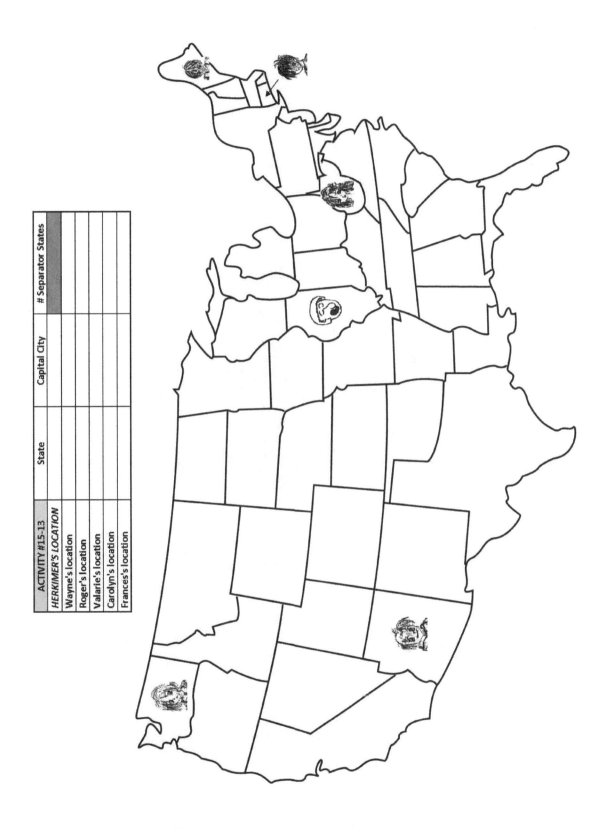

ACTIVITY #15-13	State	Capital City	# Separator States
HERKIMER'S LOCATION			
Wayne's location			
Roger's location			
Valarie's location			
Carolyn's location			
Frances's location			

On the previous page Herkimer
began his U.S. journeys in the state of
ILLINOIS

Lines from the ILLINOIS state song

By the rivers gently flowing, Illinois, Illinois,
O'er thy prairies verdant growing, Illinois, Illinois,
Comes an echo on the breeze, rustling through the leafy trees,
and its mellow tones are these, Illinois, Illinois.

82

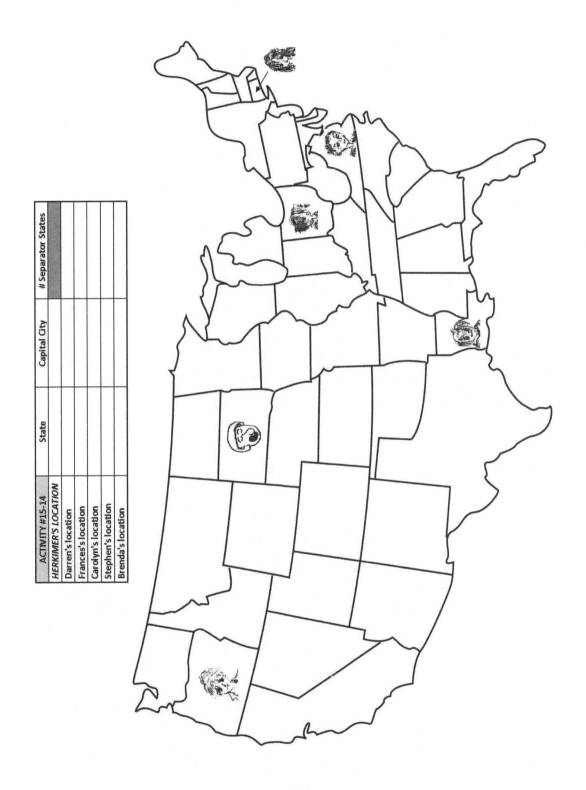

ACTIVITY #15-14	State	Capital City	# Separator States
HERKIMER'S LOCATION			
Darren's location			
Frances's location			
Carolyn's location			
Stephen's location			
Brenda's location			

On the previous page Herkimer
began his U.S. journeys in the state of
SOUTH DAKOTA

Lines from the SOUTH DAKOTA state song

Hail! South Dakota, a great state of the land
Health, wealth and beauty, that's what makes her grand;
She has Black Hills, and mines with gold so rare,
And with her scenery, no other state can compare.

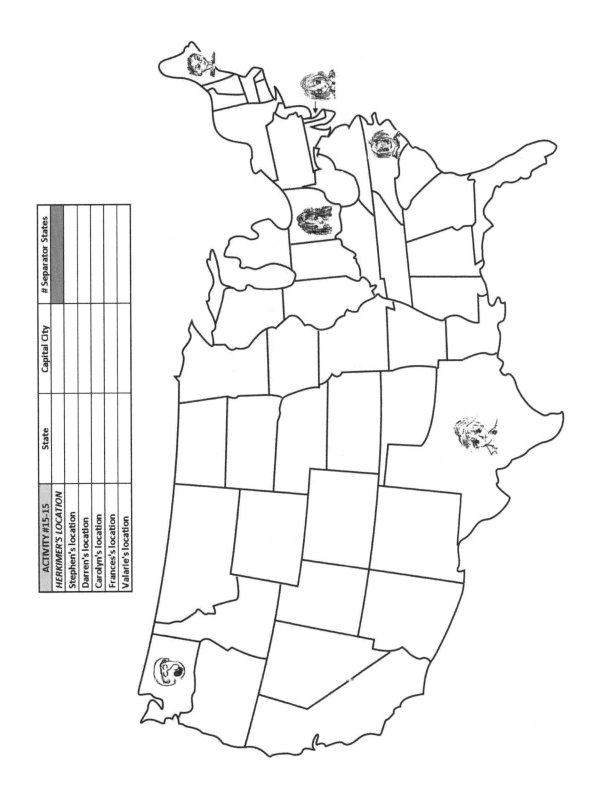

ACTIVITY #15-15	State	Capital City	# Separator States
HERKIMER'S LOCATION			
Stephen's location			
Darren's location			
Carolyn's location			
Frances's location			
Valarie's location			

On the previous page Herkimer
began his U.S. journeys in the state of
WASHINGTON

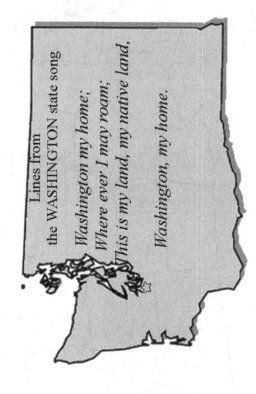

Lines from
the WASHINGTON state song

Washington my home;
Where ever I may roam;
This is my land, my native land,

Washington, my home.

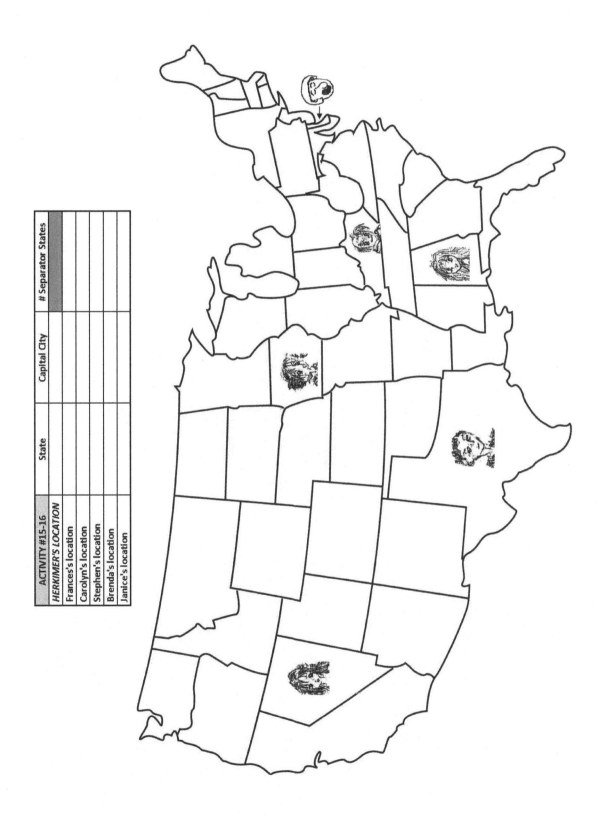

ACTIVITY #15-16	State	Capital City	# Separator States
HERKIMER'S LOCATION			
Frances's location			
Carolyn's location			
Stephen's location			
Brenda's location			
Janice's location			

On the previous page Herkimer
began his U.S. journeys in the state of
DELAWARE

Lines from the DELAWARE state song

Of the gardens and the hedges,
And the welcome waiting there,
For the loyal son that pledges
Faith to good old Delaware.

88

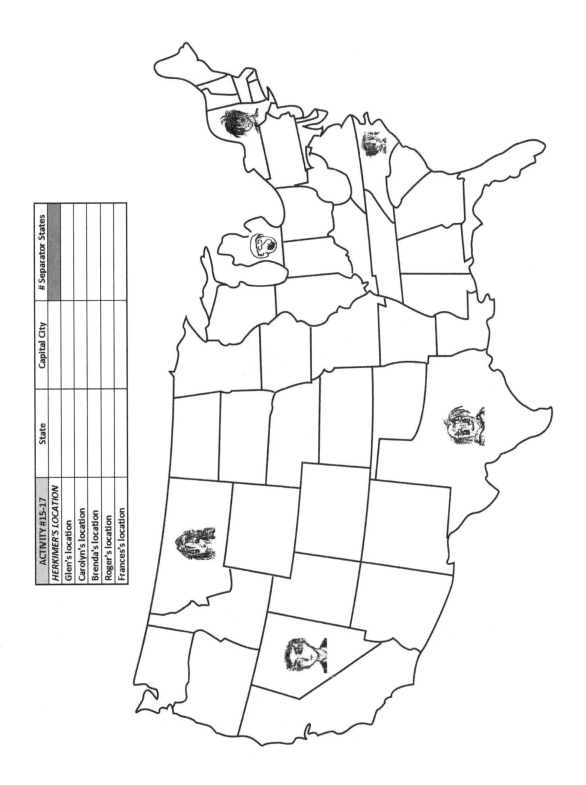

ACTIVITY #15-17	State	Capital City	# Separator States
HERKIMER'S LOCATION			
Glen's location			
Carolyn's location			
Brenda's location			
Roger's location			
Frances's location			

On the previous page Herkimer
began his U.S. journeys in the state of
MICHIGAN

Lines from the MICHIGAN state song

The whisper of the forest tree,
The thunder of the inland sea,
Unite in one grand symphony
Of Michigan, my Michigan.

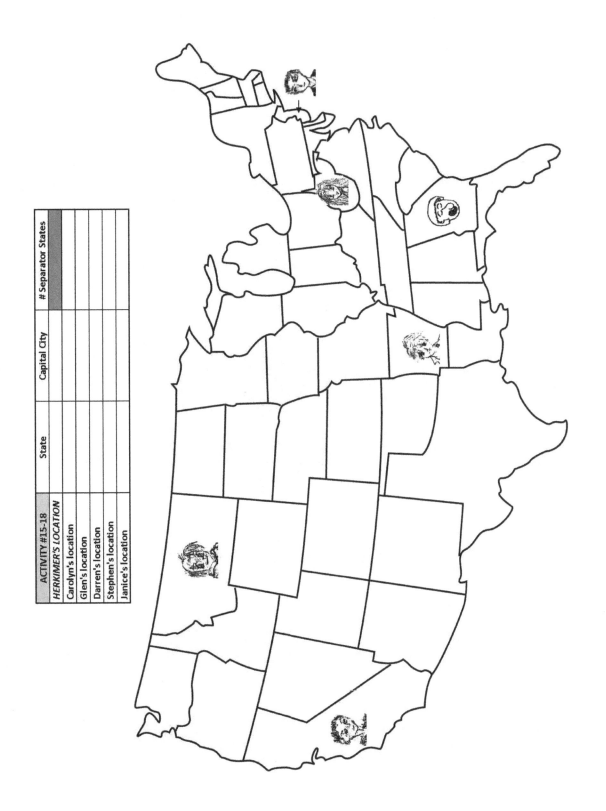

ACTIVITY #15-18	State	Capital City	# Separator States
HERKIMER'S LOCATION			
Carolyn's location			
Glen's location			
Darren's location			
Stephen's location			
Janice's location			

On the previous page Herkimer
began his U.S. journeys in the state of
GEORGIA

Lines from the GEORGIA state song

Georgia, Georgia, the whole day through
Just an old sweet song keeps Georgia on my mind.
Georgia, Georgia, a song of you
Comes as sweet and clear as moonlight through the pines.

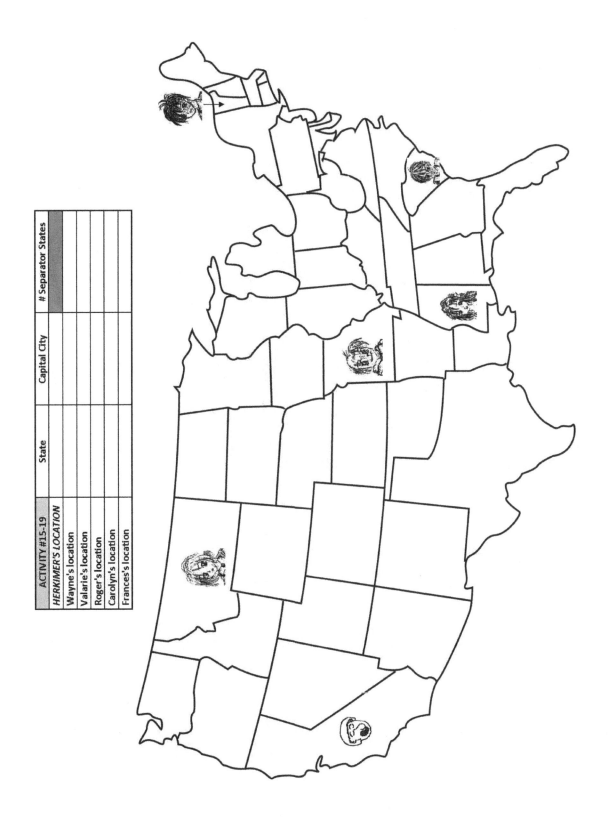

ACTIVITY #15-19	State	Capital City	# Separator States
HERKIMER'S LOCATION			
Wayne's location			
Valarie's location			
Roger's location			
Carolyn's location			
Frances's location			

On the previous page Herkimer
began his U.S. journeys in the state of
CALIFORNIA

Lines from the CALIFORNIA state song

I love you, California, you're the greatest state of all
I love you in the winter, summer, spring, and in the fall.
I love your fertile valleys; your dear mountains I adore.
I love your grand old ocean and I love her rugged shore.

94

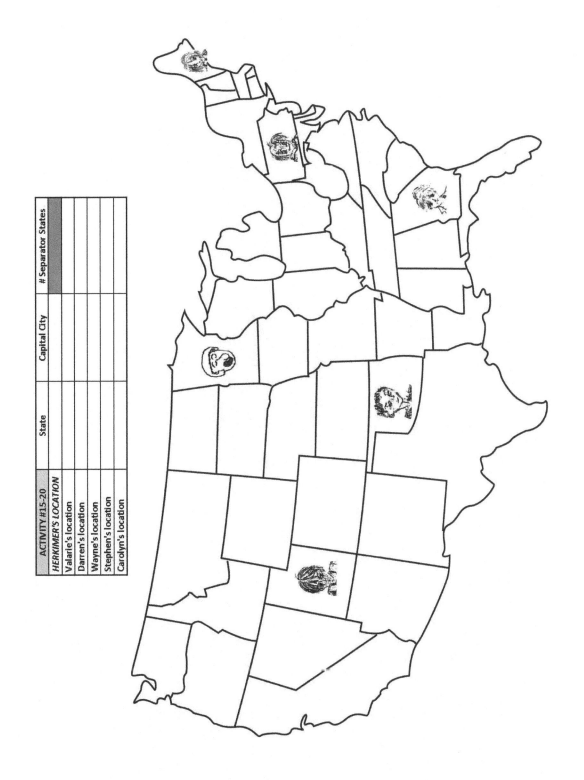

ACTIVITY #15-20	State	Capital City	# Separator States
HERKIMER'S LOCATION			
Valarie's location			
Darren's location			
Wayne's location			
Stephen's location			
Carolyn's location			

On the previous page Herkimer
began his U.S. journeys in the state of
MINNESOTA

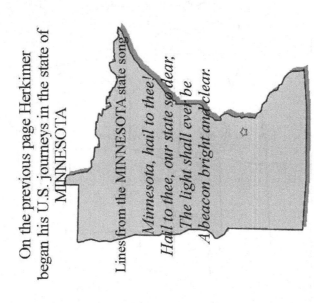

Lines from the MINNESOTA state song

Minnesota, hail to thee!
Hail to thee, our state so dear,
The light shall ever be
A beacon bright and clear.

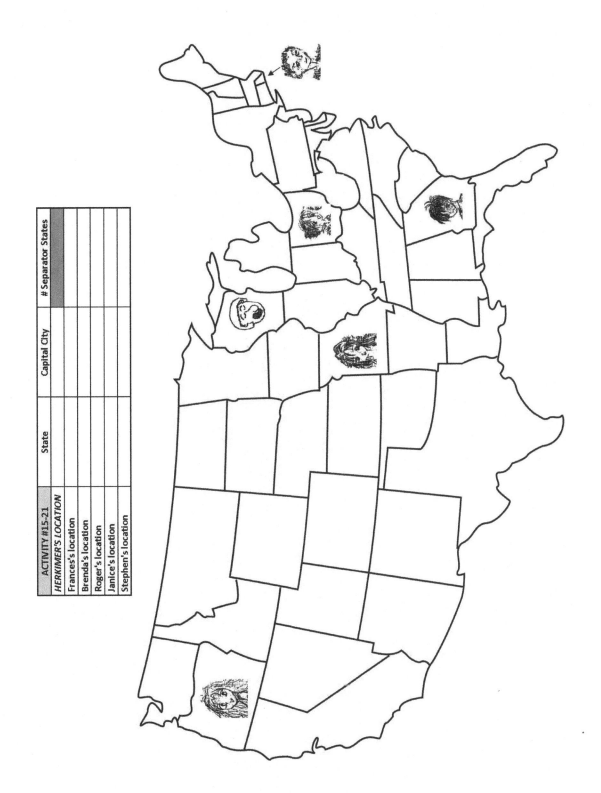

ACTIVITY #15-21	State	Capital City	# Separator States
HERKIMER'S LOCATION			
Frances's location			
Brenda's location			
Roger's location			
Janice's location			
Stephen's location			

On the previous page Herkimer
began his U.S. journeys in the state of
WISCONSIN

Lines from the WISCONSIN state song

On, Wisconsin! On Wisconsin!
Grand old badger state!
We, thy loyal sons and daughters,
Hail thee, good and great.

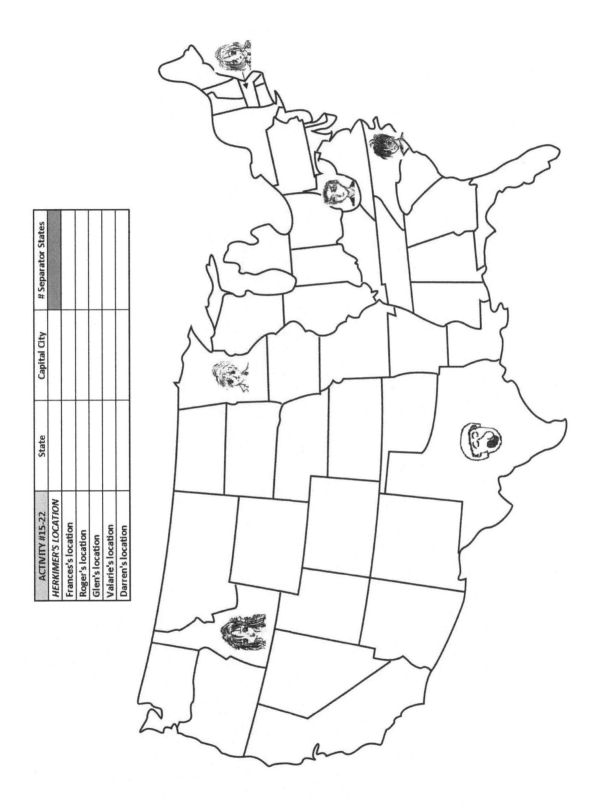

ACTIVITY #15-22	State	Capital City	# Separator States
HERKIMER'S LOCATION			
Frances's location			
Roger's location			
Glen's location			
Valarie's location			
Darren's location			

99

On the previous page Herkimer
began his U.S. journeys in the state of
TEXAS

Lines from the TEXAS state song

Texas, Our Texas! All hail the mighty State!
Texas, Our Texas! So wonderful and great!
Boldest and grandest, withstanding ev'ry test
O Empire wide and glorious, you stand extremely blest.

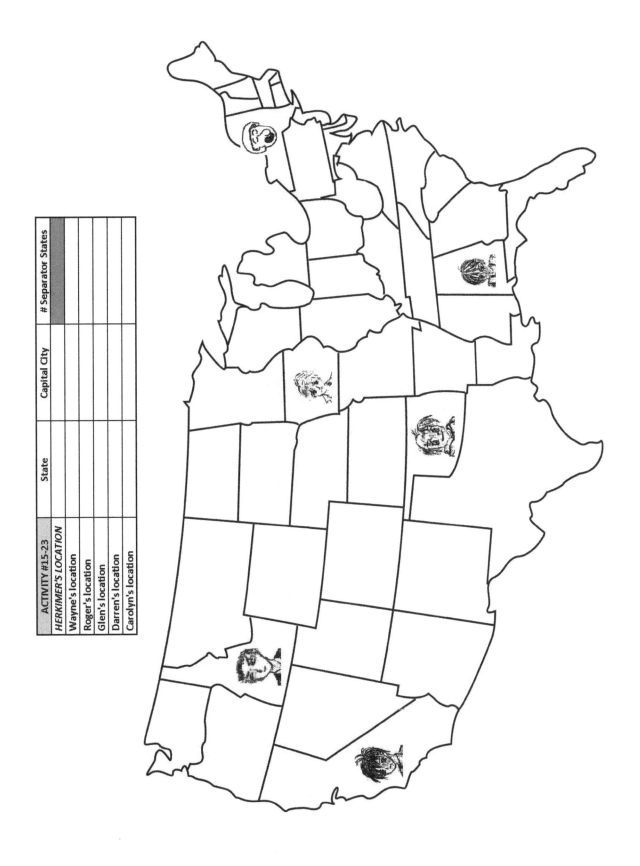

ACTIVITY #15-23	State	Capital City	# Separator States
HERKIMER'S LOCATION			
Wayne's location			
Roger's location			
Glen's location			
Darren's location			
Carolyn's location			

On the previous page Herkimer
began his U.S. journeys in the state of
NEW YORK

Lines from the NEW YORK state song

There isn't another like it
No matter where you go.
And nobody can compare it;
It's win and place and show.

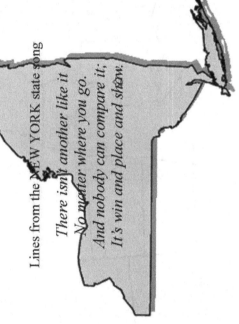

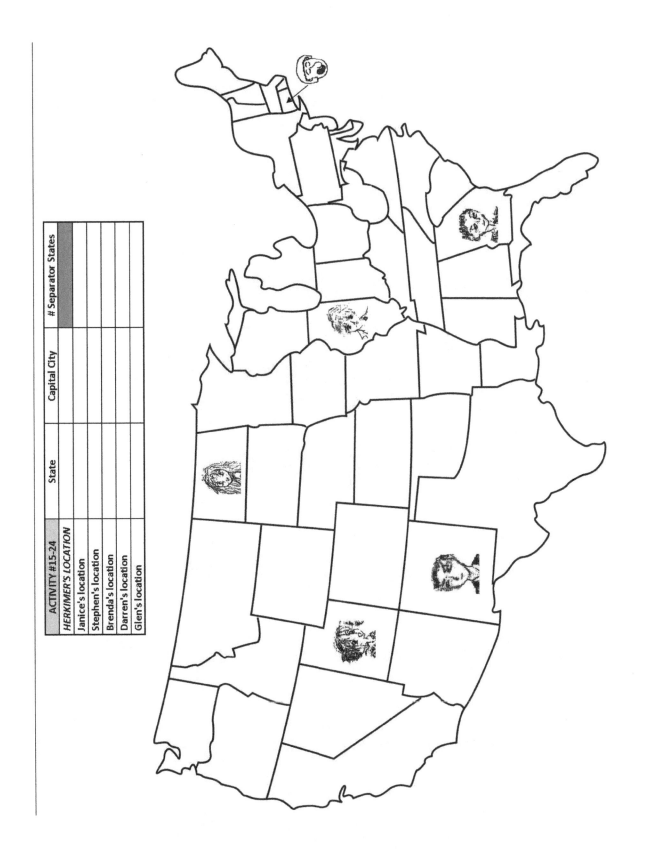

ACTIVITY #15-24	State	Capital City	# Separator States
HERKIMER'S LOCATION			
Janice's location			
Stephen's location			
Brenda's location			
Darren's location			
Glen's location			

On the previous page Herkimer
began his U.S. journeys in the state of
CONNECTICUT

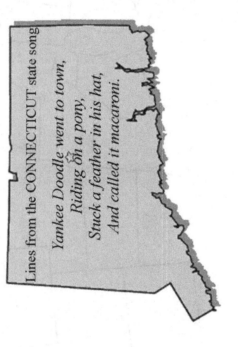

Lines from the CONNECTICUT state song

Yankee Doodle went to town,
Riding on a pony,
Stuck a feather in his hat,
And called it macaroni.

ACTIVITY #15-25	State	Capital City	# Separator States
HERKIMER'S LOCATION			
Wayne's location			
Frances's location			
Stephen's location			
Glen's location			
Valarie's location			

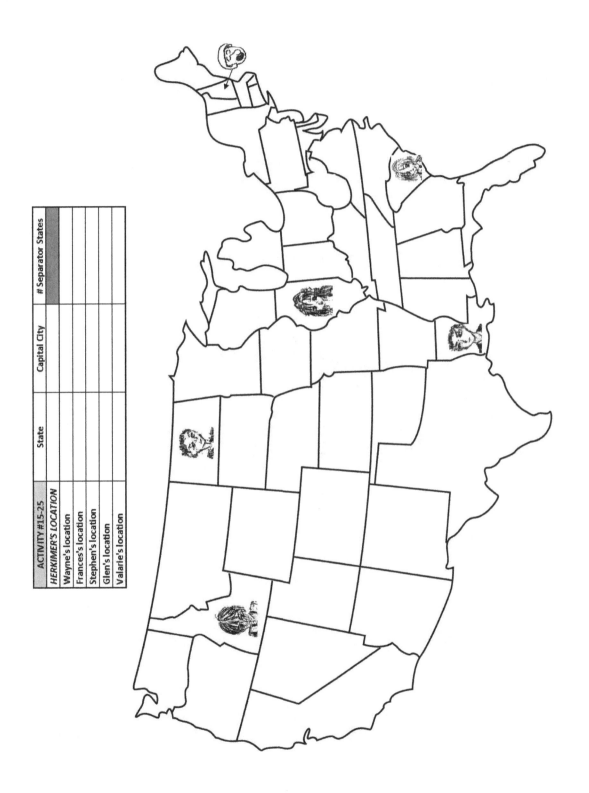

On the previous page Herkimer
began his U.S. journeys in the state of
NEW HAMPSHIRE

Lines from the NEW HAMPSHIRE state song

Old New Hampshire, Old New Hampshire
Old New Hampshire Grand and Great
We will sing of Old New Hampshire,
Of the dear old Granite State.

106

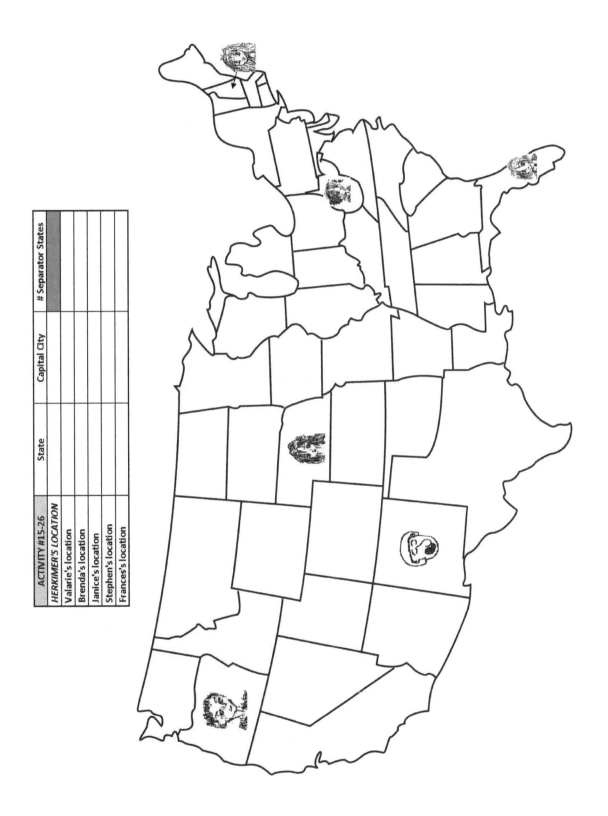

ACTIVITY #15-26	State	Capital City	# Separator States
HERKIMER'S LOCATION			
Valarie's location			
Brenda's location			
Janice's location			
Stephen's location			
Frances's location			

On the previous page Herkimer
began his U.S. journeys in the state of
NEW MEXICO

Lines from the NEW MEXICO state song

O, Fair New Mexico
We love, we love you so,
Our hearts with pride o'reflow
No matter where we go.

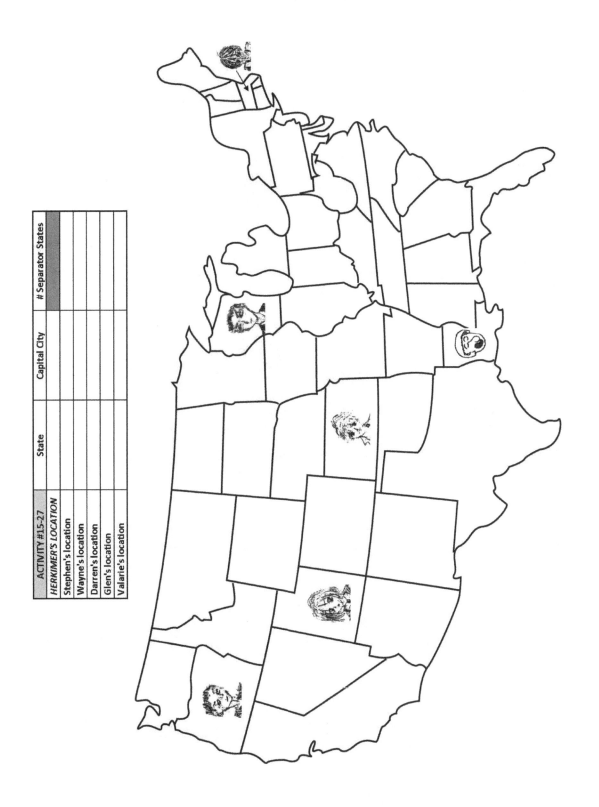

ACTIVITY #15-27	State	Capital City	# Separator States
HERKIMER'S LOCATION			
Stephen's location			
Wayne's location			
Darren's location			
Glen's location			
Valarie's location			

109

On the previous page Herkimer
began his U.S. journeys in the state of
LOUISIANA

Lines from the LOUISIANA state song

Give me Louisiana,
The state where I was born,
The land of snowy cotton,
The best I've ever known.

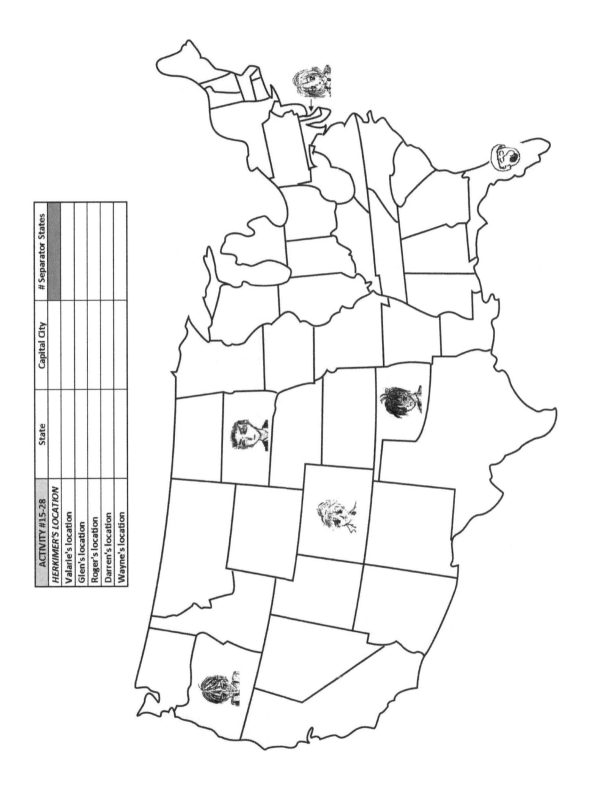

ACTIVITY #15-28	State	Capital City	# Separator States
HERKIMER'S LOCATION			
Valarie's location			
Glen's location			
Roger's location			
Darren's location			
Wayne's location			

111

On the previous page Herkimer
began his U.S. journeys in the state of
FLORIDA

Lines from the FLORIDA state song

All the world is sad and dreary
Everywhere I roam.
O dear ones, how my heart grows weary,
Far from the old folks at home.

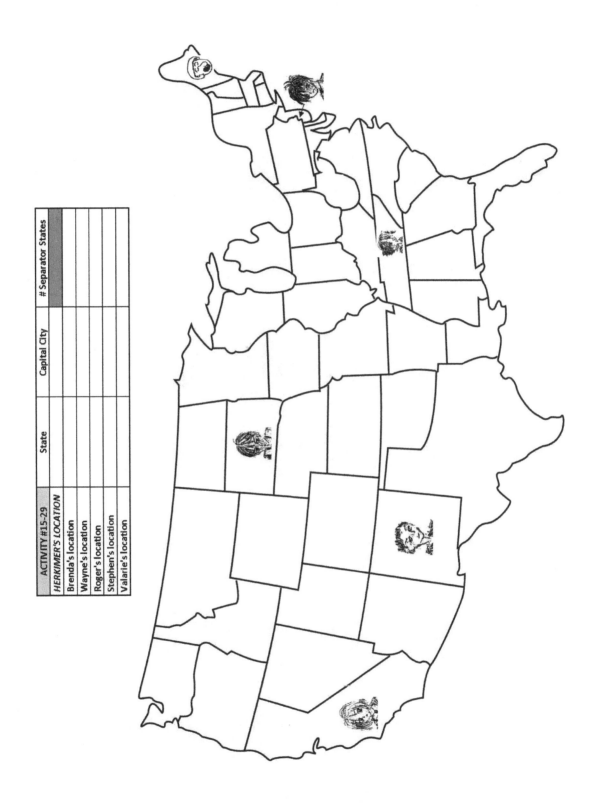

ACTIVITY #15-29	State	Capital City	# Separator States
HERKIMER'S LOCATION			
Brenda's location			
Wayne's location			
Roger's location			
Stephen's location			
Valarie's location			

On the previous page Herkimer
began his U.S. journeys in the state of
MAINE

Lines from the MAINE state song

And tho'we seek far and wide
Our search will be in vain
To find a fairer spot on earth
Then Maine! Maine! Maine!

114

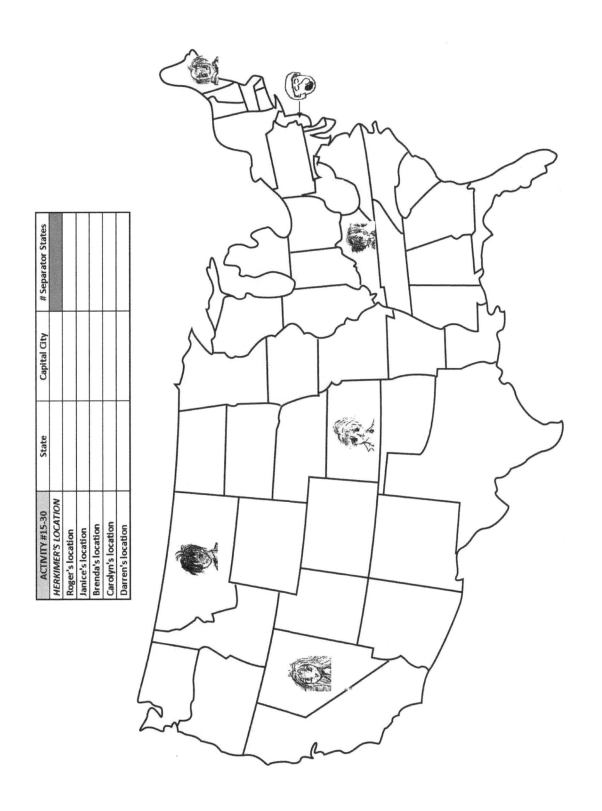

ACTIVITY #15-30	State	Capital City	# Separator States
HERKIMER'S LOCATION			
Roger's location			
Janice's location			
Brenda's location			
Carolyn's location			
Darren's location			

On the previous page Herkimer
began his U.S. journeys in the state of
NEW JERSEY

Lines from the NEW JERSEY state song

I'm from New Jersey and I'm proud about it,
I love the Garden State.
I'm from New Jersey and I want to shout it,
I think it's simply great.

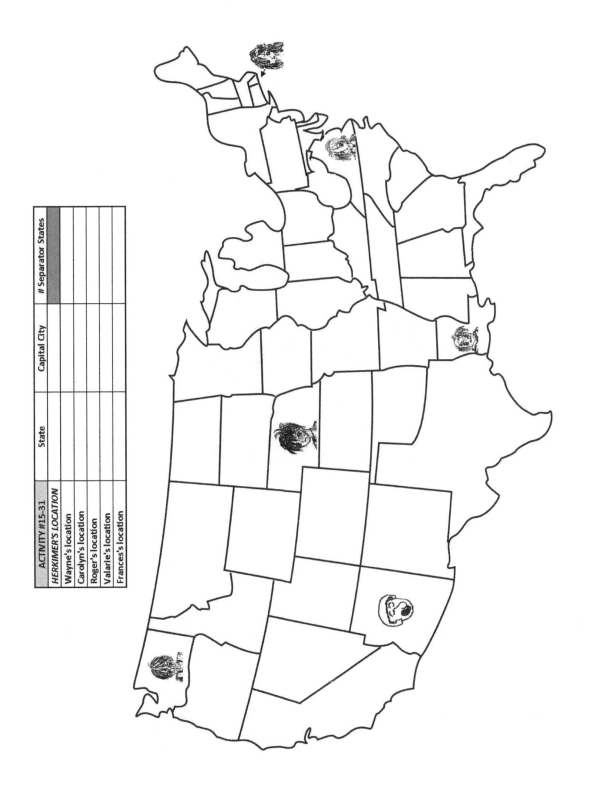

ACTIVITY #15-31	State	Capital City	# Separator States
HERKIMER'S LOCATION			
Wayne's location			
Carolyn's location			
Roger's location			
Valarie's location			
Frances's location			

On the previous page Herkimer
began his U.S. journeys in the state of
ARIZONA

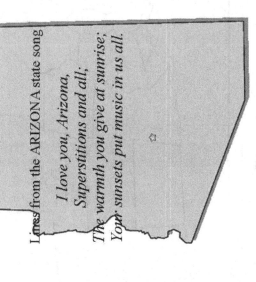

Lines from the ARIZONA state song

I love you, Arizona,
Superstitions and all;
The warmth you give at sunrise;
Your sunsets put music in us all.

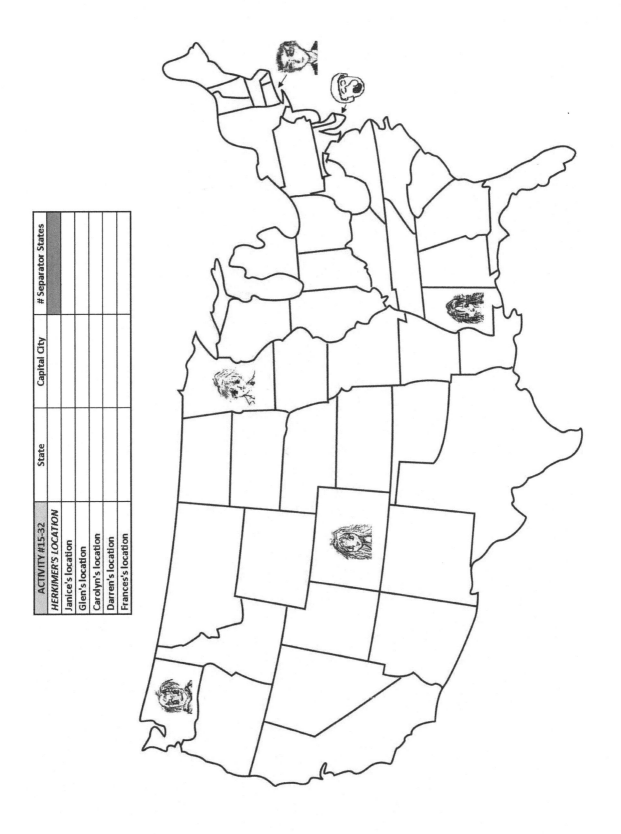

ACTIVITY #15-32	State	Capital City	# Separator States
HERKIMER'S LOCATION			
Janice's location			
Glen's location			
Carolyn's location			
Darren's location			
Frances's location			

On the previous page Herkimer
began his U.S. journeys in the state of
MARYLAND

Lines from the MARYLAND state song

For life and death, from woe and weal,
Thy peerless chivalry reveal,
And grid thy beauteous limbs with steel,
Maryland! My Maryland.

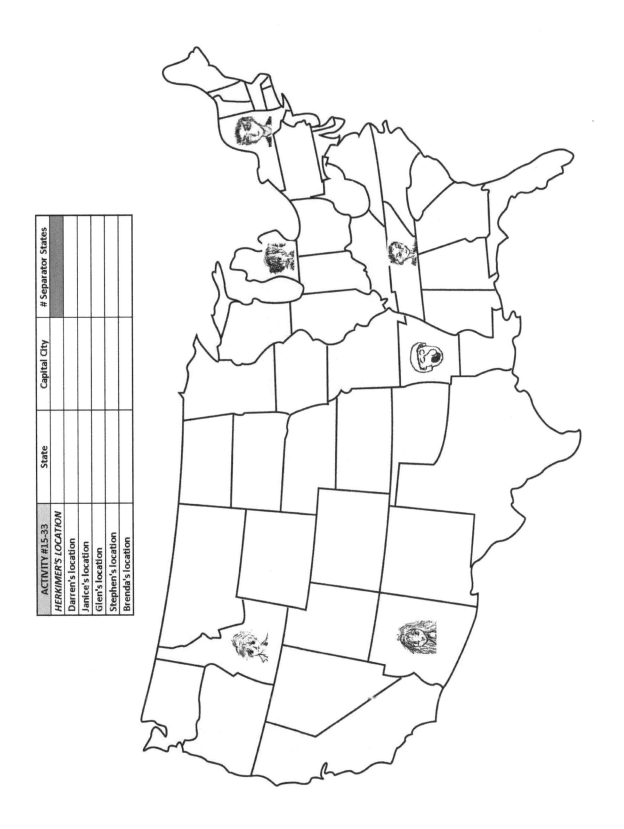

ACTIVITY #15-33	State	Capital City	# Separator States
HERKIMER'S LOCATION			
Darren's location			
Janice's location			
Glen's location			
Stephen's location			
Brenda's location			

On the previous page Herkimer
began his U.S. journeys in the state of
ARKANSAS

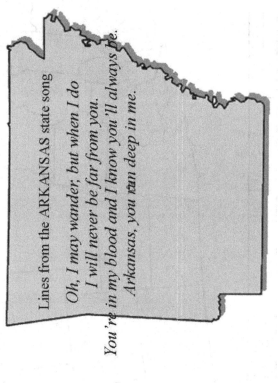

Lines from the ARKANSAS state song

Oh, I may wander, but when I do
I will never be far from you.
You're in my blood and I know you'll always be.
Arkansas, you run deep in me.

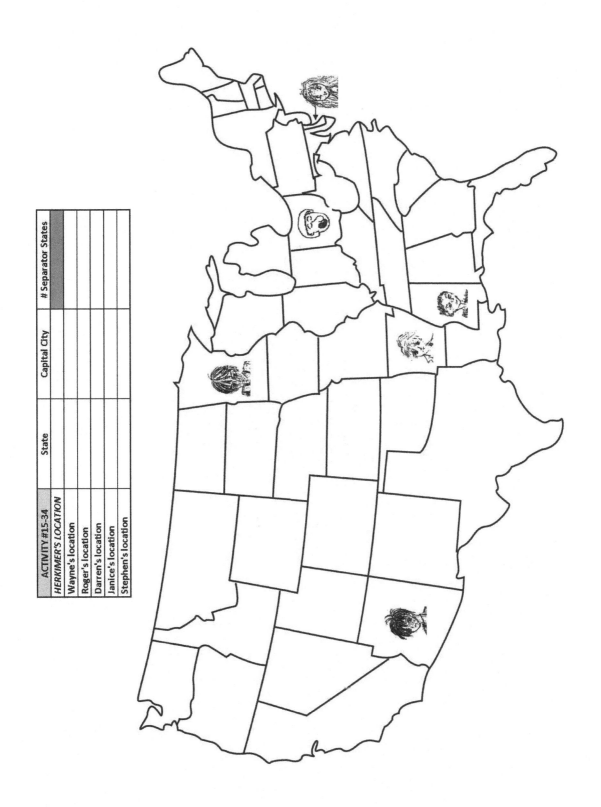

ACTIVITY #15-34	State	Capital City	# Separator States
HERKIMER'S LOCATION			
Wayne's location			
Roger's location			
Darren's location			
Janice's location			
Stephen's location			

On the previous page Herkimer
began his U.S. journeys in the state of
OHIO

Lines from the OHIO state song

Freedom is supreme in this majestic land;
Mighty factories seem to hum a tune, so grand.
Beautiful Ohio, thy wonders are in view,
Land where my dreams all come true.

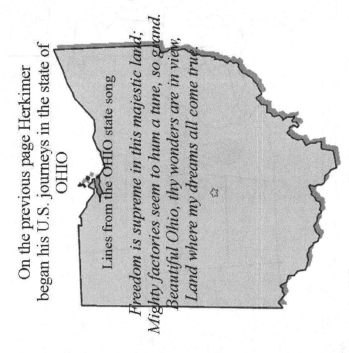

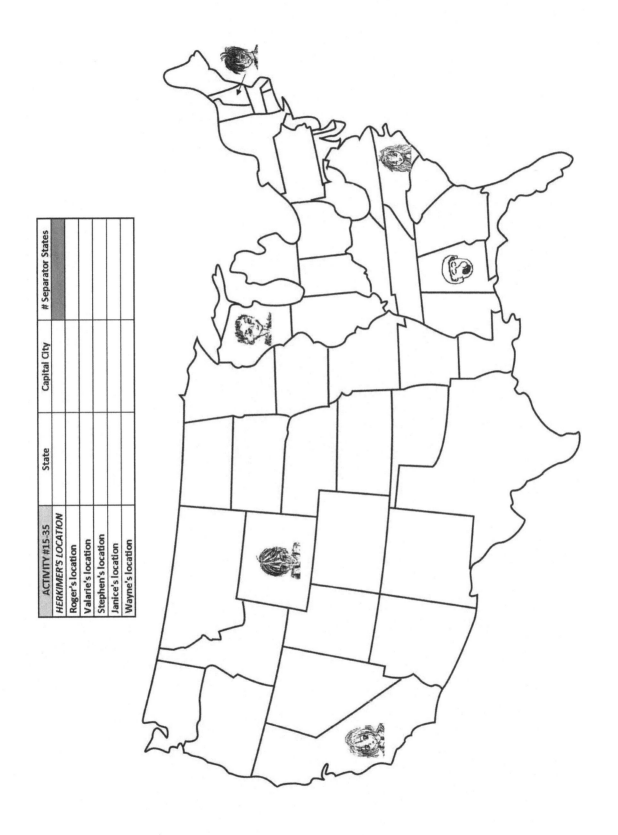

ACTIVITY #15-35	State	Capital City	# Separator States
HERKIMER'S LOCATION			
Roger's location			
Valarie's location			
Stephen's location			
Janice's location			
Wayne's location			

On the previous page Herkimer began his U.S. journeys in the state of ALABAMA

Lines from the ALABAMA state song

Strong-armed miners, sturdy farmers;
Loyal hears what'er we be
Alabama, Alabama
We will aye be true to thee!

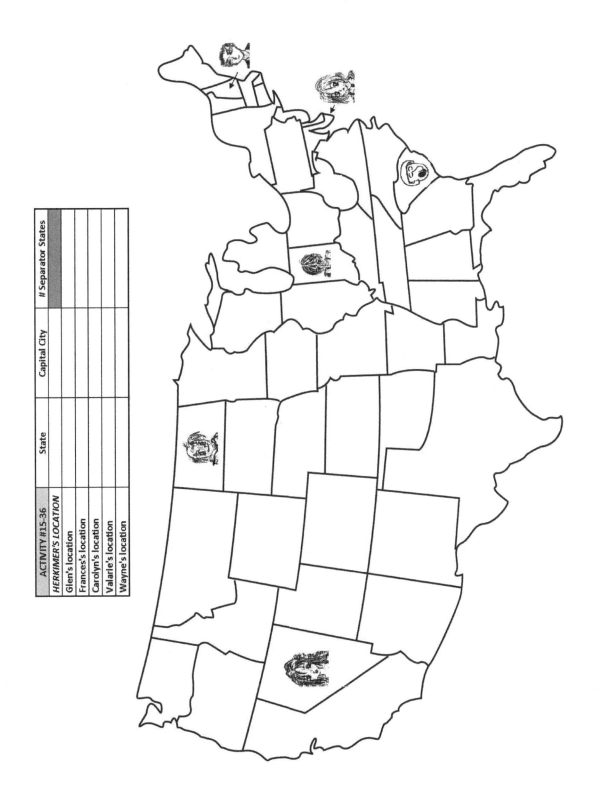

ACTIVITY #15-36	State	Capital City	# Separator States
HERKIMER'S LOCATION			
Glen's location			
Frances's location			
Carolyn's location			
Valarie's location			
Wayne's location			

On the previous page Herkimer
began his U.S. journeys in the state of
SOUTH CAROLINA

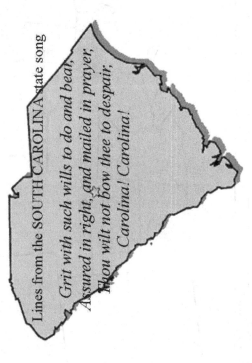

Lines from the SOUTH CAROLINA state song

Grit with such wills to do and bear,
Assured in right, and mailed in prayer,
Thou wilt not bow thee to despair,
Carolina! Carolina!

128

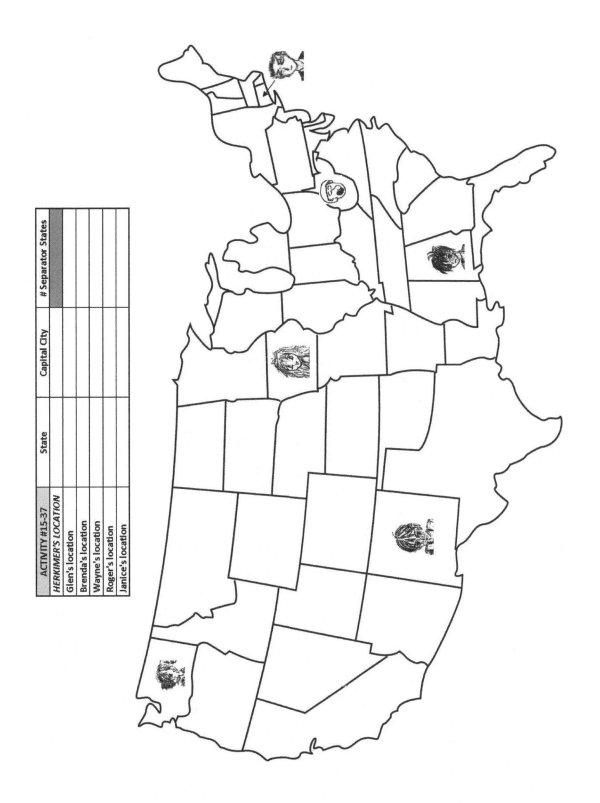

ACTIVITY #15-37	State	Capital City	# Separator States
HERKIMER'S LOCATION			
Glen's location			
Brenda's location			
Wayne's location			
Roger's location			
Janice's location			

On the previous page Herkimer began his U.S. journeys in the state of WEST VIRGINIA

Lines from the WEST VIRGINIA state song

Oh, the hills, beautiful hills,
How I love those West Virginia hills,
If o're sea o're land I roam, still I think of happy home,
And my friends among the West Virginia hills.

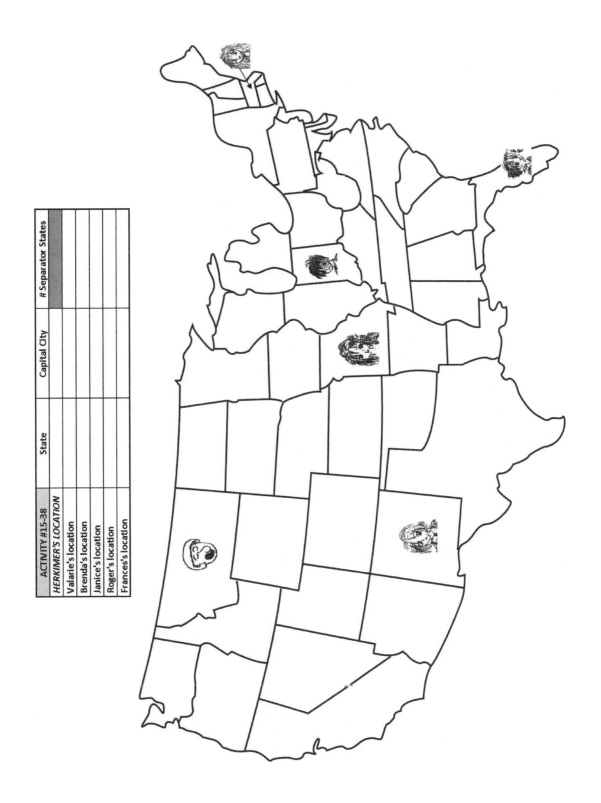

ACTIVITY #15-38	State	Capital City	# Separator States
HERKIMER'S LOCATION			
Valarie's location			
Brenda's location			
Janice's location			
Roger's location			
Frances's location			

On the previous page Herkimer
began his U.S. journeys in the state of
MONTANA

Lines from the MONTANA state song

Montana, Montana,
Glory of the West
Of all the states from coast to coast,
You're easily the best.

ACTIVITY #15-39	State	Capital City	# Separator States
HERKIMER'S LOCATION			
Wayne's location			
Brenda's location			
Janice's location			
Carolyn's location			
Stephen's location			

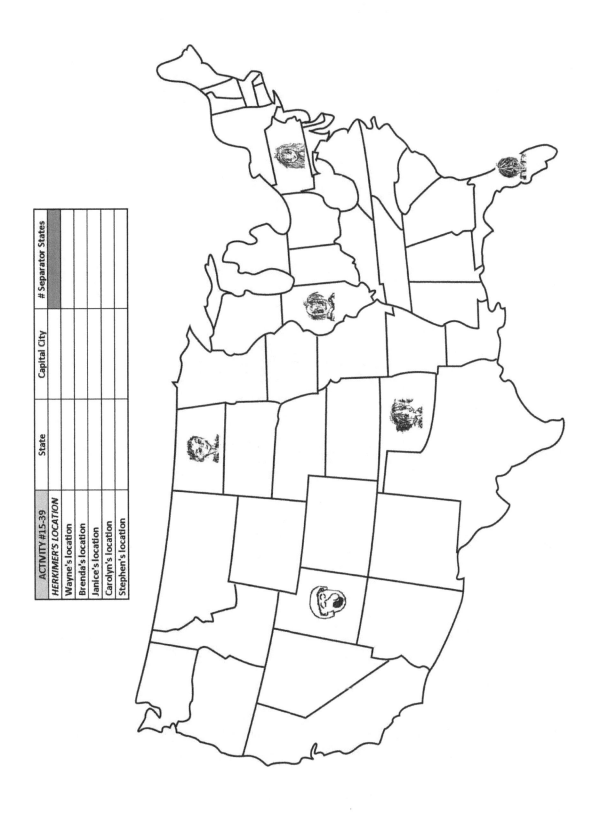

On the previous page Herkimer
began his U.S. journeys in the state of
UTAH

Lines from the UTAH state song

Utah! With its mountains and valleys.
Utah! With its canyons and streams.
You can go anywhere, but there's none that compare.
This is the place!

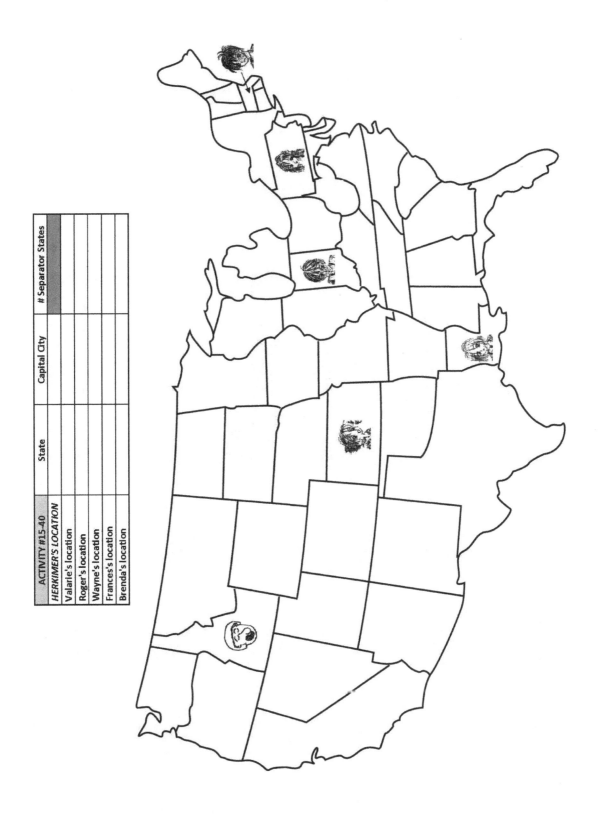

ACTIVITY #15-40	State	Capital City	# Separator States
HERKIMER'S LOCATION			
Valarie's location			
Roger's location			
Wayne's location			
Frances's location			
Brenda's location			

On the previous page Herkimer
began his U.S. journeys in the state of
IDAHO

Lines from the IDAHO state song

And here we have Idaho
Winning her way to fame.
Silver and gold in the sunlight blaze,
And romance lies in her name.

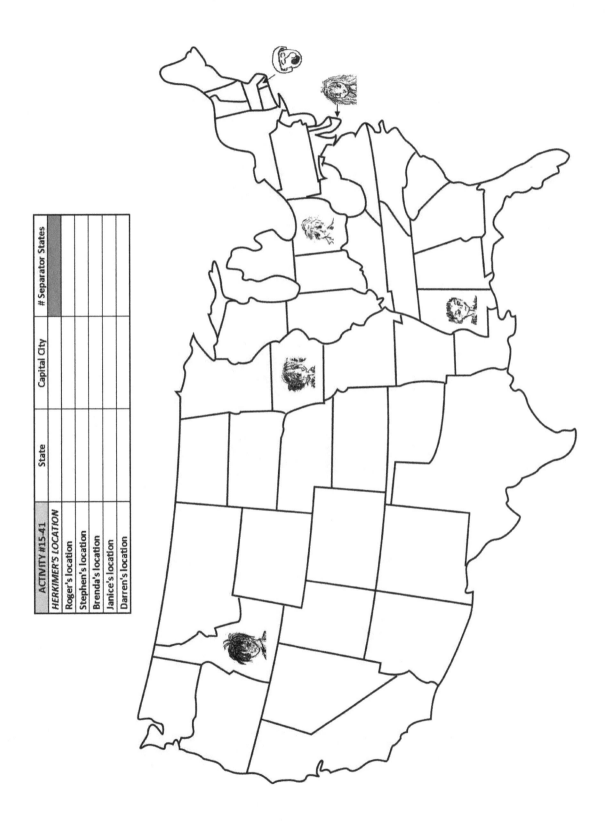

ACTIVITY #15-41	State	Capital City	# Separator States
HERKIMER'S LOCATION			
Roger's location			
Stephen's location			
Brenda's location			
Janice's location			
Darren's location			

On the previous page Herkimer
began his U.S. journeys in the state of
RHODE ISLAND

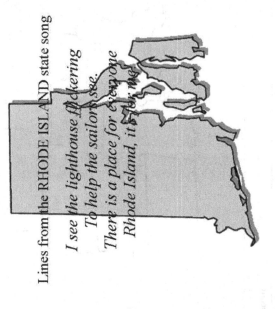

Lines from the RHODE ISLAND state song

I see the lighthouse flickering
To help the sailors see.
There is a place for everyone
Rhode Island, it's for me.

ACTIVITY #15-42	State	Capital City	# Separator States
HERKIMER'S LOCATION			
Valarie's location			
Glen's location			
Carolyn's location			
Roger's location			
Wayne's location			

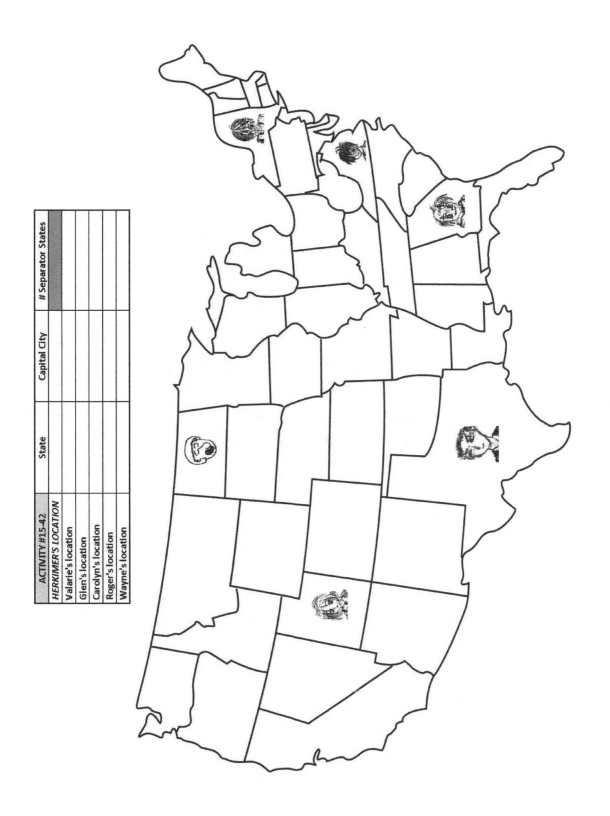

On the previous page Herkimer
began his U.S. journeys in the state of
NORTH DAKOTA

Lines from the NORTH DAKOTA state song

North Dakota, North Dakota,
With thy prairies wide and free,
All thy sons and daughters love thee,
Fairest state from sea to sea.

ACTIVITY #15-43	State	Capital City	# Separator States
HERKIMER'S LOCATION			
Darren's location			
Stephen's location			
Frances's location			
Brenda's location			
Janice's location			

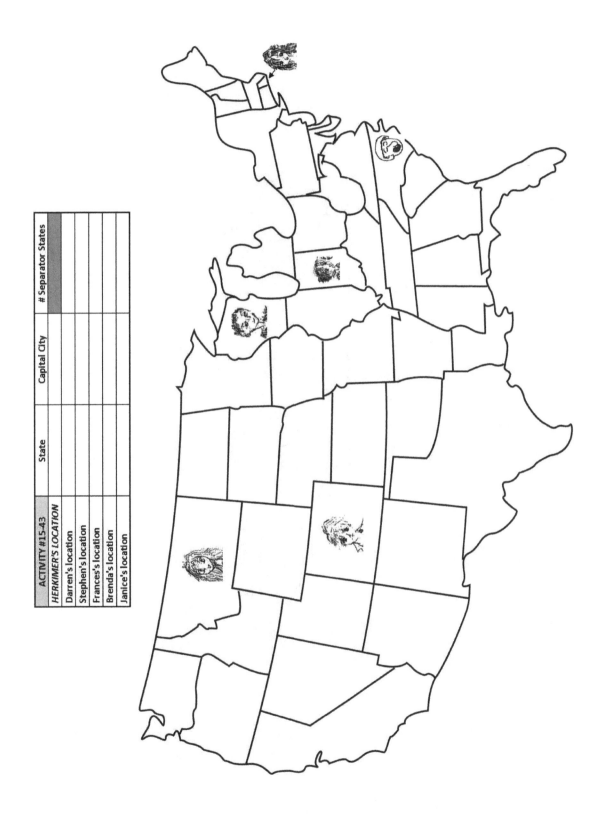

On the previous page Herkimer
began his U.S. journeys in the state of
NORTH CAROLINA

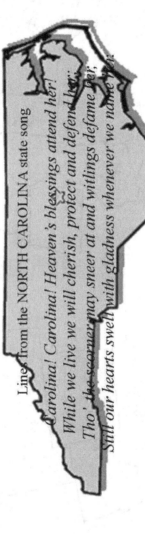

Lines from the NORTH CAROLINA state song

Carolina! Carolina! Heaven's blessings attend her!
While we live we will cherish, protect and defend her;
Tho' the scorner may sneer at and witlings defame her,
Still our hearts swell with gladness whenever we name her.

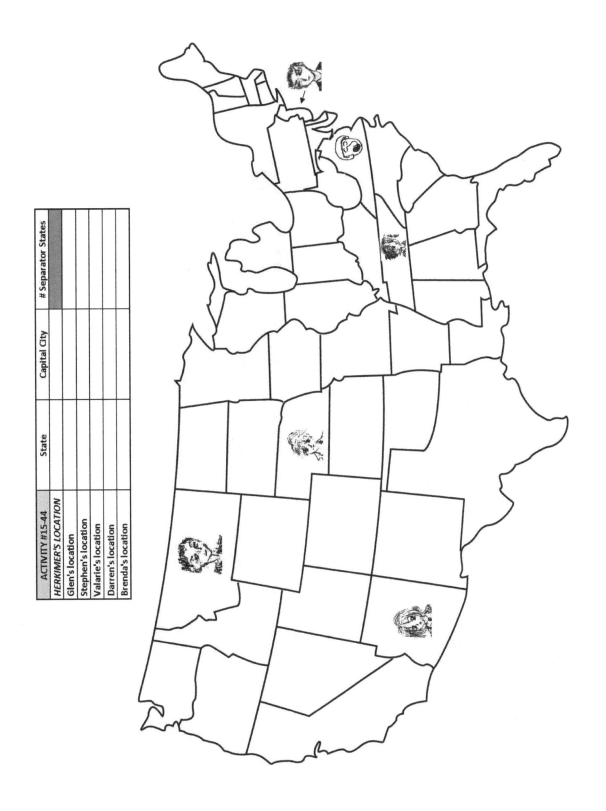

ACTIVITY #15-44	State	Capital City	# Separator States
HERKIMER'S LOCATION			
Glen's location			
Stephen's location			
Valarie's location			
Darren's location			
Brenda's location			

On the previous page Herkimer
began his U.S. journeys in the state of
VIRGINIA

Lines from the VIRGINIA state song

Carry me back to old Virginny,
There's were the cotton and the corn and tatoes grow,
There's where the bird warble sweet in the springtime,
There's were this old darkey's heart am long,d to go.

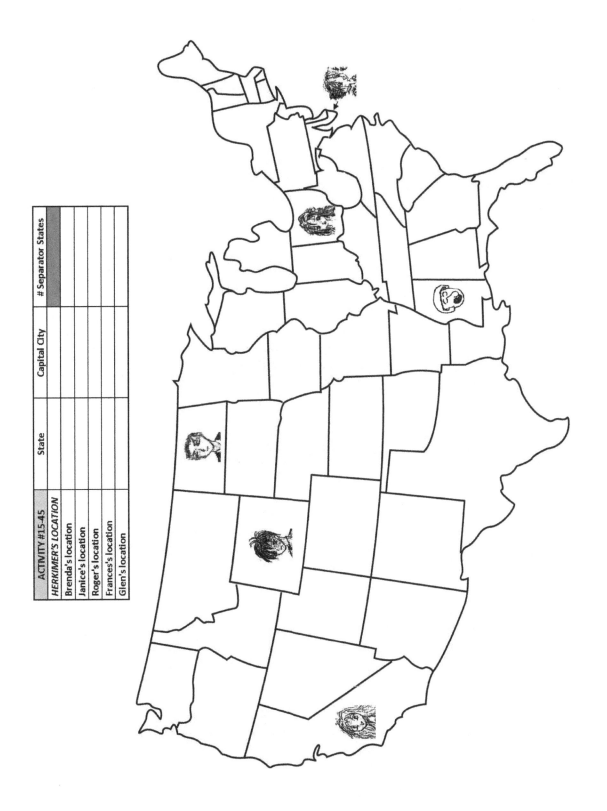

ACTIVITY #15-45	State	Capital City	# Separator States
HERKIMER'S LOCATION			
Brenda's location			
Janice's location			
Roger's location			
Frances's location			
Glen's location			

On the previous page Herkimer
began his U.S. journeys in the state of
MISSISSIPPI

Lines from the MISSISSIPPI state song

Go, Mississippi, get up and go,
Go, Mississippi, let the world know,
That our Mississippi is leading the show,
M-I-S-S-I-S-S-I-P-P-I

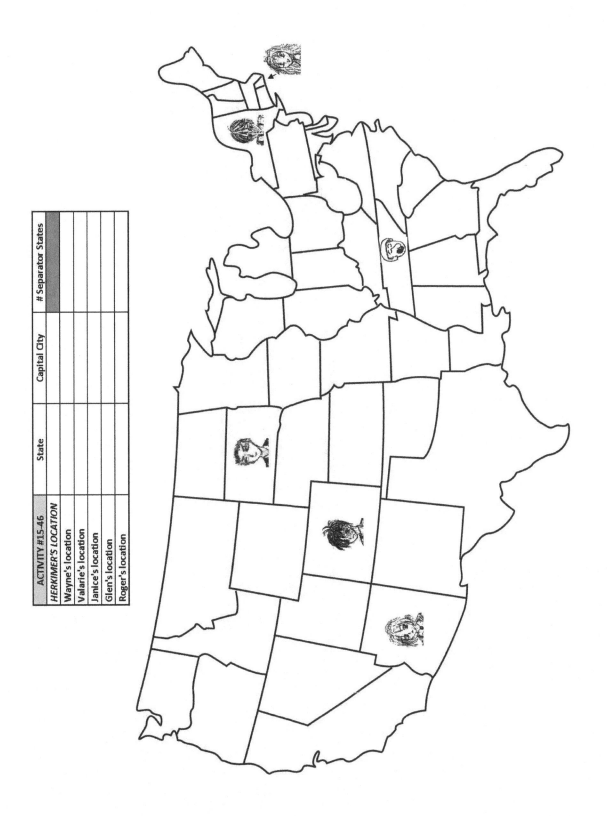

ACTIVITY #15-46	State	Capital City	# Separator States
HERKIMER'S LOCATION			
Wayne's location			
Valarie's location			
Janice's location			
Glen's location			
Roger's location			

On the previous page Herkimer
began his U.S. journeys in the state of
TENNESSEE

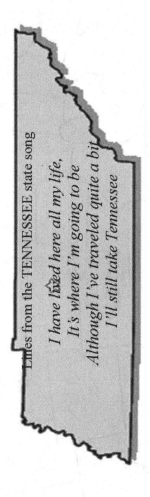

Lines from the TENNESSEE state song

I have lived here all my life,
It's where I'm going to be
Although I've traveled quite a bit
I'll still take Tennessee

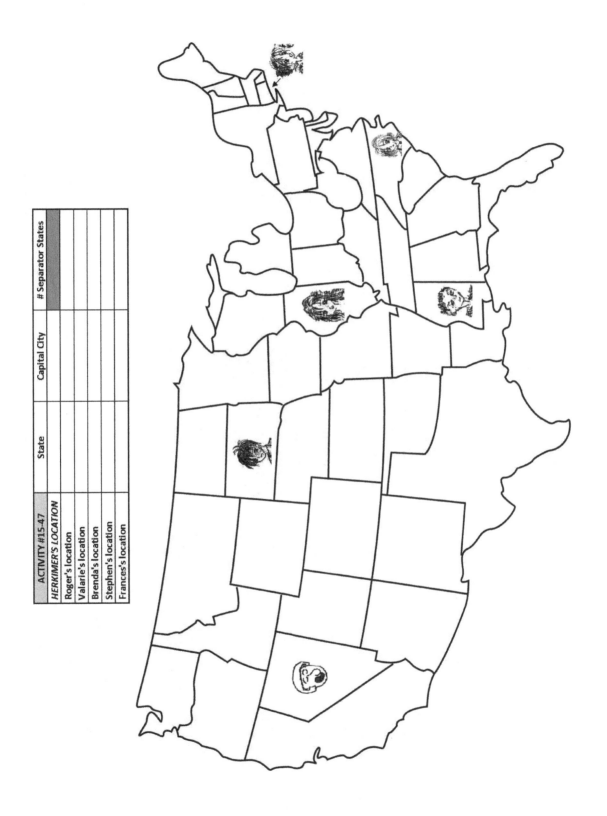

ACTIVITY #15-47	State	Capital City	# Separator States
HERKIMER'S LOCATION			
Roger's location			
Valarie's location			
Brenda's location			
Stephen's location			
Frances's location			

On the previous page Herkimer
began his U.S. journeys in the state of
NEVADA

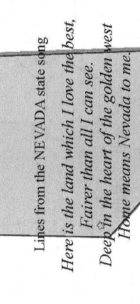

Lines from the NEVADA state song

Here is the land which I love the best,
Fairer than all I can see.
Deep in the heart of the golden west
Home means Nevada to me.

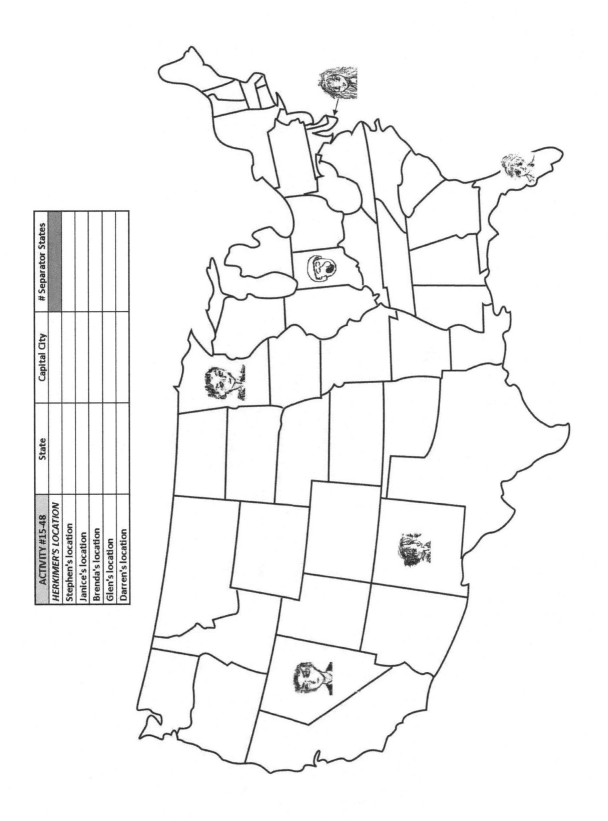

ACTIVITY #15-48	State	Capital City	# Separator States
HERKIMER'S LOCATION			
Stephen's location			
Janice's location			
Brenda's location			
Glen's location			
Darren's location			

151

On the previous page Herkimer
began his U.S. journeys in the state of
INDIANA

Lines from the INDIANA state song

Oh, the moonlight's fair tonight along the Wabsah,
From the fields there comes the breath of newmown hay.
Through the sycamores the candle lights are gleaming,
On the banks of the Wabash, far away.

The largest state of all had no bordering states.
It is the amazing state of
ALASKA

Lines from the ALASKA state song

The great North Star with its steady light,
Over land and sea a beacon bright.
Alaska's flag – to Alaskans dear,
The simple flag of a last frontier.

This wonderful state has no bordering state and is made up of many islands. This is the state of
HAWAII

Lines from the HAWAII state song

Hawaii's own true sons, be loyal to your chief
Your country's liege and lord the Alii.[1]
Father above us all, Kamehameha.[2]
Who guarded in the war with his ihe[3]

1. Alii (ah-lee-ee): Sovereign.
2. Kamehameha (Kah-may'-ha-may'-ha): King who first united the islands,
3. Ihe (ee-hay): Spear

> ## You can't get there from here.
>
> **(Old New England saying)**

But Herkimer sez:

Oh yes, you can! If you completed all 48 separator state challenge activities you discovered some amazing facts about travel between two states in our great country. Who, for instance, would believe that you can get from NEW MEXICO to VIRGINIA by going through just 3 other states?

If you have finished with the challenges in U.S. Activity Set #15 then relax for a bit and when you're ready move right along on to the series of educational challenges that follow this page. There is more fun ahead that has been prepared by those clever students in the Stat Pack.

Lines from
THE STAR SPANGLED BANNER

And the rocket's red glare, the bombs bursting in air,
Gave proof through the night that our flag was
still there.
Oh, say does that star-spangled banner yet wave
O'er the land of the free and the home of the brave.

U. S. ACTIVITY #16

Created by all members of the STAT PACK

STATE IDENTIFICATION CHALLENGE FROM SEPARATOR STATE HISTOGRAMS

If necessary, read or reread details relating to the STATE IDENTIFICATION CHALLENGE in the Preface. States were ordered by random selection. The histograms show the separator states distribution for each of the 48 states excluding Alaska and Hawaii. Your challenge is to identify each state from the displayed provided by the Pack.

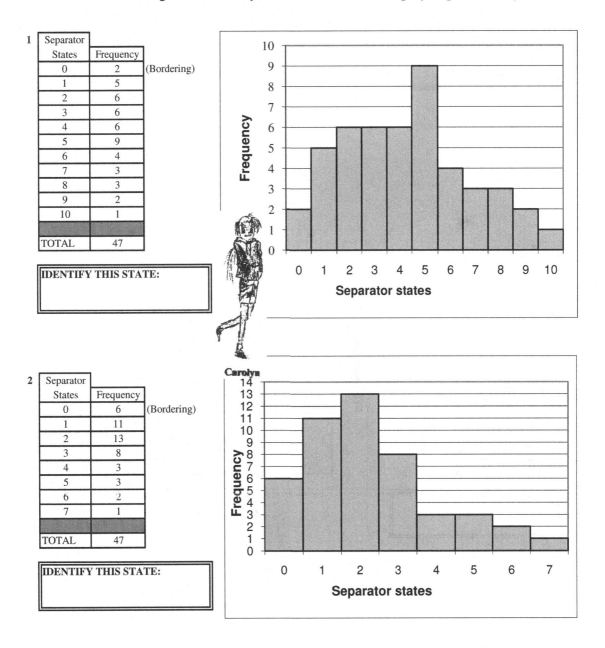

1

Separator States	Frequency	
0	2	(Bordering)
1	5	
2	6	
3	6	
4	6	
5	9	
6	4	
7	3	
8	3	
9	2	
10	1	
TOTAL	47	

IDENTIFY THIS STATE:

2

Separator States	Frequency	
0	6	(Bordering)
1	11	
2	13	
3	8	
4	3	
5	3	
6	2	
7	1	
TOTAL	47	

IDENTIFY THIS STATE:

157

3

Separator States	Frequency	
0	4	(Bordering)
1	11	
2	16	
3	7	
4	3	
5	3	
6	2	
7	1	
TOTAL	47	

IDENTIFY THIS STATE:

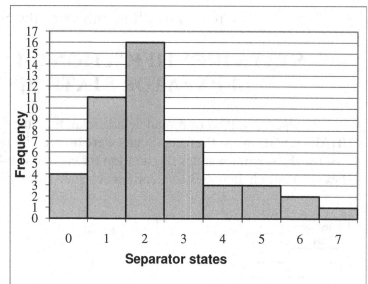

4

Separator States	Frequency	
0	3	(Bordering)
1	5	
2	6	
3	6	
4	6	
5	8	
6	4	
7	3	
8	3	
9	2	
10	1	
TOTAL	47	

IDENTIFY THIS STATE:

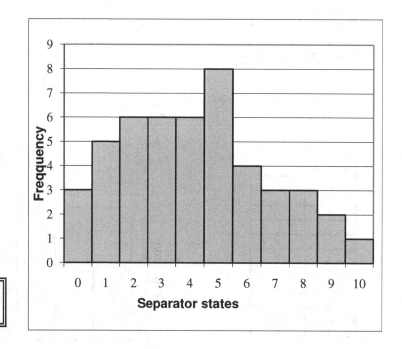

5

Separator States	Frequency	
0	8	(Bordering)
1	16	
2	10	
3	7	
4	3	
5	2	
6	1	
TOTAL	47	

IDENTIFY THIS STATE:

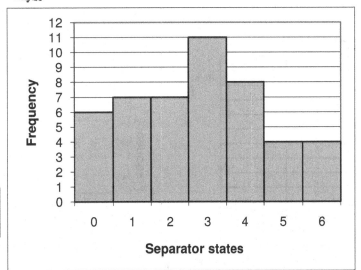

Wayne

6

Separator States	Frequency	
0	6	(Bordering)
1	7	
2	7	
3	11	
4	8	
5	4	
6	4	
TOTAL	47	

IDENTIFY THIS STATE:

7

Separator States	Frequency	
0	8	(Bordering)
1	13	
2	9	
3	7	
4	7	
5	2	
6	1	
TOTAL	47	

IDENTIFY THIS STATE:

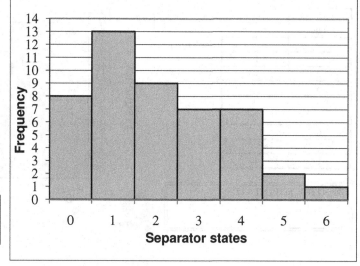

8

Separator States	Frequency	
0	3	(Bordering)
1	3	
2	2	
3	4	
4	4	
5	5	
6	10	
7	8	
8	4	
9	4	
TOTAL	47	

IDENTIFY THIS STATE:

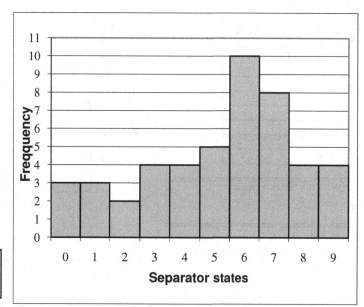

160

9

Separator States	Frequency	
0	4	(Bordering)
1	6	
2	12	
3	10	
4	6	
5	5	
6	4	
TOTAL	47	

IDENTIFY THIS STATE:

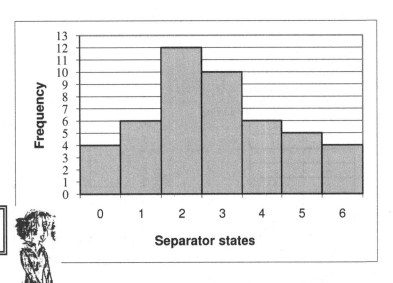

Brenda

10

Separator States	Frequency	
0	6	(Bordering)
1	7	
2	11	
3	10	
4	4	
5	3	
6	3	
7	2	
8	1	
TOTAL	47	

IDENTIFY THIS STATE:

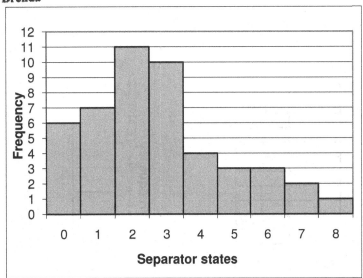

161

11

Separator States	Frequency	
0	4	(Bordering)
1	8	
2	11	
3	9	
4	7	
5	5	
6	2	
7	1	
TOTAL	47	

IDENTIFY THIS STATE:

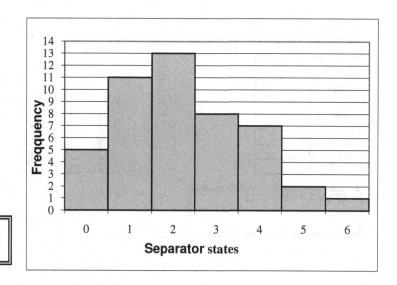

12

Separator States	Frequency	
0	5	(Bordering)
1	11	
2	13	
3	8	
4	7	
5	2	
6	1	
TOTAL	47	

IDENTIFY THIS STATE:

13

Separator States	Frequency	
0	4	(Bordering)
1	4	
2	5	
3	6	
4	6	
5	9	
6	4	
7	3	
8	3	
9	2	
10	1	
TOTAL	47	

IDENTIFY THIS STATE:

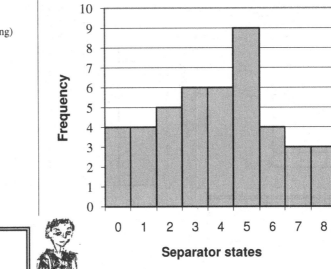

Stephen

14

Separator States	Frequency	
0	7	(Bordering)
1	13	
2	12	
3	8	
4	6	
5	1	
TOTAL	47	

IDENTIFY THIS STATE:

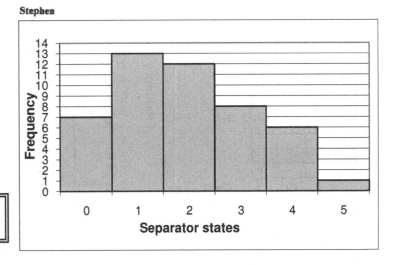

163

15

Separator States	Frequency	
0	7	(Bordering)
1	9	
2	10	
3	8	
4	4	
5	3	
6	3	
7	2	
8	1	
TOTAL	47	

IDENTIFY THIS STATE:

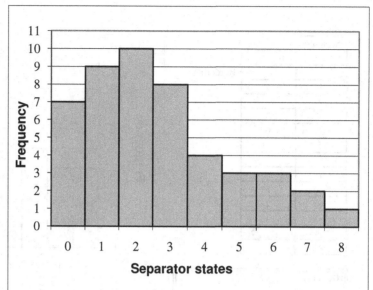

16

Separator States	Frequency	
0	5	(Bordering)
1	5	
2	11	
3	9	
4	7	
5	7	
6	2	
7	1	
TOTAL	47	

IDENTIFY THIS STATE:

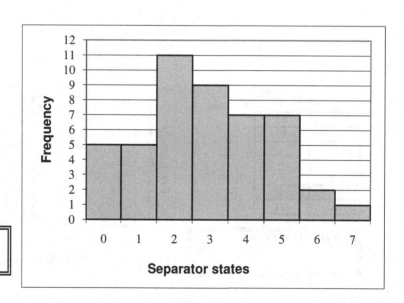

17

Separator States	Frequency	
0	4	(Bordering)
1	6	
2	10	
3	14	
4	6	
5	4	
6	2	
7	1	
TOTAL	47	

IDENTIFY THIS STATE:

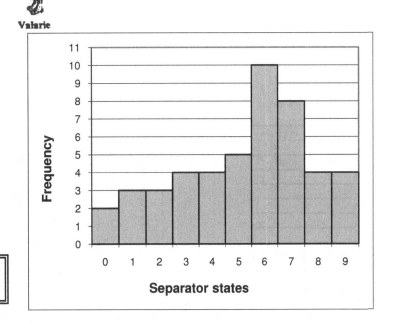

Valarie

18

Separator States	Frequency	
0	2	(Bordering)
1	3	
2	3	
3	4	
4	4	
5	5	
6	10	
7	8	
8	4	
9	4	
TOTAL	47	

IDENTIFY THIS STATE:

165

19

Separator States	Frequency	
0	4	(Bordering)
1	7	
2	10	
3	9	
4	7	
5	7	
6	2	
7	1	
TOTAL	47	

IDENTIFY THIS STATE:

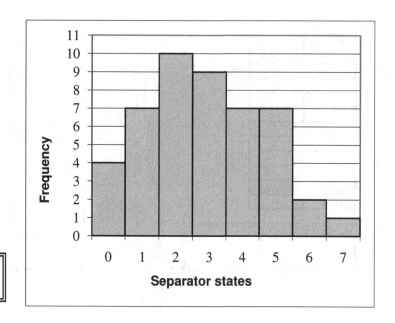

20

Separator States	Frequency	
0	4	(Bordering)
1	8	
2	11	
3	9	
4	8	
5	6	
6	1	
TOTAL	47	

IDENTIFY THIS STATE:

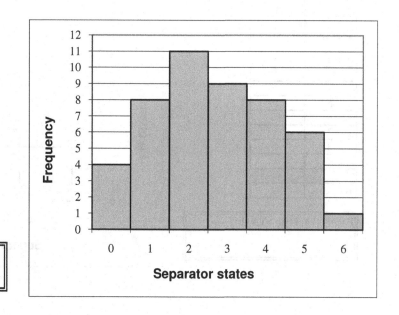

21

Separator States	Frequency	
0	6	(Bordering)
1	10	
2	14	
3	8	
4	3	
5	3	
6	2	
7	1	
TOTAL	47	

IDENTIFY THIS STATE:

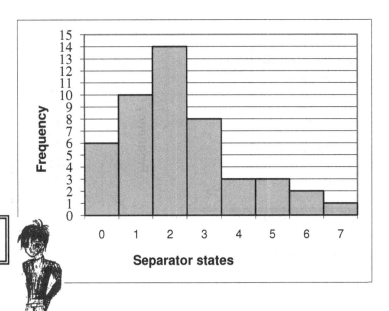

Roger

22

Separator States	Frequency	
0	6	(Bordering)
1	13	
2	15	
3	4	
4	3	
5	3	
6	2	
7	1	
TOTAL	47	

IDENTIFY THIS STATE:

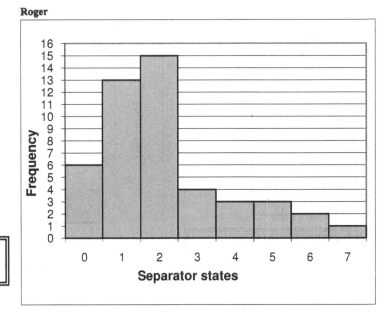

23

Separator	
States	Frequency
0	5
1	9
2	13
3	11
4	5
5	4
TOTAL	47

(Bordering)

IDENTIFY THIS STATE:

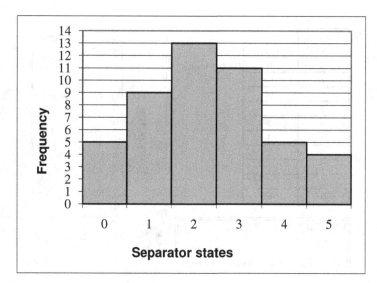

24

Separator	
States	Frequency
0	2
1	4
2	6
3	11
4	9
5	8
6	6
7	1
TOTAL	47

(Bordering)

IDENTIFY THIS STATE:

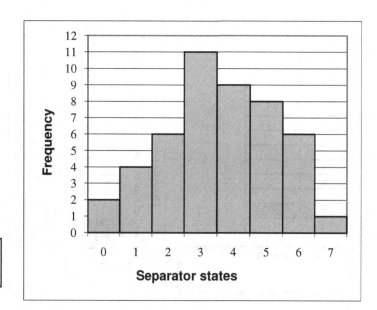

25

Separator States	Frequency	
0	6	(Bordering)
1	9	
2	6	
3	5	
4	8	
5	4	
6	3	
7	3	
8	2	
9	1	
TOTAL	47	

IDENTIFY THIS STATE:

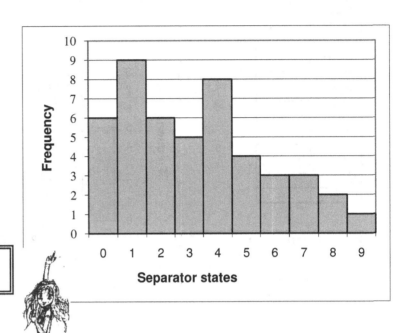

Janice

26

Separator States	Frequency	
0	5	(Bordering)
1	6	
2	5	
3	5	
4	10	
5	8	
6	4	
7	4	
TOTAL	47	

IDENTIFY THIS STATE:

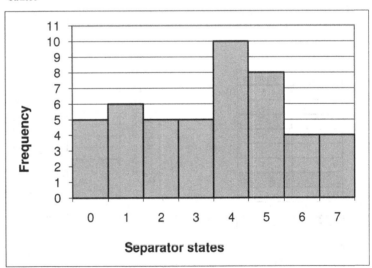

169

27

Separator States	Frequency	
0	5	(Bordering)
1	9	
2	9	
3	10	
4	5	
5	3	
6	3	
7	2	
8	1	
TOTAL	47	

IDENTIFY THIS STATE:

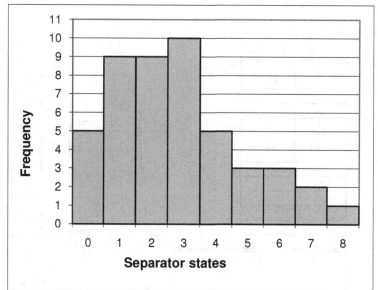

28

Separator States	Frequency	
0	5	(Bordering)
1	9	
2	13	
3	10	
4	6	
5	4	
TOTAL	47	

IDENTIFY THIS STATE:

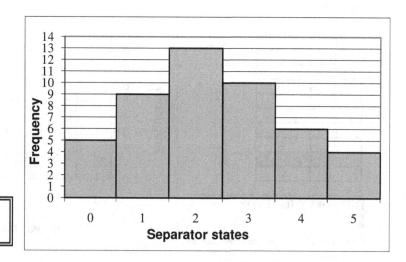

170

29

Separator States	Frequency	
0	3	(Bordering)
1	4	
2	8	
3	10	
4	9	
5	5	
6	4	
7	4	
TOTAL	47	

IDENTIFY THIS STATE:

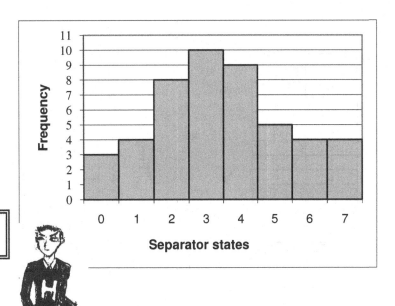

Glen

30

Separator States	Frequency	
0	3	(Bordering)
1	5	
2	9	
3	9	
4	9	
5	6	
6	3	
7	2	
8	1	
TOTAL	47	

IDENTIFY THIS STATE:

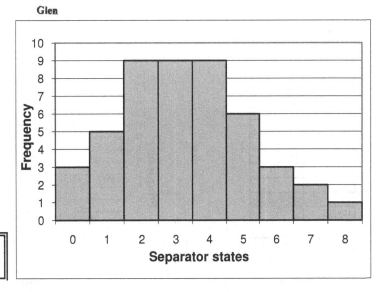

31

Separator States	Frequency	
0	4	(Bordering)
1	7	
2	10	
3	14	
4	9	
5	2	
6	1	
TOTAL	47	

IDENTIFY THIS STATE:

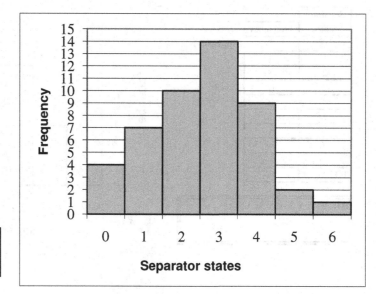

32

Separator States	Frequency	
0	3	(Bordering)
1	6	
2	10	
3	13	
4	10	
5	5	
TOTAL	47	

IDENTIFY THIS STATE:

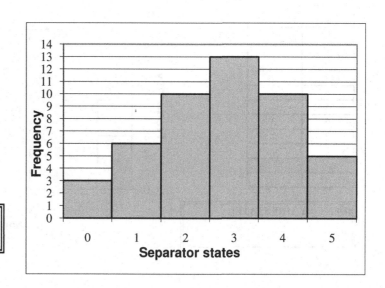

33

Separator States	Frequency	
0	6	(Bordering)
1	11	
2	7	
3	10	
4	4	
5	3	
6	3	
7	2	
8	1	
TOTAL	47	

IDENTIFY THIS STATE:

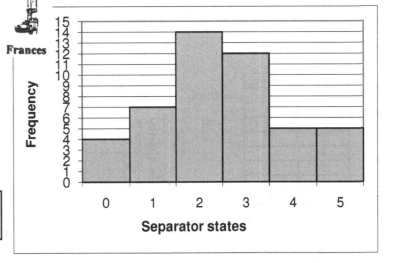

Frances

34

Separator States	Frequency	
0	4	(Bordering)
1	7	
2	14	
3	12	
4	5	
5	5	
TOTAL	47	

IDENTIFY THIS STATE:

35

Separator States	Frequency	
0	3	(Bordering)
1	6	
2	6	
3	6	
4	10	
5	8	
6	4	
7	4	
TOTAL	47	

IDENTIFY THIS STATE:

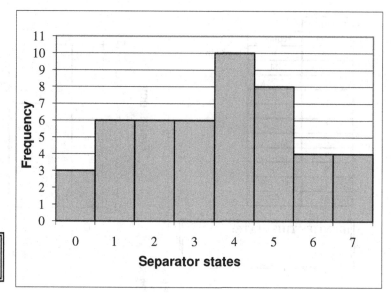

36

Separator States	Frequency	
0	6	(Bordering)
1	11	
2	12	
3	8	
4	4	
5	3	
6	2	
7	1	
TOTAL	47	

IDENTIFY THIS STATE:

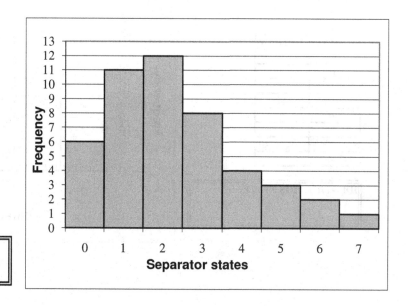

37

Separator States	Frequency	
0	3	(Bordering)
1	5	
2	4	
3	4	
4	5	
5	10	
6	8	
7	4	
8	4	
TOTAL	47	

IDENTIFY THIS STATE:

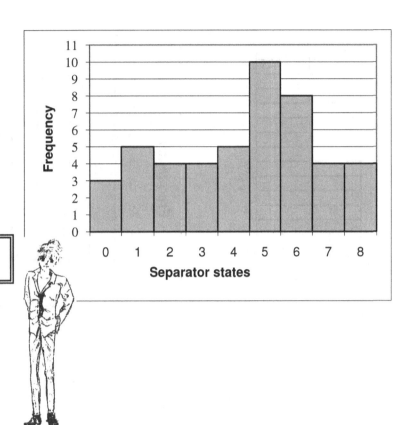

Darren

38

Separator States	Frequency	
0	1	(Bordering)
1	2	
2	3	
3	2	
4	4	
5	4	
6	5	
7	10	
8	8	
9	4	
10	4	
TOTAL	47	

IDENTIFY THIS STATE:

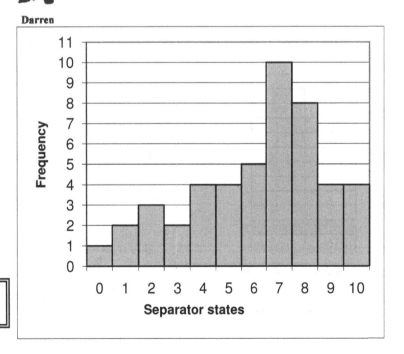

39

Separator States	Frequency	
0	5	(Bordering)
1	5	
2	6	
3	5	
4	5	
5	8	
6	4	
7	3	
8	3	
9	2	
10	1	
TOTAL	47	

IDENTIFY THIS STATE:

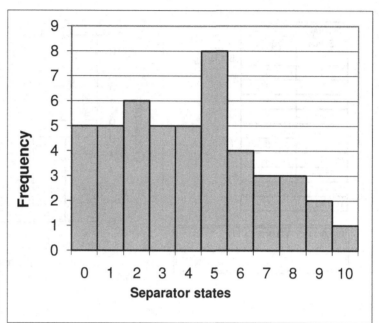

40

Separator States	Frequency	
0	5	(Bordering)
1	3	
2	4	
3	4	
4	5	
5	10	
6	8	
7	4	
8	4	
TOTAL	47	

IDENTIFY THIS STATE:

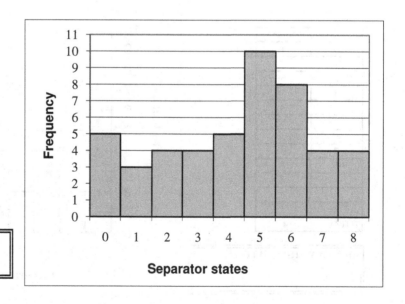

176

41

Separator States	Frequency	
0	3	(Bordering)
1	5	
2	12	
3	12	
4	7	
5	2	
6	3	
7	2	
8	1	
TOTAL	47	

IDENTIFY THIS STATE:

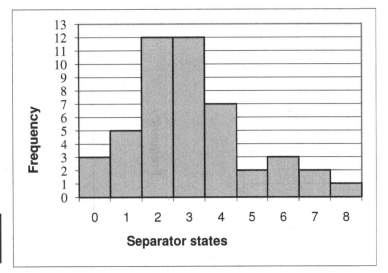

42

Separator States	Frequency	
0	2	(Bordering)
1	4	
2	5	
3	10	
4	9	
5	7	
6	7	
7	2	
8	1	
TOTAL	47	

IDENTIFY THIS STATE:

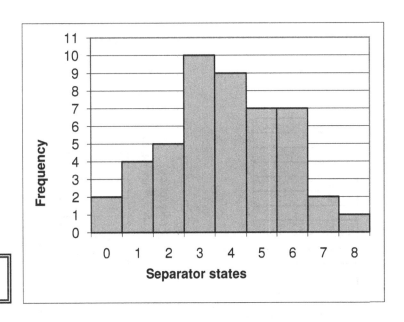

43

Separator States	Frequency	
0	4	(Bordering)
1	8	
2	8	
3	6	
4	8	
5	4	
6	3	
7	3	
8	2	
9	1	
TOTAL	47	

IDENTIFY THIS STATE:

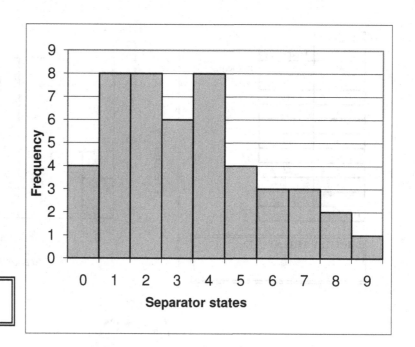

44

Separator States	Frequency	
0	3	(Bordering)
1	4	
2	5	
3	4	
4	5	
5	10	
6	8	
7	4	
8	4	
TOTAL	47	

IDENTIFY THIS STATE:

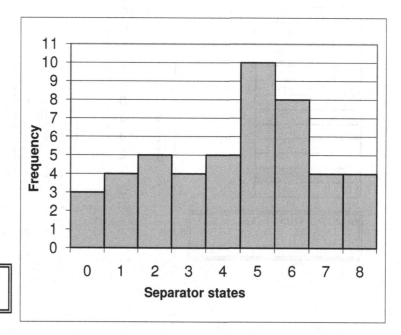

178

45

Separator States	Frequency	
0	5	(Bordering)
1	7	
2	7	
3	7	
4	8	
5	4	
6	3	
7	3	
8	2	
9	1	
TOTAL	47	

IDENTIFY THIS STATE:

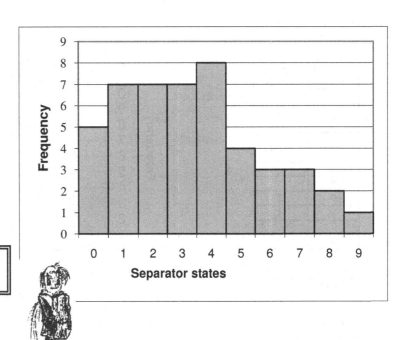

Carolyn

46

Separator States	Frequency	
0	6	(Bordering)
1	7	
2	6	
3	6	
4	9	
5	4	
6	3	
7	3	
8	2	
9	1	
TOTAL	47	

IDENTIFY THIS STATE:

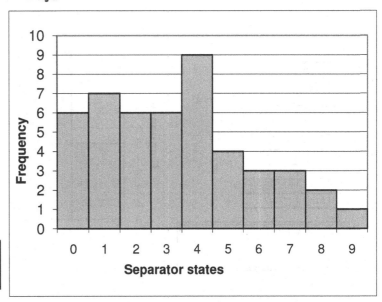

179

47

Separator States	Frequency	
0	4	(Bordering)
1	7	
2	12	
3	12	
4	4	
5	2	
6	3	
7	2	
8	1	
TOTAL	47	

IDENTIFY THIS STATE:

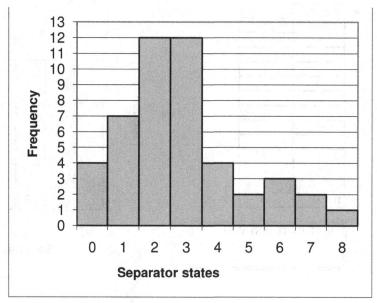

48

Separator States	Frequency	
0	5	(Bordering)
1	11	
2	11	
3	8	
4	7	
5	5	
TOTAL	47	

IDENTIFY THIS STATE:

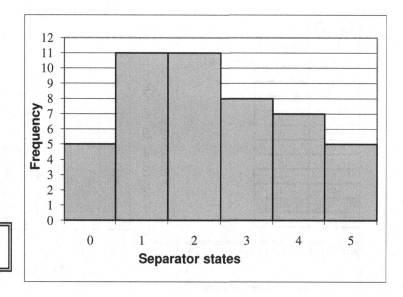

> *You can't head off a man who won't quit.*
>
> **(Ken Alstad,** *Savvy Sayin's)*

Herkimer sez:

Hey, you've got this far! Well done! I bet you have increased your knowledge of the United States considerably as a result of your participation in the activities that have been presented in this book. Now move ahead to the fun
United States trivia quiz
created by those neat young students
in the Stat Pack.

Answers to questions written in **bold** type can be found in this book.

Answers to questions written in *italics* might require a bit of outside research.

Good luck and have fun with it!

Lines from
THE MARINE'S HYMN

From the Halls of Montezuma
To the shores of Tripoli
We fight our country's battles
In the air, on land, and sea.

United States Trivia Quiz

1	*Which state is the #1 producer of peanuts, pecans, and peaches?*
2	**Consider the letter x. If you add the number of state names containing the letter and the number of capital city names containing the letter, what is the total?**
3	*Which state capital city is on the Delaware River?*
4	**How many state names contain the letter b?**
5	**Which are the only two states whose names begin with double consonants?**
6	*In which major U.S. City do the Monongahela and Allegheny Rivers meet to form the Ohio River?*
7	*On which river is Washington, D.C. located?*
8	*Which is the only state bordered by the rivers on both its east and west boundaries?*
9	*Which east coast state has the shortest coastline?*
10	*How many states have no counties?*
11	**Which states have fewer representatives than senators in Congress?**
12	*Which is the only state to have different designs on the two sides of its state flag?*
13	**Which 11-letter state name contains only 4 letters of the alphabet?**
14	**How many states were named after a U. S. President?**
15	*Which state capital city is named in honor of the third president of the U.S.?*
16	**How many states have more than 1,000 people per square mile?**
17	**Which state name contains only 3 letters of the alphabet?**
18	*Which state has a coastline that is longer than the length of all other state coastlines combined?*
19	**Which four state names have the same first letter as their respective capital cities?**
20	*Which of the contiguous 48 states has the northernmost land location?*
21	**Which is the only state whose name begins with the letter A but does not end with the letter a?**
22	*Which state contains the oldest state university in the United States?*
23	*Which is the only state whose flag is not rectangular?*
24	**How many states have a shoreline along at least one of the five Great Lakes?**
25	**Which state has the largest number of bordering states?**
26	**Which state is the only one whose name has just one syllable?**
27	*Which state was the first to give women the right to vote?*
28	*Which state capital city has the highest elevation?*
29	**How many state names contain a specific letter at least three times?**
30	*Which state has no location that is more than 345 feet above sea level?*
31	**How many states were named in honor of a person?**
32	*In which state was the first intercollegiate football game played?*
33	*Which state contains the tallest building on the North American continent?*
34	*Which state has 2 non-connecting rivers with the same name?*
35	*Which is the only state that borders 3 Canadian provinces?*

36	**How many state names contain the letter y?**
37	*"Home on the Range" is the official state song of which state?*
38	**Which state has the greatest percentage of its border as coastline?**
39	**In terms of population, which is the smallest state capital city?**
40	*The praying mantis is the state insect of which state?*
41	*Which capital city originally had the word "Great" as part of its name?*
42	**How many state names contain the letter f?**
43	*Which inland state has the most shoreline?*
44	**How many states have less than 10 people per square mile?**
45	*In which state was Elvis Presley born?*
46	**How many of the Great Lakes have only U. S. coastlines?**
47	*Which large U.S. City, not a state capital, is known as "the City of Roses?"*
48	**The roadrunner is the official bird of which state?**
49	*Which are the northernmost, westernmost, easternmost and southernmost states?*
50	**How many state names contain the letter k more than once?**
51	**Which letter is the most common first letter in state capital city names?**
52	*Which is the only state whose entire border has no straight line section?*
53	*Which state capital city is known as the Sailing Capital of the world?*
54	*Which four state capital cities are named after cities in England?*
55	*Which state contains the town of Dixon, the boyhood home of President Ronald Reagan?*
56	*Which state has more mountain ranges than any other state?*
57	**How many names of state capital cities begin with the letter C?**
58	**How many states share a border with Tennessee?**
59	**How many states share a border with California?**
60	*The name of which state capital means "sheltered harbor"?*
61	**How many states share a border with Canada?**
62	**Which is the only state whose name has no common letters with the name of its capital city?**
63	**Which four states share a common boundary?**
64	**Which state name is the only one starting with two vowels?**
65	**(a) How many state names begin with the letter J? (b) How many state capital city names begin with the letter J?**
66	*Which state capital is the home of the National Cowboy Hall of Fame?*
67	**How many states have borders that are just four straight sides?**
68	**How many states have a direction in their names?**
69	**How many states share a border with South Carolina?**
70	*Which state raises more turkeys than any other state?*
71	**How many state names contain only one of the vowels *a, e, i, o, u*?**
72	**How many state names contain a specific letter 4 times?**
73	**How many states have the word "New" in their names?**
74	**How many state capital city names contain 3 words?**

75	**How many states share a border with Michigan?**
76	**How many states entered the union before 1900?**
77	*Which state contains 75% of the land in the U.S. with an altitude exceeding 10,000 feet?*
78	*Which state has more miles of river than any other state?*
79	*How many islands make up the state of Hawaii?*
80	**How many states share a border with Mexico?**
81	**How many state capital cities have a population exceeding one million?**
82	**Which two states border Washington, D.C.?**
83	*Which state has a town called Hell?*
84	*Which state has the largest lake entirely within its borders?*
85	*Which state has 75% of its land area covered by forests?*
86	**How many state names contain two words?**
87	*What is the actual color of bluegrass in Kentucky, the Bluegrass State?*
88	*Which state has milk as its official beverage?*
89	**Which state shares a border with just one other state?**
90	*How many states have their lowest elevation point below sea level?*
91	**In a listing of the 50 state names, how many letters of the alphabet appear only once in the entire list?**
92	**In the list of 50 state names, which letter occurs most frequently?**
93	**Which state has the most people per square mile?**
94	**In a listing of the 50 state names, which letter occurs the least number of times?**
95	**In a listing of the 50 state capital city names, how many times does the letter Q appear?**
96	**How many state capital city names contain the word "City"?**
97	*In which state is the Pro Football Hall of Fame located?*
98	**In terms of land area, which are the three largest states?**
99	*Which state produces, by far, the most blueberries?*
100	**Which state has the property that one can get into any of its 6 bordering states by going directly south from somewhere in the state?**

United States

185

Lines from
THE UNITED STATES AIR FORCE THEME SONG

Off we go into the wild blue yonder,
Climbing high into the sun,
Here they come, zooming to meet our
thunder;
At 'em boys, give 'er the gun!

SOLUTIONS

FOR

SELECTED

ACTIVITIES

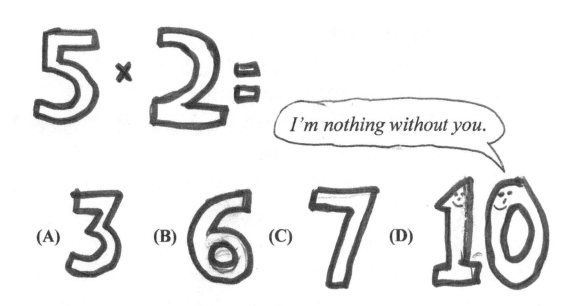

5 × 2 =

I'm nothing without you.

(A) 3   (B) 6   (C) 7   (D) 10

13 stars

15 stars

U.S. ACTIVITY #1 SOLUTIONS

Number of state names beginning with alphabetic letter

Letter	#	State names beginning with letter
A	4	ALABAMA, ALASKA, ARIZONA, ARKANSAS
B	0	
C	3	CALFORNIA,COLORADO, CONNECTICUT
D	1	DELAWARE
E	0	
F	1	FLORIDA
G	1	GEORGIA
H	1	HAWAII
I	4	IDAHO, ILLINOIS, INDIANA, IOWA
J	0	
K	2	KANSAS, KENTUCKY
L	1	LOUISIANA
M	8	MAINE, MARYLAND, MASSACHUSETTS, MICHIGAN, MINNESOTA, MISSISSIPPI, MISSOURI, MONTANA
N	8	NEBRASKA, NEVADA, NEW HAMPSHIRE, NEW JERSEY, NEW MEXICO, NEW YORK, NORTH CAROLINA, NORTH DAKOTA
O	3	OHIO, OKLAHOMA, OREGON
P	1	PENNSYLVANIA
Q	0	
R	1	RHODE ISLAND
S	2	SOUTH CAROLINA, SOUTH DAKOTA
T	2	TENNESSEE, TEXAS
U	1	UTAH
V	2	VERMONT, VIRGINIA
W	4	WASHINGTON, WEST VIRGINIA, WISCONSIN, WYOMING
X	0	
Y	0	
Z	0	

20 stars

21 stars

U. S. ACTIVITY #2 SOLUTIONS

NUMBER OF LETTERS IN STATE NAME

Spreadsheet by Valarie and Darren

In the frequency histogram below fill the 50 rectangles with the 50 state names so they are correctly categorized by the number of letters in the name.

FREQUENCY

NUMBER OF LETTERS IN STATE NAME	States (stacked from bottom)	Frequency
4	IOWA, OHIO, UTAH	3
5	IDAHO, MAINE, TEXAS	3
6	ALASKA, HAWAII, KANSAS, NEVADA, OREGON	5
7	ALABAMA, ARIZONA, FLORIDA, GEORGIA, INDIANA, MONTANA, NEW YORK, VERMONT, WYOMING	9
8	ARKANSAS, COLORADO, DELAWARE, ILLINOIS, KENTUCKY, MARYLAND, MICHIGAN, MISSOURI, NEBRASKA, OKLAHOMA, VIRGINIA	11
9	LOUISIANA, MINNESOTA, NEW JERSEY, NEW MEXICO, TENNESSEE, WISCONSIN	6
10	CALIFORNIA, WASHINGTON	2
11	CONNECTICUT, MISSISSIPPI, NORTH DAKOTA, RHODE ISLAND, SOUTH DAKOTA	5
12	NEW HAMPSHIRE, PENNSYLVANIA, WEST VIRGINIA	3
13	MASSACHUSETTS, NORTH CAROLINA, SOUTH CAROLINA	3

NUMBER OF LETTERS IN STATE NAME

23 stars

24 stars

U.S. ACTIVITY #3 SOLUTIONS

Number of state names containing alphabetic letter

Letter	#	State names with letter
A	36	ALABAMA, ALASKA, ARIZONA, ARKANSAS, CALIFORNIA, COLORADO, DELAWARE, FLORIDA, GEORGIA, HAWAII, IDAHO, INDIANA, IOWA, KANSAS, LOUISIANA, MAINE, MARYLAND, MASSACHUSETTS, MICHIGAN, MINNESOTA, MONTANA, NEBRASKA, NEVADA, NEW HAMPSHIRE, NORTH CAROLINA, NORTH DAKOTA, OKLAHOMA, PENNSYLVANIA, RHODE ISLAND, SOUTH CAROLINA, SOUTH DAKOTA, TEXAS, UTAH, VIRGINIA, WASHINGTON, WEST VIRGINIA,
B	2	ALABAMA, NEBRASKA
C	10	CALIFORNIA, COLORADO, CONNECTICUT, KENTUCKY, MASSACHUSETTS, MICHIGAN, NEW MEXICO, NORTH CAROLINA, SOUTH CAROLINA, WISCONSIN
D	10	COLORADO, DELAWARE, FLORIDA, IDAHO, INDIANA, MARYLAND, NEVADA, NORTH DAKOTA, RHODE ISLAND, SOUTH DAKOTA
E	20	CONNECTICUT, DELAWARE, GEORGIA, KENTUCKY, MAINE, MASSACHUSETTS, MINNESOTA, NEBRASKA, NEVADA, NEW HAMPSHIRE, NEW JERSEY, NEW MEXICO, NEW YORK, OREGON, PENNSYLVANIA, RHODE ISLAND, TENNESSEE, TEXAS, VERMONT, WEST VIRGINIA,
F	2	CALIFORNIA, FLORIDA
G	7	GEORGIA, MICHIGAN, OREGON, VIRGINIA, WASHINGTON, WEST VIRGINIA, WYOMING
H	14	HAWAII, IDAHO, MASSACHUSETTS, MICHIGAN, NEW HAMPSHIRE, NORTH CAROLINA, NORTH DAKOTA, OHIO, OKLAHOMA, RHODE ISLAND, SOUTH CAROLINA, SOUTH DAKOTA, UTAH, WASHINGTON
I	28	ARIZONA, CALIFORNIA, CONNECTICUT, FLORIDA, GEORGIA, HAWAII, IDAHO, ILLINOIS, INDIANA, IOWA, LOUISIANA, MAINE, MICHIGAN, MINNESOTA, MISSISSIPPI, MISSOURI, NEW HAMPSHIRE, NEW MEXICO, NORTH CAROLINA, OHIO, PENNSYLVANIA, RHODE ISLAND, SOUTH CAROLINA, VIRGINIA, WASHINGTON, WEST VIRGINIA, WISCONSIN, WYOMING
J	1	NEW JERSEY
K	9	ALASKA, ARKANSAS, KANSAS, KENTUCKY, NEBRASKA, NEW YORK, NORTH DAKOTA, OKLAHOMA, SOUTH DAKOTA
L	14	ALABAMA, ALASKA, CALIFORNIA, COLORADO, DELAWARE, FLORIDA, ILLINOIS, LOUISIANA, MARYLAND, NORTH CAROLINA, OKLAHOMA, PENNSYLVANIA, RHODE ISLAND, SOUTH CAROLINA
M	14	ALABAMA, MAINE, MARYLAND, MASSACHUSETTS, MICHIGAN, MINNESOTA, MISSISSIPPI, MISSOURI, MONTANA, NEW HAMPSHIRE, NEW MEXICO, OKLAHOMA, VERMONT, WYOMING
N	33	ARIZONA, ARKANSAS, CALIFORNIA, CONNECTICUT, ILLINOIS, INDIANA, KANSAS, KENTUCKY, LOUISIANA, MAINE, MARYLAND, MICHIGAN, MINNESOTA, MONTANA, NEBRASKA, NEVADA, NEW HAMPSHIRE, NEW JERSEY, NEW MEXICO, NEW YORK, NORTH CAROLINA, NORTH DAKOTA, OREGON, PENNSYLVANIA, RHODE ISLAND, SOUTH CAROLINA, TENNESSEE, VERMONT, VIRGINIA, WASHINGTON, WEST VIRGINIA, WISCONSIN, WYOMING.
O	27	ARIZONA, CALIFORNIA, COLORADO, CONNECTICUT, FLORIDA, GEORGIA, IDAHO, ILLINOIS, IOWA, LOUISIANA, MINNESOTA, MISSOURI, MONTANA, NEW MEXICO, NEW YORK, NORTH CAROLINA, NORTH DAKOTA, OHIO, OKLAHOMA, OREGON, RHODE ISLAND, SOUTH CAROLINA, SOUTH DAKOTA, VERMONT, WASHINGTON, WISCONSIN, WYOMING
P	3	MISSISSIPPI, NEW HAMPSHIRE, PENNSYLVANIA
Q	0	
R	21	ARIZONA, ARKANSAS, CALIFORNIA, COLORADO, DELAWARE, FLORIDA, GEORGIA, MARYLAND, MISSOURI, NEBRASKA, NEW HAMPSHIRE, NEW JERSEY, NEW YORK, NORTH CAROLINA, NORTH DAKOTA, OREGON, RHODE ISLAND, SOUTH CAROLINA, VERMONT, VIRGINIA, WEST VIRGINIA
S	21	ALASKA, ARKANSAS, ILLINOIS, KANSAS, LOUISIANA, MASSACHUSETTS, MINNESOTA, MISSISSIPPI, MISSOURI, NEBRASKA, NEW HAMPSHIRE, NEW JERSEY, PENNSYLVANIA, RHODE ISLAND, SOUTH CAROLINA, SOUTH DAKOTA, TENNESSEE, TEXAS, WASHINGTON, WEST VIRGINIA, WISCONSIN
T	15	CONNECTICUT, KENTUCKY, MASSACHUSETTS, MINNESOTA, MONTANA, NORTH CAROLINA, NORTH DAKOTA, SOUTH CAROLINA, SOUTH DAKOTA, TENNESSEE, TEXAS, UTAH, VERMONT, WASHINGTON, WEST VIRGINIA
U	8	CONNECTICUT, KENTUCKY, LOUISIANA, MASSACHUSETTS, MISSOURI, SOUTH CAROLINA, SOUTH DAKOTA, UTAH
V	5	NEVADA, PENNSYLVANIA, VERMONT, VIRGINIA, WEST VIRGINIA
W	11	DELAWARE, HAWAII, IOWA, NEW HAMPSHIRE, NEW JERSEY, NEW MEXICO, NEW YORK, WASHINGTON, WEST VIRGINIA, WISCONSIN, WYOMING
X	2	NEW MEXICO, TEXAS
Y	6	KENTUCKY, MARYLAND, NEW JERSEY, NEW YORK, PENNSYLVANIA, WYOMING
Z	1	ARIZONA

25 stars

26 stars

U.S. ACTIVITY #4 SOLUTIONS

Number of state names containing alphabetic letter more than once

Letter	#	State names with letter more than once
A	21	ALABAMA, ALASKA, ARIZONA, ARKANSAS, CALIFORNIA, DELAWARE, HAWAII, INDIANA, KANSAS, LOUISIANA, MARYLAND, MASSACHUSETTS, MONTANA, NEBRASKA, NEVADA, NORTH CAROLINA, NORTH DAKOTA, OKLAHOMA, PENNSYLVANIA, SOUTH CAROLINA, SOUTH DAKOTA
B	0	
C	1	CONNECTICUT
D	1	RHODE ISLAND
E	5	DELAWARE, NEW HAMPSHIRE, NEW JERSEY, NEW MEXICO, TENNESSEE
F	0	
G	1	GEORGIA
H	1	NEW HAMPSHIRE
I	11	CALIFORNIA, HAWAII, ILLINOIS, INDIANA, LOUISIANA, MICHIGAN, MISSISSIPPI, MISSOURI, VIRGINIA, WEST VIRGINIA, WISCONSIN
J	0	
K	1	KENTUCKY
L	1	ILLINOIS
M	0	
N	9	CONNECTICUT, INDIANA, MINNESOTA, MONTANA, NORTH CAROLINA, PENNSYLVANIA, TENNESSEE, WASHINGTON, WISCONSIN
O	8	COLORADO, NORTH CAROLINA, NORTH DAKOTA, OHIO, OKLAHOMA, OREGON, SOUTH CAROLINA, SOUTH DAKOTA
P	1	MISSISSIPPI
Q	0	
R	1	NORTH CAROLINA
S	7	ARKANSAS, KANSAS, MASSACHUSETTS, MISSISSIPPI, MISSOURI, TENNESSEE, WISCONSIN
T	4	CONNECTICUT, MASSACHUSETTS, NORTH DAKOTA, SOUTH DAKOTA
U	0	
V	0	
W	0	
X	0	
Y	0	
Z	0	

27 stars

28 stars

U.S. ACTIVITY #5 SOLUTIONS

Number of state capital names beginning with alphabetic letter

Letter	#	State capital names beginning with letter
A	5	Albany, Annapolis, Atlanta, Augusta, Austin
B	4	Baton Rouge, Bismarck, Boise, Boston
C	6	Carson City, Charleston, Cheyenne, Columbia, Columbus, Concord
D	3	Denver, Des Moines, Dover
E	0	
F	1	Frankfort
G	0	
H	4	Harrisburg, Hartford, Helena, Honolulu
I	1	Indianapolis
J	3	Jackson, Jefferson City, Juneau
K	0	
L	3	Lansing, Lincoln, Little Rock
M	3	Madison, Montgomery, Montpelier
N	1	Nashville
O	2	Oklahoma City, Olympia
P	3	Phoenix, Pierre, Providence
Q	0	
R	2	Raleigh, Richmond
S	6	Sacramento, Salem, Salt Lake City, Santa Fe, Springfield, St. Paul
T	3	Tallahassee, Topeka, Trenton
U	0	
V	0	
W	0	
X	0	
Y	0	
Z	0	

29 stars

30 stars

U. S. ACTIVITY #6 SOLUTIONS

COMPLETE THE STATEHOOD CHART (10 YEAR INTERVALS)

SPREADSHEET CONSTRUCTED BY FRANCES AND WAYNE

Put state names in the appropriate 10-year time interval during which statehood was attained.

As an extra challenge, put names in the order in which statehood was attained.

	1	2	3	4	5	6	7	8	9	10	11	12	13
1770-1779													
1780-1789	DELAWARE	PENNSYLVANIA	NEW JERSEY	GEORGIA	CONNECTICUT	MASSACHUSETTS	MARYLAND	SOUTH CAROLINA	NEW HAMPSHIRE	VIRGINIA	NEW YORK	NORTH CAROLINA	
1790-1799	RHODE ISLAND	VERMONT	KENTUCKY	TENNESSEE									
1800-1809	OHIO												
1810-1819	LOUISIANA	INDIANA	MISSISSIPPI	ILLINOIS	ALABAMA								
1820-1829	MAINE	MISSOURI											
1830-1839	ARKANSAS	MICHIGAN											
1840-1849	FLORIDA	TEXAS	IOWA	WISCONSIN									
1850-1859	CALIFORNIA	MINNESOTA	OREGON										
1860-1869	KANSAS	WEST VIRGINIA	NEVADA	NEBRASKA									
1870-1879	COLORADO												
1880-1889	NORTH DAKOTA	SOUTH DAKOTA	MONTANA	WASHINGTON									
1890-1899	IDAHO	WYOMING	UTAH										
1900-1909	OKLAHOMA												
1910-1919	NEW MEXICO	ARIZONA											
1920-1929													
1930-1939													
1940-1949													
1950-1959	ALASKA	HAWAII											
1960-1969													

31 *stars*

32 *stars*

U. S. ACTIVITY #7 SOLUTIONS

	Scrambled State and Capital City		Unscrambled
1	GTAGAENAORILAT	1	ATLANTA, GEORGIA
2	EFKTFOKURKNYANCTR	2	FRANKFORT, KENTUCKY
3	NNASOESUTLIAMPT	3	ST. PAUL, MINNESOTA
4	GNHNIACIMALSNGI	4	LANSING, MICHIGAN
5	NNLMEOHAANAET	5	HELENA, MONTANA
6	AMRSIRKDAOTBTHANKO	6	BISMARK, NORTH DAKOTA
7	ANXMCSINEETOFEWA	7	SANTA FE, NEW MEXICO
8	WROEEOHNRCAINDHCMPS	8	CONCORD, NEW HAMPSHIRE
9	AADPONRIANMNLYASL	9	ANNAPOLIS, MARYLAND
10	RIHINAIVDMNGCOIR	10	RICHMOND, VIRGINIA
11	DAVERLCRODEONO	11	DENVER, COLORADO
12	TRWNCRSELGIASIEANTOHIV	12	CHARLESTON, WEST VIRGINIA
13	NGSIAAEAUMTU	13	AUGUSTA, MAINE
14	KYAKOHAMLLATOHCMIOAO	14	OKLAHOMA CITY, OKLAHOMA
15	WLAOILHOHNAUUI	15	HONOLULU, HAWAII
16	TTDIFNURNORACTHOCEC	16	HARTFORD, CONNECTICUT
17	SIMNOOIWDEEAS	17	DES MOINES, IOWA
18	KYYAALERBNOWN	18	ALBANY, NEW YORK
19	UIOAMIOTSCHARUONLCLBA	19	COLUMBIA, SOUTH CAROLINA
20	TLOAILLSAEFSHRDAAE	20	TALLAHASSEE, FLORIDA
21	KURIOHEATRDTAPSEO	21	PIERRE, SOUTH DAKOTA
22	ENOEWRNNSERETTYJ	22	TRENTON, NEW JERSEY
23	SANSSEHBCOTUMOTTSSA	23	BOSTON, MASSACHUSETTS
24	KSUEAJLNAAUA	24	JUNEAU, ALASKA
25	DLPGIFLRNIOIISNLIES	25	SPRINGFIELD, ILLINOIS
26	SAXTEUITSAN	26	AUSTIN, TEXAS
27	IUSOFRECRSTSOYENFMIJI	27	JEFFERSON CITY, MISSOURI
28	NAHEOXIIONZARP	28	PHOENIX, ARIZONA
29	ESNKOASAPTKA	29	TOPEKA, KANSAS
30	SDHIBAOOIE	30	BOISE, IDAHO
31	WOPMLHONATIYSANGI	31	OLYMPIA, WASHINGTON
32	NKSTRATEAICSKRLOLA	32	LITTLE ROCK, ARKANSAS
33	SOSCISWMNDOINAIN	33	MADISON, WISCONSIN
34	AAOERINRIOHLNHCLTRAG	34	RALEIGH, NORTH CAROLINA
35	NDNCAYCVITESRAOA	35	CARSON CITY, NEVADA
36	AITLNORUSOUIGAOAEBN	36	BATON ROUGE, LOUISIANA
37	GOLSAENREMO	37	SALEM, OREGON
38	ARRGBRNVINHLEPNUSIASYA	38	HARRISBURG, PENNSYLVANIA
39	RAOOMAAYMLGNTAMEB	39	MONTGOMERY, ALABAMA
40	EVIELSTSNENESALNEH	40	NASHVILLE, TENNESSEE
41	TROMAONLNIAAESICRCFA	41	SACRAMENTO, CALIFORNIA
42	AEVODEWDRRLAE	42	DOVER, DELAWARE
43	PKIASMSJSPSISIOINC	43	JACKSON, MISSISSIPPI
44	OENNEMIYNEYWHGC	44	CHEYENNE, WYOMING
45	AONNSIAENKRLBLC	45	LINCOLN, NEBRASKA
46	INLVRHIENRDEPOCEDOADS	46	PROVIDENCE, RHODE ISLAND
47	ATTTHLSUYELCAAKI	47	SALT LAKE CITY, UTAH
48	ANALNAIISOIDDPAINNI	48	INDIANAPOLIS, INDIANA
49	ETMRMIROVELTONNPE	49	MONTPELIER, VERMONT
50	HUCIBLOUSOMO	50	COLUMBUS, OHIO

201

33 stars

34 stars

U. S. ACTIVITY #10 SOLUTIONS

STATES SORTED BY POPULATION RANK

	State	State population
1	CALIFORNIA	36,962,000
2	TEXAS	24,783,000
3	NEW YORK	19,542,000
4	FLORIDA	18,538,000
5	ILLINOIS	12,911,000
6	PENNSYLVANIA	12,605,000
7	OHIO	11,543,000
8	MICHIGAN	9,970,000
9	GEORGIA	9,830,000
10	NORTH CAROLINA	9,381,000
11	NEW JERSEY	8,708,000
12	VIRGINIA	7,883,000
13	WASHINGTON	6,665,000
14	ARIZONA	6,596,000
15	MASSACHUSETTS	6,594,000
16	INDIANA	6,424,000
17	TENNESSEE	6,297,000
18	MISSOURI	5,988,000
19	MARYLAND	5,700,000
20	WISCONSIN	5,655,000
21	MINNESOTA	5,267,000
22	COLORADO	5,025,000
23	ALABAMA	4,710,000
24	SOUTH CAROLINA	4,562,000
25	LOUISIANA	4,493,000
26	KENTUCKY	4,315,000
27	OREGON	3,826,000
28	OKLAHOMA	3,688,000
29	CONNECTICUT	3,519,000
30	IOWA	3,008,000
31	MISSISSIPPI	2,952,000
32	ARKANSAS	2,890,000
33	KANSAS	2,819,000
34	UTAH	2,785,000
35	NEVADA	2,644,000
36	NEW MEXICO	2,010,000
37	WEST VIRGINIA	1,820,000
38	NEBRASKA	1,797,000
39	IDAHO	1,546,000
40	NEW HAMPSHIRE	1,325,000
41	MAINE	1,319,000
42	HAWAII	1,296,000
43	RHODE ISLAND	1,054,000
44	MONTANA	975,000
45	DELAWARE	885,122
46	SOUTH DAKOTA	812,400
47	ALASKA	699,000
48	NORTH DAKOTA	647,000
49	VERMONT	622,000
50	WYOMING	545,000

35 stars

36 stars

U. S. ACTIVITY #11 SOLUTIONS

STATES SORTED BY POPULATION OF CAPITAL CITY

	State	Capital city	Capital city population
1	ARIZONA	Phoenix	1,512,990
2	INDIANA	Indianapolis	791,930
3	OHIO	Columbus	733,210
4	TEXAS	Austin	709,900
5	TENNESSEE	Nashville	607,420
6	MASSACHUSETTS	Boston	590,770
7	COLORADO	Denver	566,980
8	OKLAHOMA	Oklahoma City	541,510
9	GEORGIA	Atlanta	486,420
10	CALIFORNIA	Sacramento	467,350
11	NORTH CAROLINA	Raleigh	380,180
12	HAWAII	Honolulu	377,360
13	MINNESOTA	St. Paul	287,160
14	NEBRASKA	Lincoln	225,590
15	LOUISIANA	Baton Rouge	224,100
16	WISCONSIN	Madison	221,560
17	IOWA	Des Moines	209,130
18	ARKANSAS	Little Rock	204,380
19	IDAHO	Boise	201,290
20	ALABAMA	Montgomery	200,130
21	VIRGINIA	Richmond	195,260
22	MISSISSIPPI	Jackson	184,260
23	UTAH	Salt Lake City	181,750
24	RHODE ISLAND	Providence	176,870
25	FLORIDA	Tallahassee	168,980
26	OREGON	Salem	149,310
27	CONNECTICUT	Hartford	124,400
28	SOUTH CAROLINA	Columbia	122,820
29	KANSAS	Topeka	122,330
30	MICHIGAN	Lansing	119,130
31	ILLINOIS	Springfield	116,490
32	NEW YORK	Albany	96,000
33	NEW JERSEY	Trenton	84,640
34	NEW MEXICO	Santa Fe	70,631
35	NEVADA	Carson City	57,710
36	NORTH DAKOTA	Bismark	55,540
37	WYOMING	Cheyenne	55,370
38	WEST VIRGINIA	Charleston	52,710
39	PENNSYLVANIA	Harrisburg	48,960
40	WASHINGTON	Olympia	42,520
41	NEW HAMPSHIRE	Concord	42,230
42	MISSOURI	Jefferson City	39,640
43	MARYLAND	Annapolis	36,220
44	DELAWARE	Dover	32,140
45	ALASKA	Juneau	30,990
46	KENTUCKY	Frankfort	27,750
47	MONTANA	Helena	25,790
48	MAINE	Augusta	18,570
49	SOUTH DAKOTA	Pierre	13,880
50	VERMONT	Montpelier	8,040

37 stars

38 stars

U. S. ACTIVITY #12 SOLUTIONS

ORDER OF ENTRANCE INTO UNION

Rank	State	Year entered union
1	DELAWARE	1787
2	PENNSYLVANIA	1787
3	NEW JERSEY	1787
4	GEORGIA	1788
5	CONNECTICUT	1788
6	MASSACHUSETTS	1788
7	MARYLAND	1788
8	SOUTH CAROLINA	1788
9	NEW HAMPSHIRE	1788
10	VIRGINIA	1788
11	NEW YORK	1788
12	NORTH CAROLINA	1789
13	RHODE ISLAND	1790
14	VERMONT	1791
15	KENTUCKY	1792
16	TENNESSEE	1796
17	OHIO	1803
18	LOUISIANA	1812
19	INDIANA	1816
20	MISSISSIPPI	1817
21	ILLINOIS	1818
22	ALABAMA	1819
23	MAINE	1820
24	MISSOURI	1821
25	ARKANSAS	1836
26	MICHIGAN	1837
27	FLORIDA	1845
28	TEXAS	1845
29	IOWA	1846
30	WISCONSIN	1848
31	CALIFORNIA	1850
32	MINNESOTA	1858
33	OREGON	1859
34	KANSAS	1861
35	WEST VIRGINIA	1863
36	NEVADA	1864
37	NEBRASKA	1867
38	COLORADO	1876
39	NORTH DAKOTA	1889
40	SOUTH DAKOTA	1899
41	MONTANA	1889
42	WASHINGTON	1889
43	IDAHO	1890
44	WYOMING	1890
45	UTAH	1896
46	OKLAHOMA	1907
47	NEW MEXICO	1912
48	ARIZONA	1912
49	ALASKA	1959
50	HAWAII	1959

43 stars

44 stars

U. S. ACTIVITY #13 SOLUTIONS

STATES SORTED BY AREA

	State	Area (sq. miles)
1	ALASKA	570,374
2	TEXAS	261,914
3	CALIFORNIA	155,973
4	MONTANA	145,556
5	NEW MEXICO	121,365
6	ARIZONA	113,641
7	NEVADA	109,806
8	COLORADO	103,730
9	WYOMING	97,105
10	OREGON	93,003
11	IDAHO	82,751
12	UTAH	82,168
13	KANSAS	81,823
14	MINNESOTA	79,617
15	NEBRASKA	76,878
16	SOUTH DAKOTA	75,898
17	NORTH DAKOTA	70,704
18	MISSOURI	68,898
19	OKLAHOMA	68,679
20	WASHINGTON	66,582
21	GEORGIA	57,919
22	MICHIGAN	56,809
23	IOWA	55,875
24	ILLINOIS	55,053
25	WISCONSIN	54,314
26	FLORIDA	54,153
27	ALABAMA	50,750
28	ARKANSAS	50,075
29	NORTH CAROLINA	48,718
30	NEW YORK	47,224
31	MISSISSIPPI	46,914
32	PENNSYLVANIA	44,820
33	LOUISIANA	43,566
34	TENNESSEE	41,220
35	OHIO	40,953
36	KENTUCKY	39,732
37	VIRGINIA	39,598
38	INDIANA	35,870
39	MAINE	30,865
40	SOUTH CAROLINA	30,111
41	WEST VIRGINIA	24,087
42	MARYLAND	9,775
43	VERMONT	9,249
44	NEW HAMPSHIRE	8,969
45	MASSACHUSETTS	7,838
46	NEW JERSEY	7,419
47	HAWAII	6,423
48	CONNECTICUT	4,845
49	DELAWARE	1,955
50	RHODE ISLAND	1,045

45 stars

46 stars

U.S. ACTIVITY #14 SOLUTIONS

STATES SORTED BY # PEOPLE PER SQUARE MILE

	State	State population	Area (sq. miles)	# people per square mile
1	NEW JERSEY	8,708,000	7,419	**1,173.7**
2	RHODE ISLAND	1,054,000	1,045	**1,008.6**
3	MASSACHUSETTS	6,594,000	7,838	**841.3**
4	CONNECTICUT	3,519,000	4,845	**726.3**
5	MARYLAND	5,700,000	9,775	**583.1**
6	DELAWARE	885,122	1,955	**452.7**
7	NEW YORK	19,542,000	47,224	**413.8**
8	FLORIDA	18,538,000	54,153	**342.3**
9	OHIO	11,543,000	40,953	**281.9**
10	PENNSYLVANIA	12,605,000	44,820	**281.2**
11	CALIFORNIA	36,962,000	155,973	**237.0**
12	ILLINOIS	12,911,000	55,053	**234.5**
13	HAWAII	1,296,000	6,423	**201.8**
14	VIRGINIA	7,883,000	39,598	**199.1**
15	NORTH CAROLINA	9,381,000	48,718	**192.6**
16	INDIANA	6,424,000	35,870	**179.1**
17	MICHIGAN	9,970,000	56,809	**175.5**
18	GEORGIA	9,830,000	57,919	**169.7**
19	TENNESSEE	6,297,000	41,220	**152.8**
20	SOUTH CAROLINA	4,562,000	30,111	**151.5**
21	NEW HAMPSHIRE	1,325,000	8,969	**147.7**
22	KENTUCKY	4,315,000	39,732	**108.6**
23	WISCONSIN	5,655,000	54,314	**104.1**
24	LOUISIANA	4,493,000	43,566	**103.1**
25	WASHINGTON	6,665,000	66,582	**100.1**
26	TEXAS	24,783,000	261,914	**94.6**
27	ALABAMA	4,710,000	50,750	**92.8**
28	MISSOURI	5,988,000	68,898	**86.9**
29	WEST VIRGINIA	1,820,000	24,087	**75.6**
30	VERMONT	622,000	9,249	**67.3**
31	MINNESOTA	5,267,000	79,617	**66.2**
32	MISSISSIPPI	2,952,000	46,914	**62.9**
33	ARIZONA	6,596,000	113,641	**58.0**
34	ARKANSAS	2,890,000	50,075	**57.7**
35	IOWA	3,008,000	55,875	**53.8**
36	OKLAHOMA	3,688,000	68,679	**53.7**
37	COLORADO	5,025,000	103,730	**48.4**
38	MAINE	1,319,000	30,865	**42.7**
39	OREGON	3,826,000	93,003	**41.1**
40	KANSAS	2,819,000	81,823	**34.5**
41	UTAH	2,785,000	82,168	**33.9**
42	NEVADA	2,644,000	109,806	**24.1**
43	NEBRASKA	1,797,000	76,878	**23.4**
44	IDAHO	1,546,000	82,751	**18.7**
45	NEW MEXICO	2,010,000	121,365	**16.6**
46	SOUTH DAKOTA	812,400	75,898	**10.7**
47	NORTH DAKOTA	647,000	70,704	**9.2**
48	MONTANA	975,000	145,556	**6.7**
49	WYOMING	545,000	97,105	**5.6**
50	ALASKA	699,000	570,374	**1.2**

48 stars

49 stars

50 stars

212

> *The person who says it can't be done
> should not interrupt the person doing it.*
>
> **(Chinese proverb)**

The next 48 pages represent

U.S. ACTIVITY #15
SEPARATION STATE CHALLENGES
SOLUTIONS

Herkimer sez:

The illustrated paths on the solution pages do not necessarily represent the only possible route that would achieve the stated objective of getting from one state to another by traveling through a minimum number of other states. That is, there might be other travel routes that would accomplish that goal.

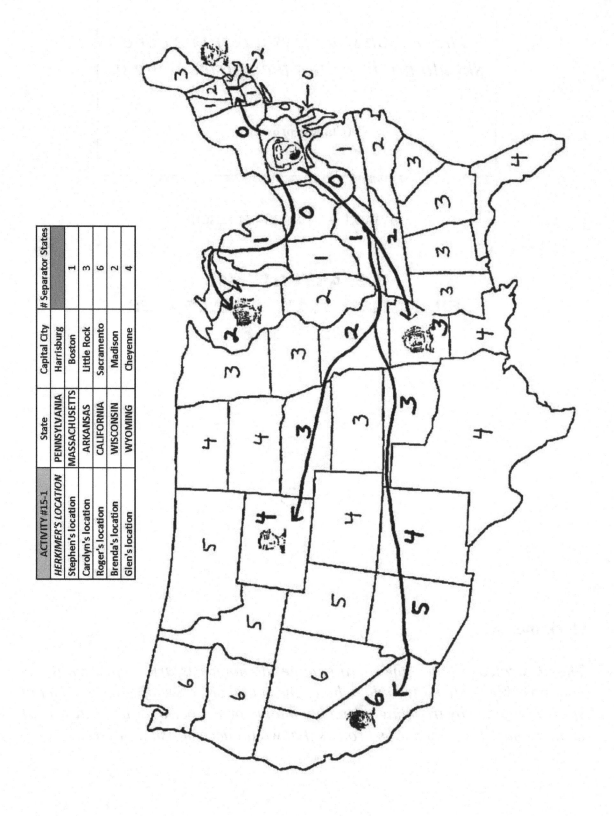

ACTIVITY #15-1	State	Capital City	# Separator States
HERKIMER'S LOCATION	PENNSYLVANIA	Harrisburg	
Stephen's location	MASSACHUSETTS	Boston	1
Carolyn's location	ARKANSAS	Little Rock	3
Roger's location	CALIFORNIA	Sacramento	6
Brenda's location	WISCONSIN	Madison	2
Glen's location	WYOMING	Cheyenne	4

214

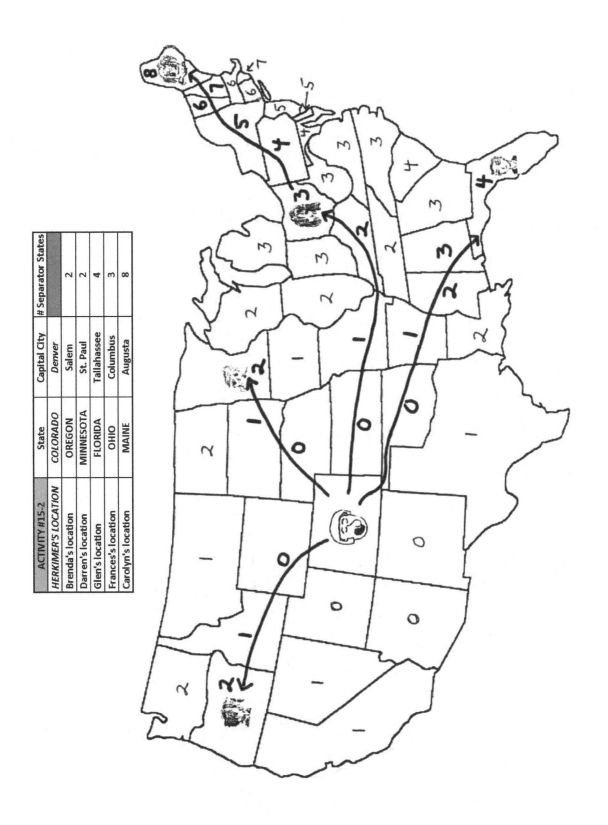

ACTIVITY #15-2	State	Capital City	# Separator States
HERKIMER'S LOCATION	*COLORADO*	*Denver*	
Brenda's location	OREGON	Salem	2
Darren's location	MINNESOTA	St. Paul	2
Glen's location	FLORIDA	Tallahassee	4
Frances's location	OHIO	Columbus	3
Carolyn's location	MAINE	Augusta	8

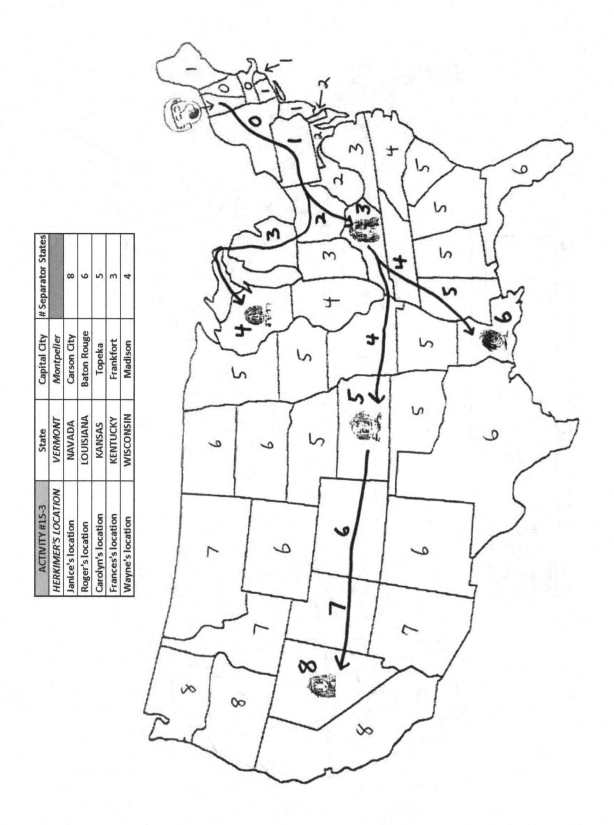

ACTIVITY #15-3	State	Capital City	# Separator States
HERKIMER'S LOCATION	VERMONT	Montpelier	
Janice's location	NAVADA	Carson City	8
Roger's location	LOUISIANA	Baton Rouge	6
Carolyn's location	KANSAS	Topeka	5
Frances's location	KENTUCKY	Frankfort	3
Wayne's location	WISCONSIN	Madison	4

216

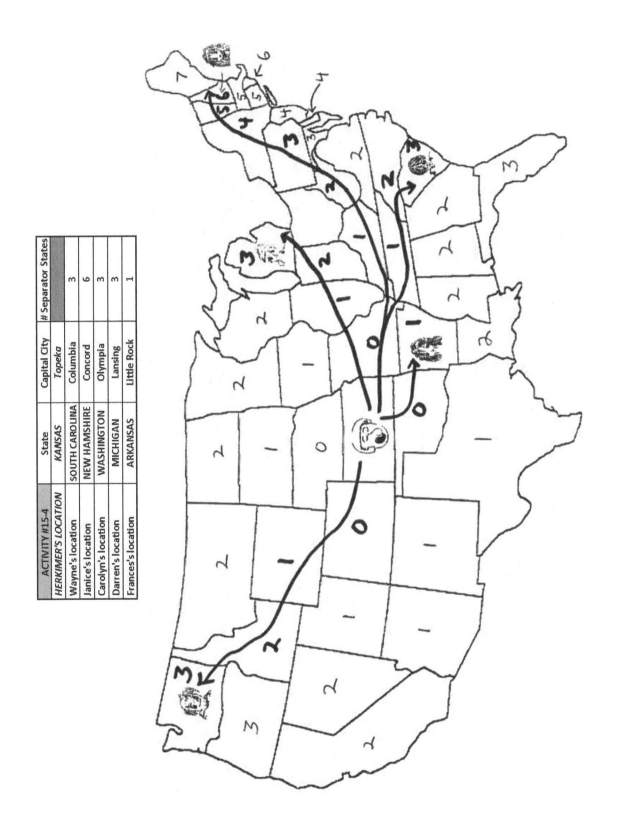

ACTIVITY #15-4	State	Capital City	# Separator States
HERKIMER'S LOCATION	KANSAS	Topeka	
Wayne's location	SOUTH CAROLINA	Columbia	3
Janice's location	NEW HAMSHIRE	Concord	6
Carolyn's location	WASHINGTON	Olympia	3
Darren's location	MICHIGAN	Lansing	3
Frances's location	ARKANSAS	Little Rock	1

ACTIVITY #15-5	State	Capital City	# Separator States
HERKIMER'S LOCATION	MISSOURI	Jefferson City	
Wayne's location	VERMONT	Montpelier	4
Carolyn's location	ARIZONA	Phoenix	2
Stephen's location	GEORGIA	Atlanta	1
Darren's location	OREGON	Salem	3
Glen's location	DELAWARE	Dover	3

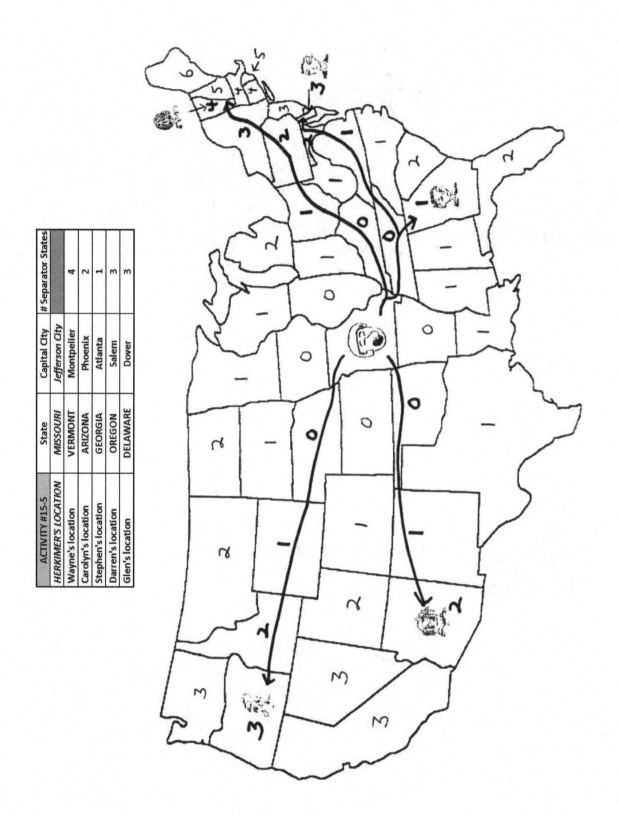

218

ACTIVITY #15-6	State	Capital City	# Separator States
HERKIMER'S LOCATION	*IOWA*	*Des Moines*	5
Valarie's location	VERMONT	Montpelier	2
Stephen's location	ALABAMA	Montgomery	2
Roger's location	IDAHO	Boise	2
Glen's location	TEXAS	Austin	2
Brenda's location	VIRGINIA	Richmond	2

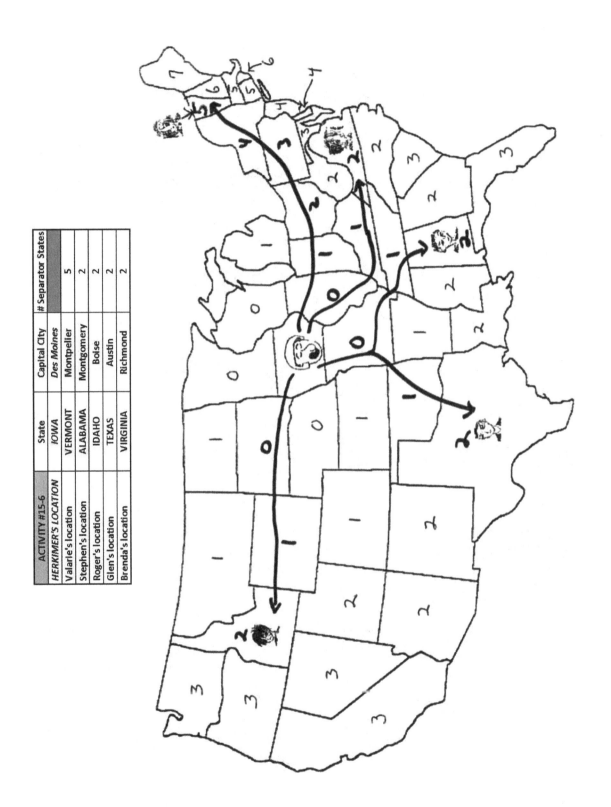

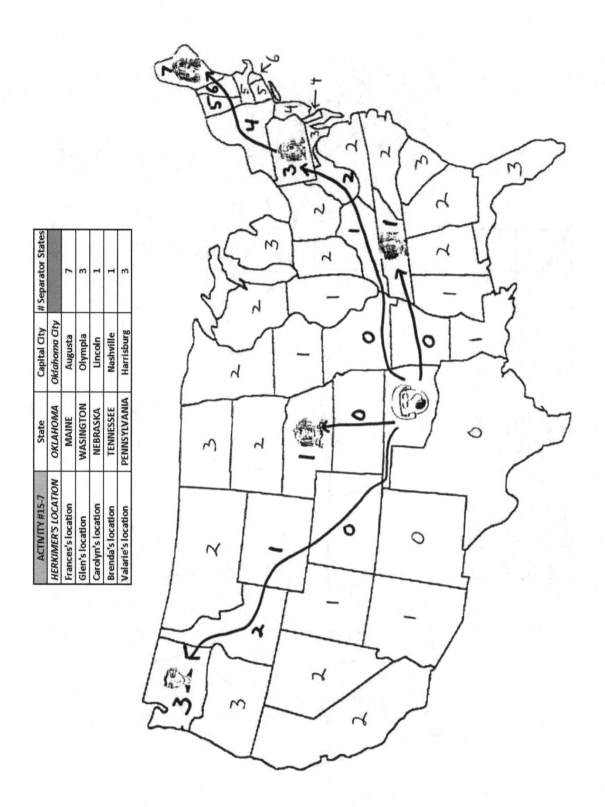

ACTIVITY #15-7			
HERKIMER'S LOCATION	OKLAHOMA	Oklahoma City	
	State	Capital City	# Separator States
Frances's location	MAINE	Augusta	7
Glen's location	WASINGTON	Olympia	3
Carolyn's location	NEBRASKA	Lincoln	1
Brenda's location	TENNESSEE	Nashville	1
Valarie's location	PENNSYLVANIA	Harrisburg	3

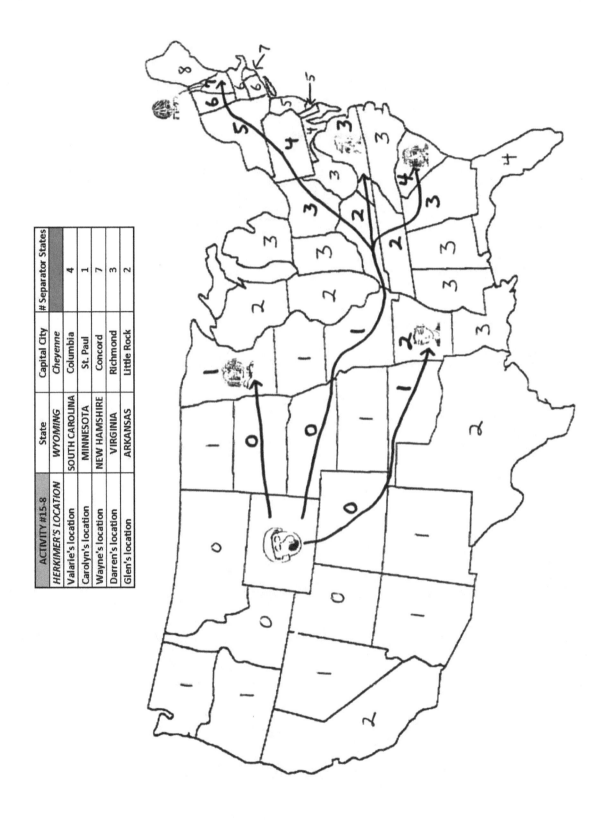

ACTIVITY #15-8			
HERKIMER'S LOCATION	State	Capital City	# Separator States
Valarie's location	WYOMING	Cheyenne	4
Carolyn's location	SOUTH CAROLINA	Columbia	1
Wayne's location	MINNESOTA	St. Paul	7
Darren's location	NEW HAMSHIRE	Concord	3
Glen's location	VIRGINIA	Richmond	3
	ARKANSAS	Little Rock	2

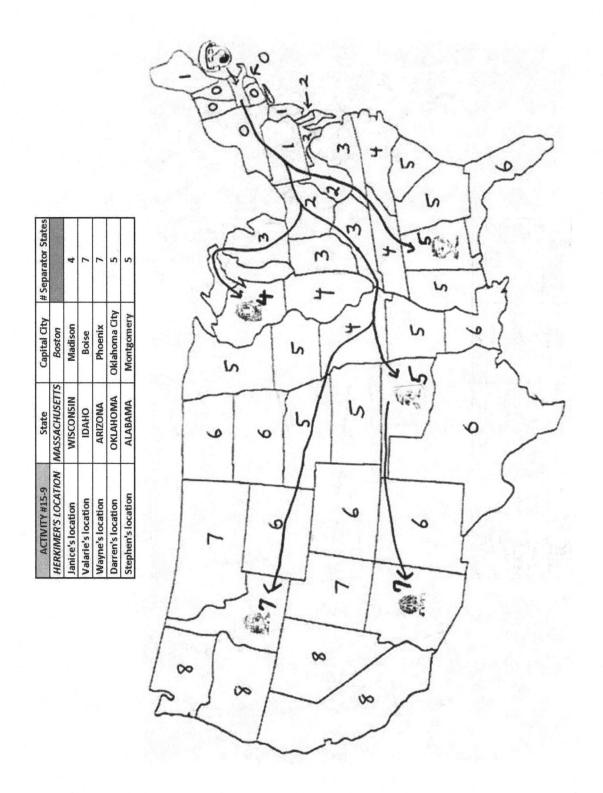

ACTIVITY #15-9			
HERKIMER'S LOCATION	MASSACHUSETTS	Boston	
	State	Capital City	# Separator States
Janice's location	WISCONSIN	Madison	4
Valarie's location	IDAHO	Boise	7
Wayne's location	ARIZONA	Phoenix	7
Darren's location	OKLAHOMA	Oklahoma City	5
Stephen's location	ALABAMA	Montgomery	5

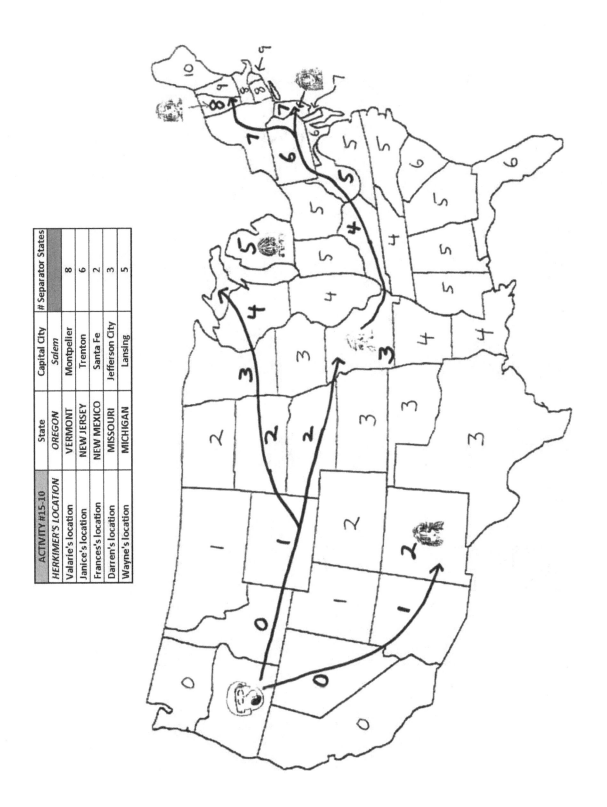

ACTIVITY #15-10	State	Capital City	# Separator States
HERKIMER'S LOCATION	*OREGON*	*Salem*	
Valarie's location	VERMONT	Montpelier	8
Janice's location	NEW JERSEY	Trenton	6
Frances's location	NEW MEXICO	Santa Fe	2
Darren's location	MISSOURI	Jefferson City	3
Wayne's location	MICHIGAN	Lansing	5

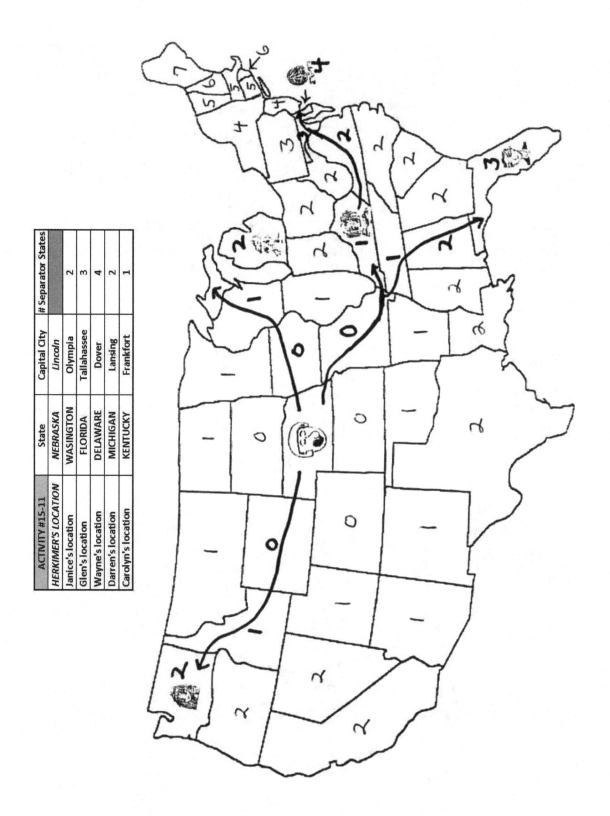

ACTIVITY #15-11	State	Capital City	# Separator States
HERKIMER'S LOCATION	*NEBRASKA*	*Lincoln*	
Janice's location	WASINGTON	Olympia	2
Glen's location	FLORIDA	Tallahassee	3
Wayne's location	DELAWARE	Dover	4
Darren's location	MICHIGAN	Lansing	2
Carolyn's location	KENTUCKY	Frankfort	1

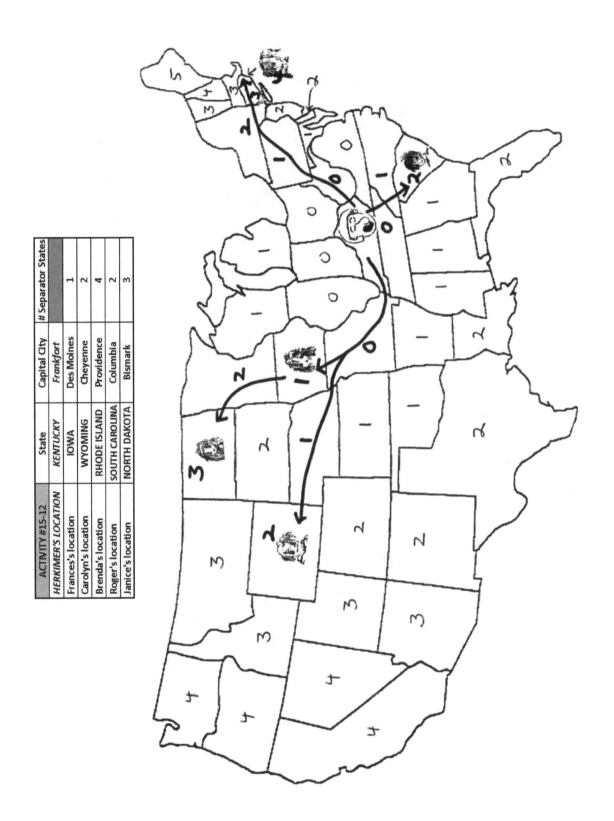

ACTIVITY #15-12	State	Capital City	# Separator States
HERKIMER'S LOCATION	KENTUCKY	Frankfort	
Frances's location	IOWA	Des Moines	1
Carolyn's location	WYOMING	Cheyenne	2
Brenda's location	RHODE ISLAND	Providence	4
Roger's location	SOUTH CAROLINA	Columbia	2
Janice's location	NORTH DAKOTA	Bismark	3

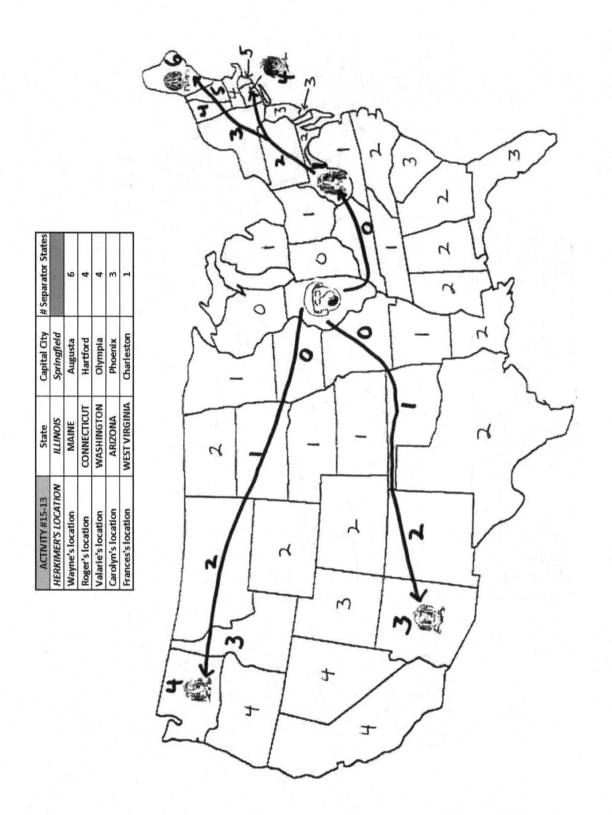

ACTIVITY #15-13	State	Capital City	# Separator States
HERKIMER'S LOCATION	ILLINOIS	Springfield	
Wayne's location	MAINE	Augusta	6
Roger's location	CONNECTICUT	Hartford	4
Valarie's location	WASHINGTON	Olympia	4
Carolyn's location	ARIZONA	Phoenix	3
Frances's location	WEST VIRGINIA	Charleston	1

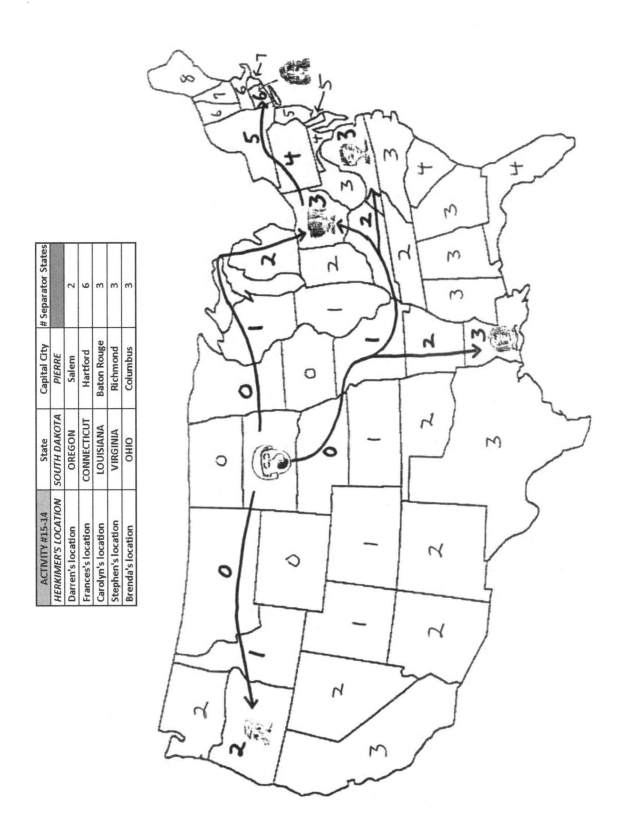

ACTIVITY #15-14	State	Capital City	# Separator States
HERKIMER'S LOCATION	SOUTH DAKOTA	PIERRE	
Darren's location	OREGON	Salem	2
Frances's location	CONNECTICUT	Hartford	6
Carolyn's location	LOUISIANA	Baton Rouge	3
Stephen's location	VIRGINIA	Richmond	3
Brenda's location	OHIO	Columbus	3

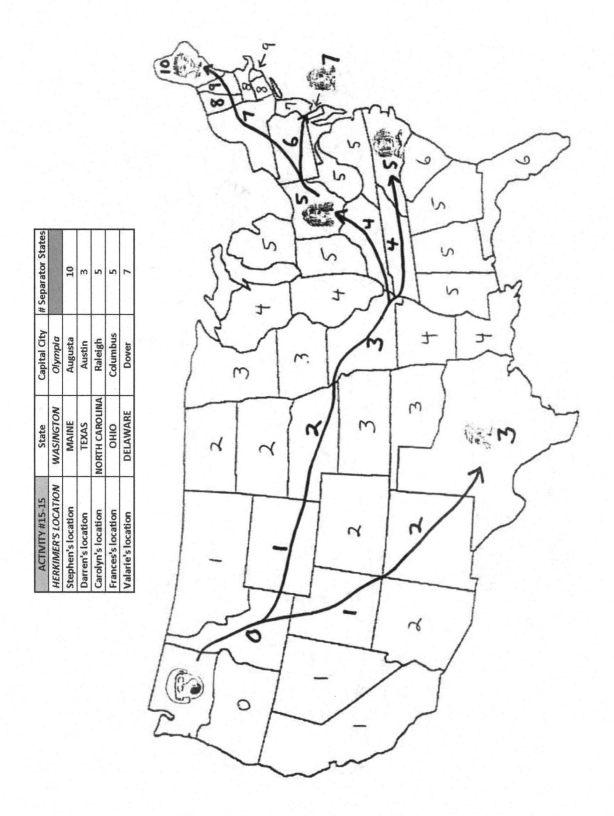

ACTIVITY #15-15	State	Capital City	# Separator States
HERKIMER'S LOCATION	WASHINGTON	Olympia	10
Stephen's location	MAINE	Augusta	3
Darren's location	TEXAS	Austin	5
Carolyn's location	NORTH CAROLINA	Raleigh	5
Frances's location	OHIO	Columbus	7
Valarie's location	DELAWARE	Dover	

228

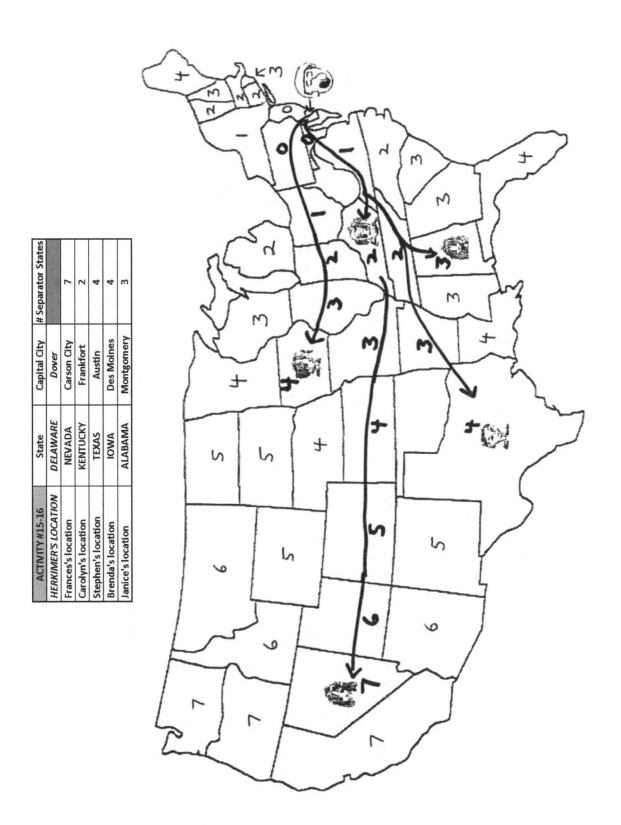

ACTIVITY #15-16	State	Capital City	# Separator States
HERKIMER'S LOCATION	DELAWARE	Dover	
Frances's location	NEVADA	Carson City	7
Carolyn's location	KENTUCKY	Frankfort	2
Stephen's location	TEXAS	Austin	4
Brenda's location	IOWA	Des Moines	4
Janice's location	ALABAMA	Montgomery	3

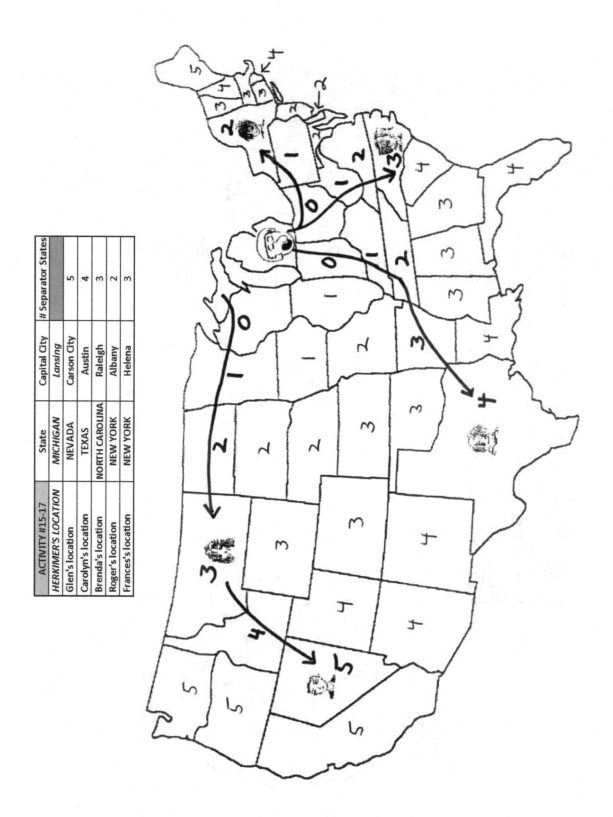

ACTIVITY #15-17			
HERKIMER'S LOCATION	State	Capital City	# Separator States
Glen's location	MICHIGAN	Lansing	5
Carolyn's location	NEVADA	Carson City	4
Brenda's location	TEXAS	Austin	3
Roger's location	NORTH CAROLINA	Raleigh	2
Frances's location	NEW YORK	Albany	2
	NEW YORK	Helena	3

ACTIVITY #15-18	State	Capital City	# Separator States
HERKIMER'S LOCATION	*GEORGIA*	*Atlanta*	
Carolyn's location	MONTANA	Helena	4
Glen's location	NEW JERSEY	Trenton	4
Darren's location	ARKANSAS	Little Rock	1
Stephen's location	CALIFORNIA	Sacramento	5
Janice's location	WEST VIRGINIA	Charleston	2

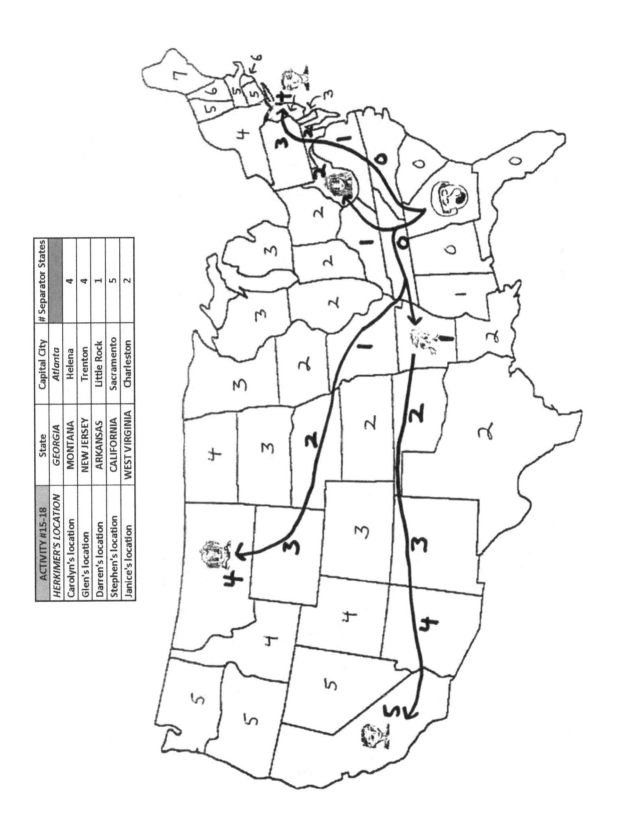

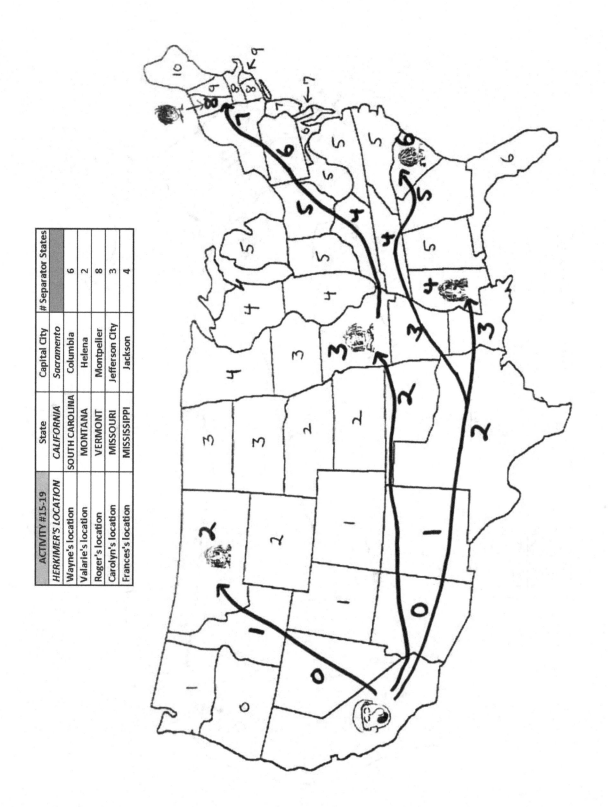

ACTIVITY #15-19	State	Capital City	# Separator States
HERKIMER'S LOCATION	*CALIFORNIA*	*Sacramento*	
Wayne's location	SOUTH CAROLINA	Columbia	6
Valarie's location	MONTANA	Helena	2
Roger's location	VERMONT	Montpelier	8
Carolyn's location	MISSOURI	Jefferson City	3
Frances's location	MISSISSIPPI	Jackson	4

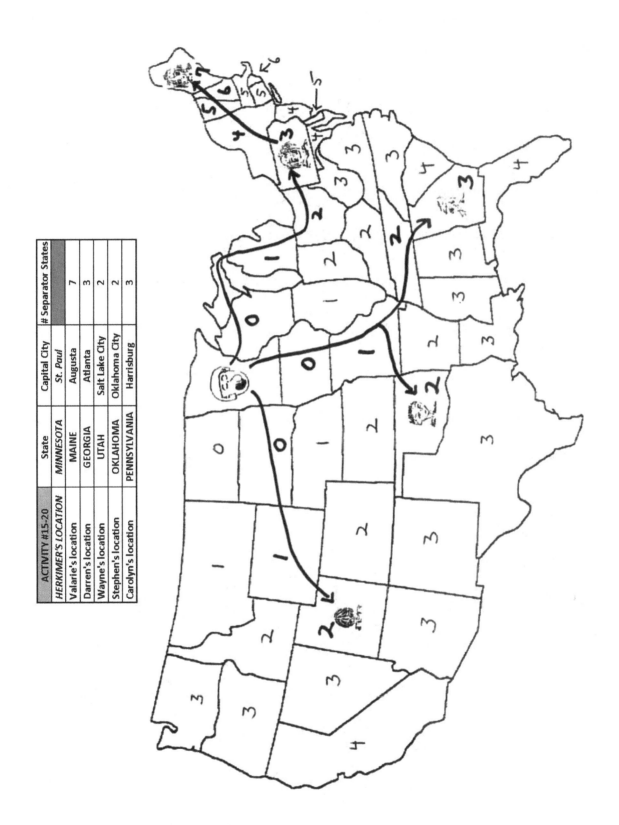

ACTIVITY #15-20	State	Capital City	# Separator States
HERKIMER'S LOCATION	*MINNESOTA*	*St. Paul*	
Valarie's location	MAINE	Augusta	7
Darren's location	GEORGIA	Atlanta	3
Wayne's location	UTAH	Salt Lake City	2
Stephen's location	OKLAHOMA	Oklahoma City	2
Carolyn's location	PENNSYLVANIA	Harrisburg	3

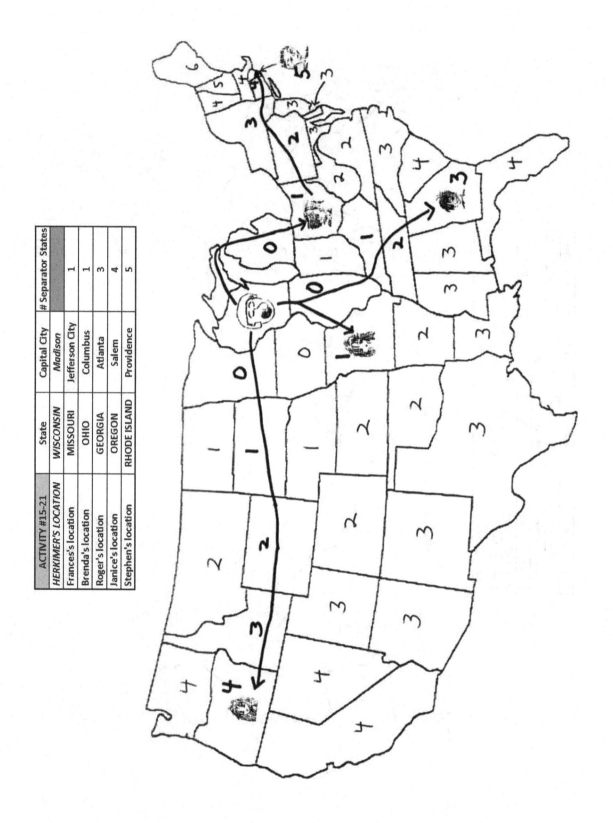

ACTIVITY #15-21	State	Capital City	# Separator States
HERKIMER'S LOCATION	WISCONSIN	Madison	
Frances's location	MISSOURI	Jefferson City	1
Brenda's location	OHIO	Columbus	1
Roger's location	GEORGIA	Atlanta	3
Janice's location	OREGON	Salem	4
Stephen's location	RHODE ISLAND	Providence	5

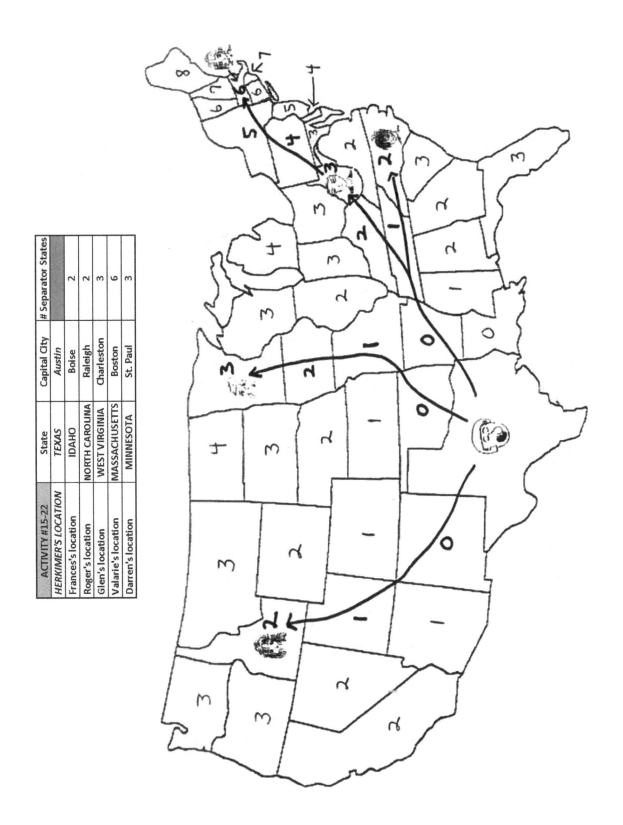

ACTIVITY #15-22	State	Capital City	# Separator States
HERKIMER'S LOCATION	*TEXAS*	*Austin*	
Frances's location	IDAHO	Boise	2
Roger's location	NORTH CAROLINA	Raleigh	2
Glen's location	WEST VIRGINIA	Charleston	3
Valarie's location	MASSACHUSETTS	Boston	6
Darren's location	MINNESOTA	St. Paul	3

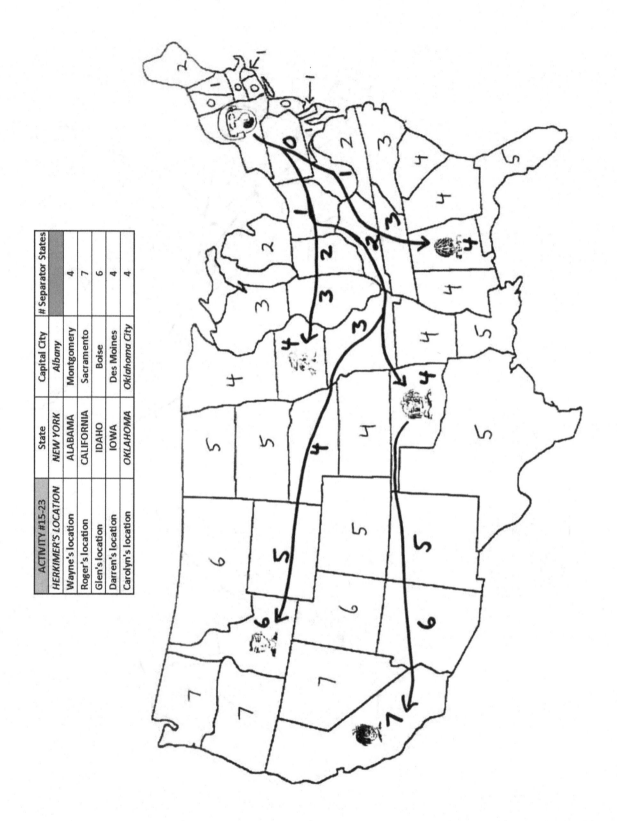

ACTIVITY #15-23			
HERKIMER'S LOCATION	State	Capital City	# Separator States
Wayne's location	*NEW YORK*	*Albany*	
Roger's location	ALABAMA	Montgomery	4
Glen's location	CALIFORNIA	Sacramento	7
Darren's location	IDAHO	Boise	6
Carolyn's location	IOWA	Des Moines	4
	OKLAHOMA	*Oklahoma City*	4

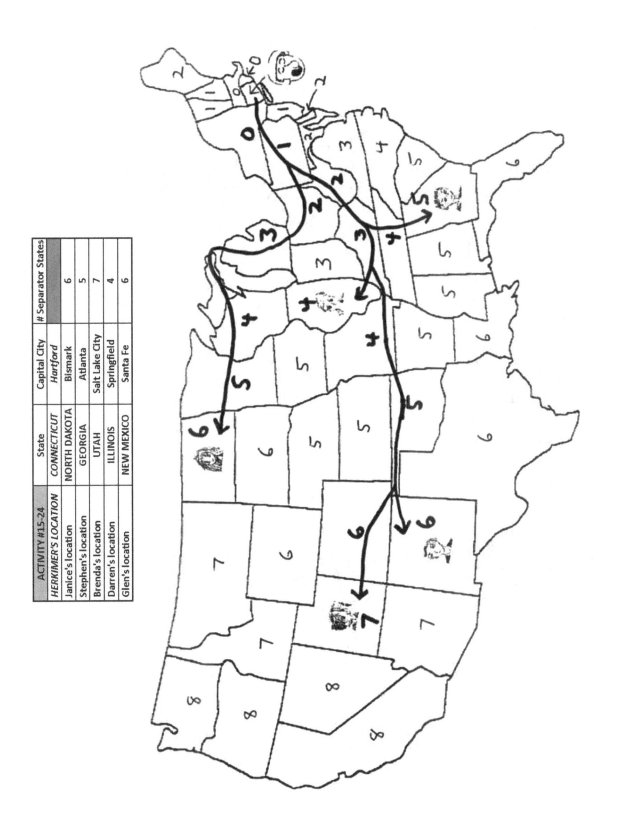

ACTIVITY #15-24			
HERKIMER'S LOCATION	State	Capital City	# Separator States
Janice's location	CONNECTICUT	Hartford	
Stephen's location	NORTH DAKOTA	Bismark	6
Brenda's location	GEORGIA	Atlanta	5
Darren's location	UTAH	Salt Lake City	7
Glen's location	ILLINOIS	Springfield	4
	NEW MEXICO	Santa Fe	6

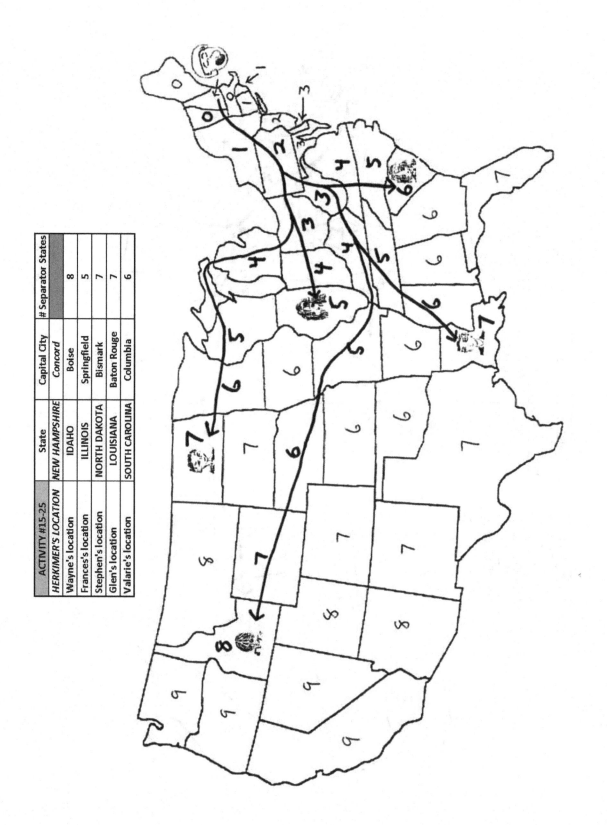

ACTIVITY #15-25	State	Capital City	# Separator States
HERKIMER'S LOCATION	NEW HAMPSHIRE	Concord	
Wayne's location	IDAHO	Boise	8
Frances's location	ILLINOIS	Springfield	5
Stephen's location	NORTH DAKOTA	Bismark	7
Glen's location	LOUISIANA	Baton Rouge	7
Valarie's location	SOUTH CAROLINA	Columbia	6

ACTIVITY #15-26			
HERKIMER'S LOCATION	State	Capital City	# Separator States
Valarie's location	NEW MEXICO	Santa Fe	4
Brenda's location	FLORIDA	Tallahassee	3
Janice's location	WEST VIRGINIA	Charleston	7
Stephen's location	NEW HAMPSHIRE	Concord	2
Frances's location	OREGON	Salem	2
	NEBRASKA	Lincoln	1

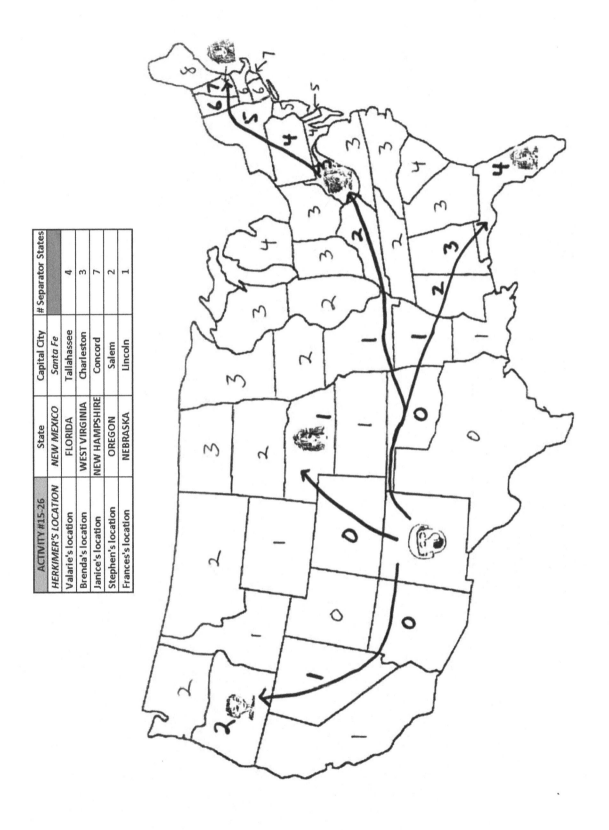

239

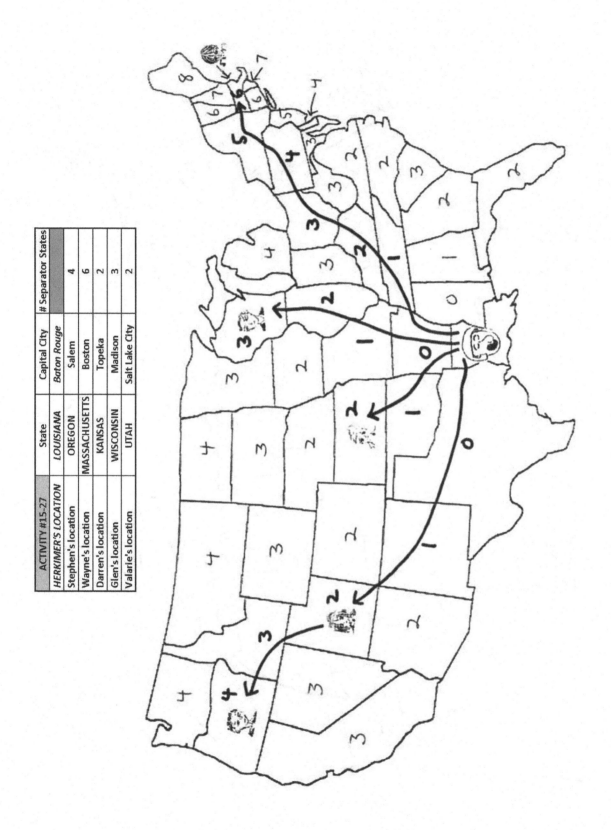

ACTIVITY #15-27	State	Capital City	# Separator States
HERKIMER'S LOCATION	*LOUISIANA*	*Baton Rouge*	
Stephen's location	OREGON	Salem	4
Wayne's location	MASSACHUSETTS	Boston	6
Darren's location	KANSAS	Topeka	2
Glen's location	WISCONSIN	Madison	3
Valarie's location	UTAH	Salt Lake City	2

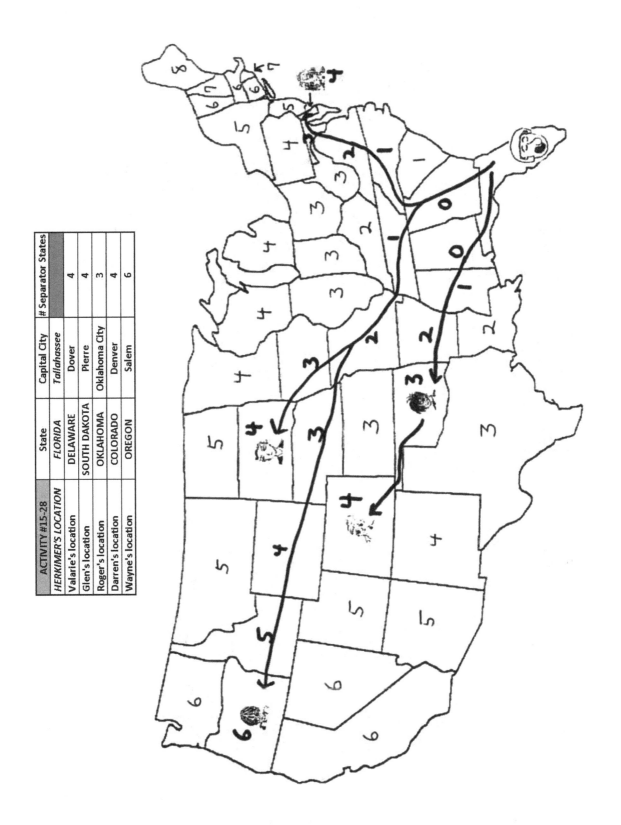

ACTIVITY #15-28	State	Capital City	# Separator States
HERKIMER'S LOCATION	FLORIDA	Tallahassee	
Valarie's location	DELAWARE	Dover	4
Glen's location	SOUTH DAKOTA	Pierre	4
Roger's location	OKLAHOMA	Oklahoma City	3
Darren's location	COLORADO	Denver	4
Wayne's location	OREGON	Salem	6

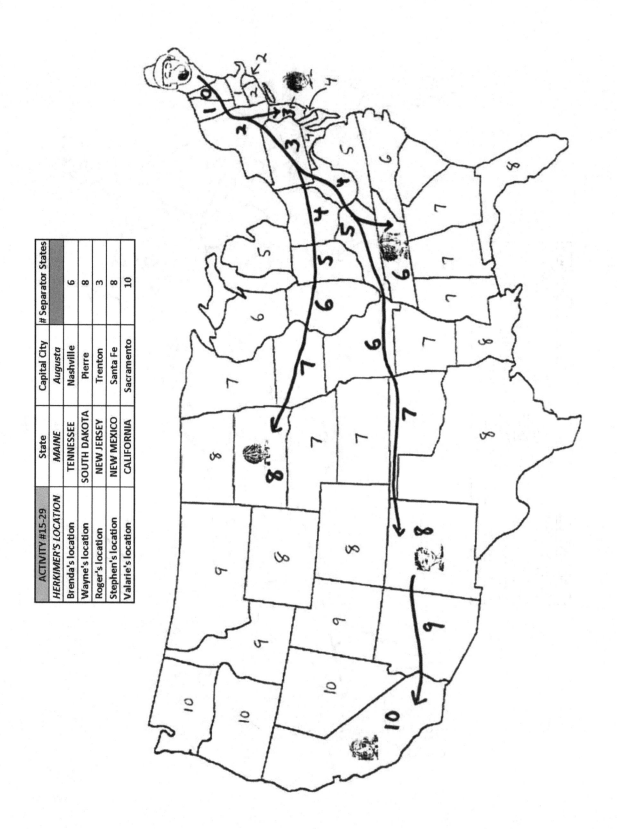

ACTIVITY #15-29	State	Capital City	# Separator States
HERKIMER'S LOCATION	MAINE	Augusta	
Brenda's location	TENNESSEE	Nashville	6
Wayne's location	SOUTH DAKOTA	Pierre	8
Roger's location	NEW JERSEY	Trenton	3
Stephen's location	NEW MEXICO	Santa Fe	8
Valarie's location	CALIFORNIA	Sacramento	10

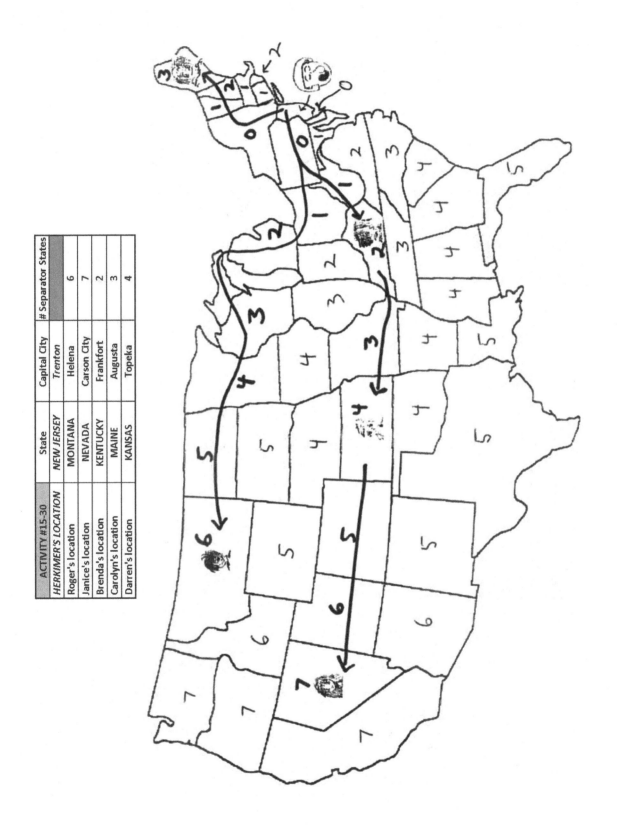

ACTIVITY #15-30	State	Capital City	# Separator States
HERKIMER'S LOCATION	*NEW JERSEY*	*Trenton*	
Roger's location	MONTANA	Helena	6
Janice's location	NEVADA	Carson City	7
Brenda's location	KENTUCKY	Frankfort	2
Carolyn's location	MAINE	Augusta	3
Darren's location	KANSAS	Topeka	4

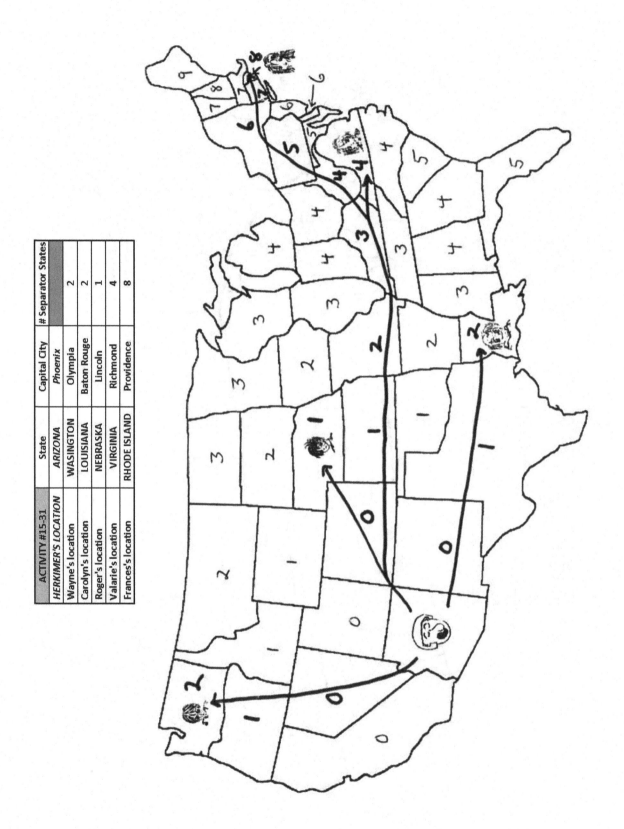

ACTIVITY #15-31	State	Capital City	# Separator States
HERKIMER'S LOCATION	*ARIZONA*	*Phoenix*	
Wayne's location	WASINGTON	Olympia	2
Carolyn's location	LOUISIANA	Baton Rouge	2
Roger's location	NEBRASKA	Lincoln	1
Valarie's location	VIRGINIA	Richmond	4
Frances's location	RHODE ISLAND	Providence	8

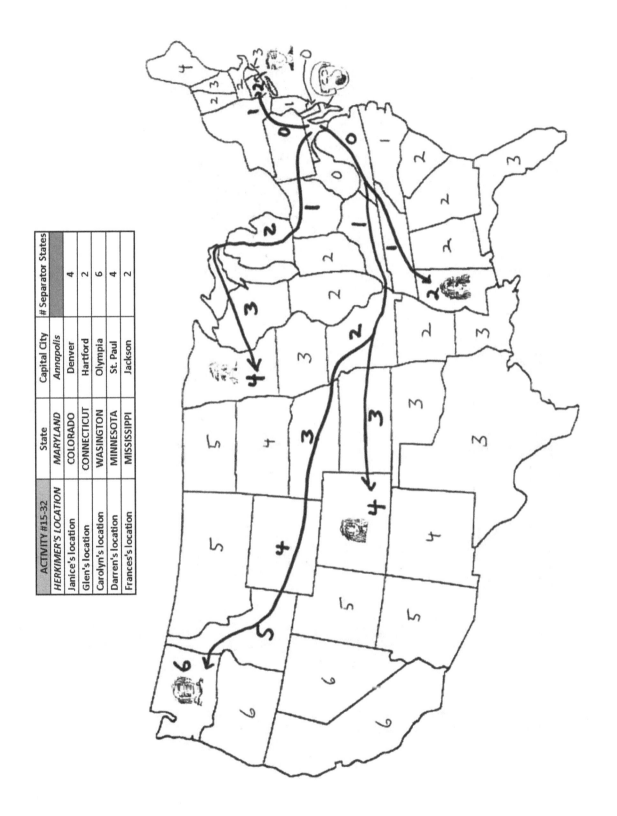

ACTIVITY #15-32			
HERKIMER'S LOCATION	State	Capital City	# Separator States
Janice's location	MARYLAND	Annapolis	
Glen's location	COLORADO	Denver	4
Carolyn's location	CONNECTICUT	Hartford	2
Darren's location	WASINGTON	Olympia	6
Frances's location	MINNESOTA	St. Paul	4
	MISSISSIPPI	Jackson	2

245

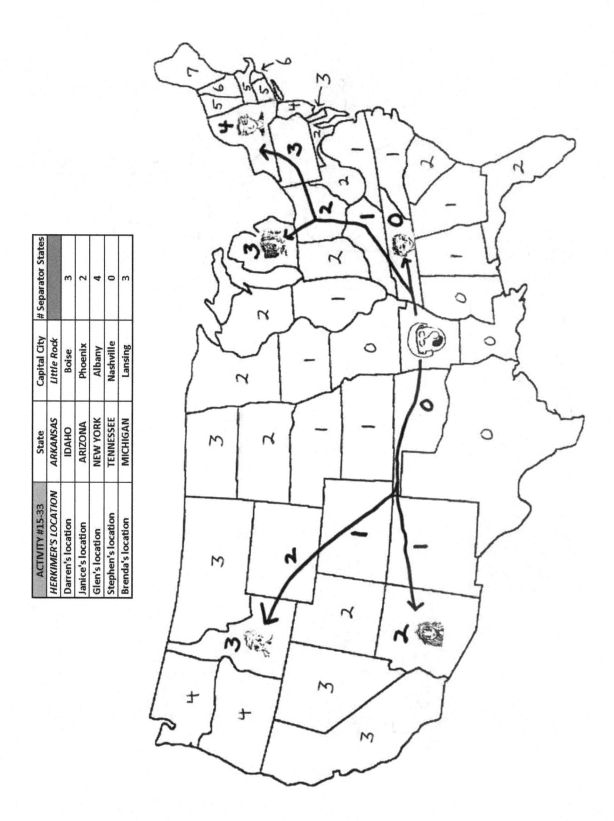

ACTIVITY #15-33	State	Capital City	# Separator States
HERKIMER'S LOCATION	*ARKANSAS*	*Little Rock*	
Darren's location	IDAHO	Boise	3
Janice's location	ARIZONA	Phoenix	2
Glen's location	NEW YORK	Albany	4
Stephen's location	TENNESSEE	Nashville	0
Brenda's location	MICHIGAN	Lansing	3

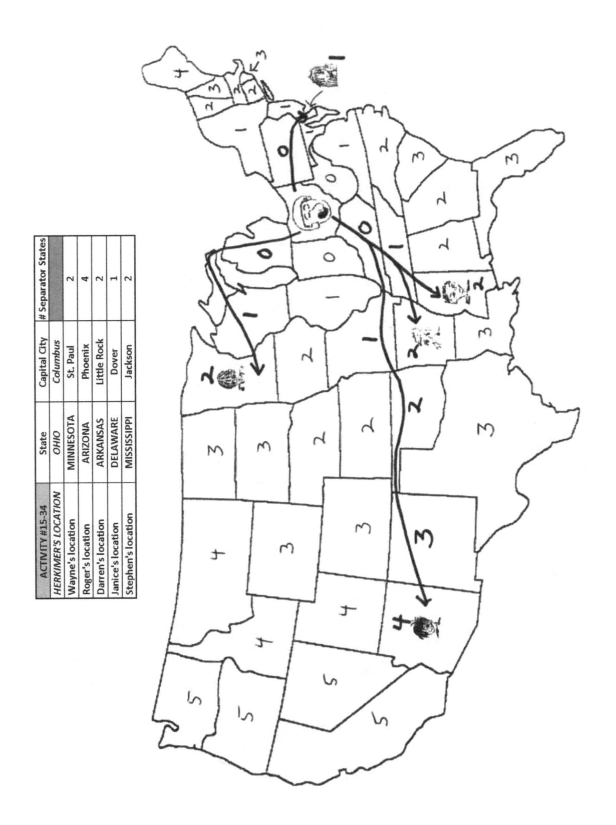

ACTIVITY #15-34			
HERKIMER'S LOCATION	State	Capital City	# Separator States
	OHIO	Columbus	
Wayne's location	MINNESOTA	St. Paul	2
Roger's location	ARIZONA	Phoenix	4
Darren's location	ARKANSAS	Little Rock	2
Janice's location	DELAWARE	Dover	1
Stephen's location	MISSISSIPPI	Jackson	2

247

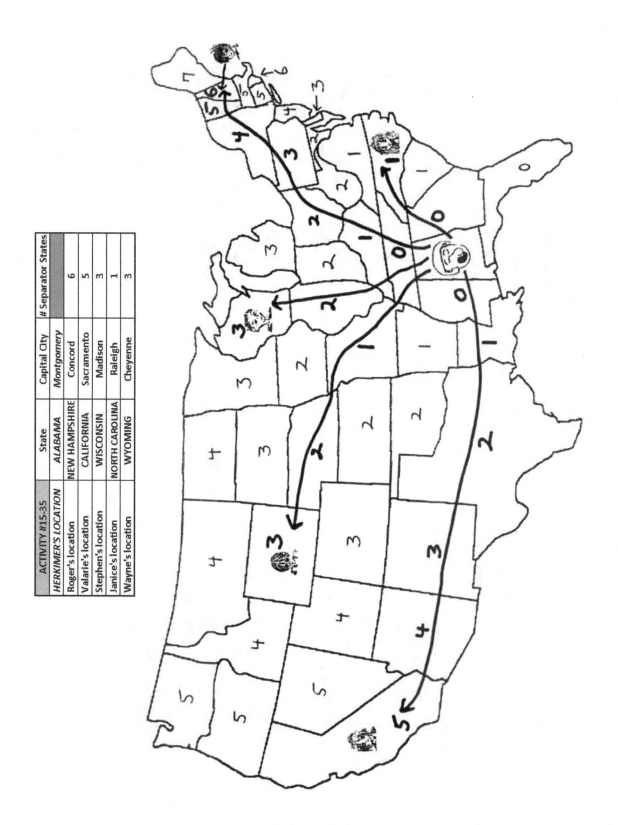

ACTIVITY #15-35	State	Capital City	# Separator States
HERKIMER'S LOCATION	*ALABAMA*	*Montgomery*	
Roger's location	NEW HAMPSHIRE	Concord	6
Valarie's location	CALIFORNIA	Sacramento	5
Stephen's location	WISCONSIN	Madison	3
Janice's location	NORTH CAROLINA	Raleigh	1
Wayne's location	WYOMING	Cheyenne	3

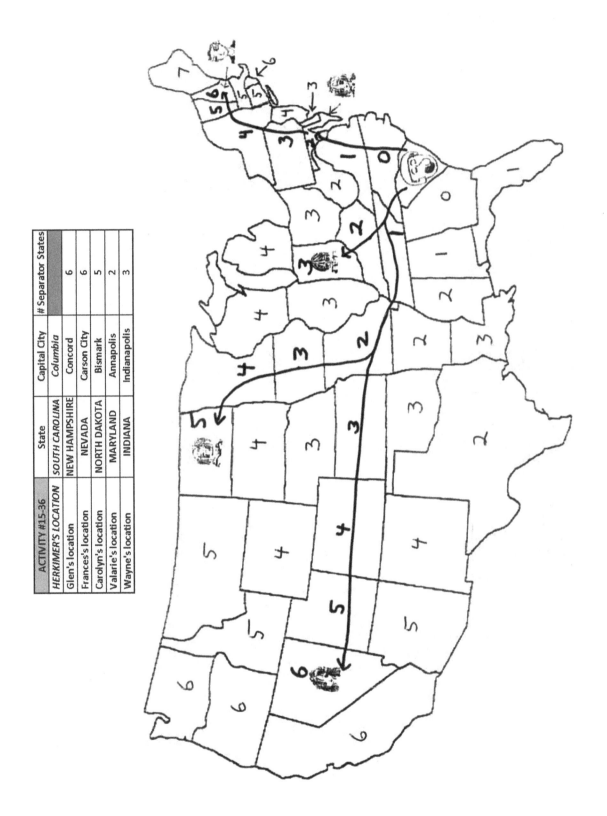

ACTIVITY #15-36	State	Capital City	# Separator States
HERKIMER'S LOCATION	*SOUTH CAROLINA*	*Columbia*	
Glen's location	NEW HAMPSHIRE	Concord	6
Frances's location	NEVADA	Carson City	6
Carolyn's location	NORTH DAKOTA	Bismark	5
Valarie's location	MARYLAND	Annapolis	2
Wayne's location	INDIANA	Indianapolis	3

249

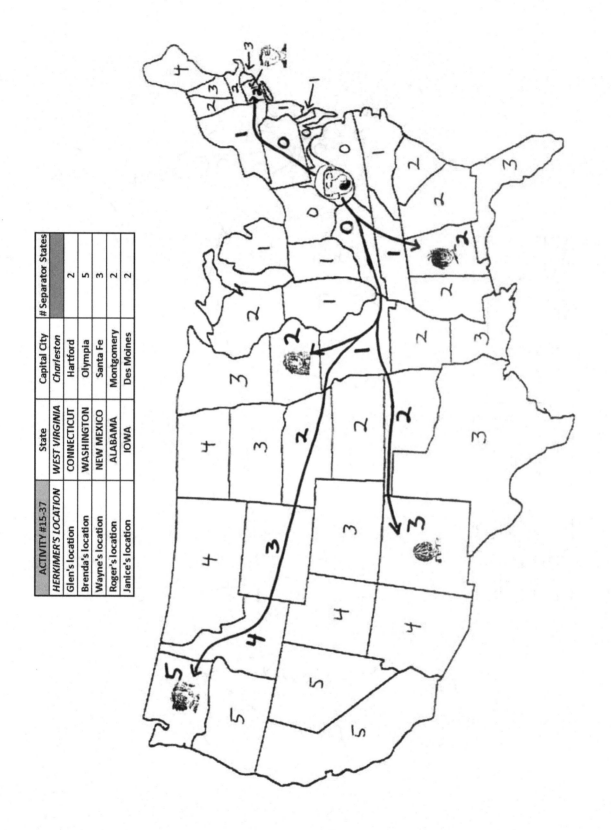

ACTIVITY #15-37			
HERKIMER'S LOCATION	State	Capital City	# Separator States
Glen's location	WEST VIRGINIA	Charleston	
Brenda's location	CONNECTICUT	Hartford	2
Wayne's location	WASHINGTON	Olympia	5
Roger's location	NEW MEXICO	Santa Fe	3
Janice's location	ALABAMA	Montgomery	2
	IOWA	Des Moines	2

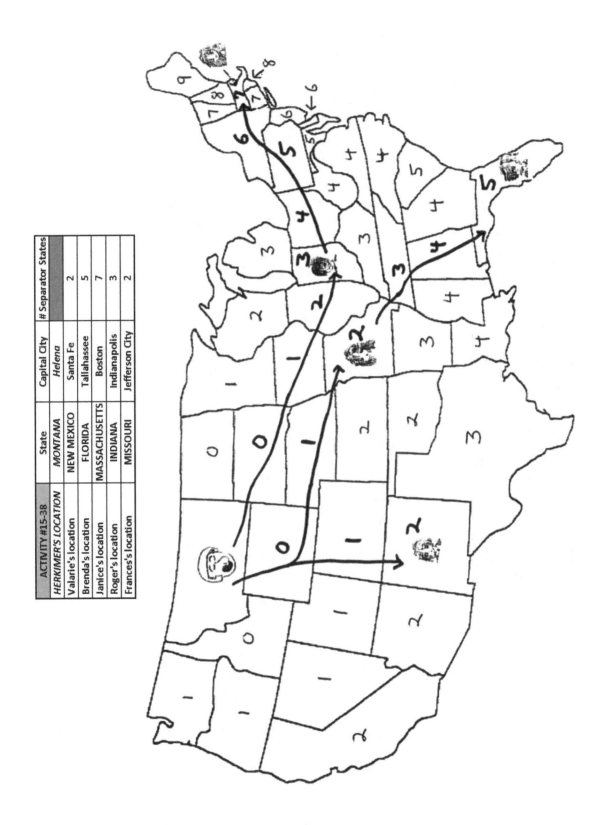

ACTIVITY #15-38	State	Capital City	# Separator States
HERKIMER'S LOCATION	*MONTANA*	*Helena*	
Valarie's location	NEW MEXICO	Santa Fe	2
Brenda's location	FLORIDA	Tallahassee	5
Janice's location	MASSACHUSETTS	Boston	7
Roger's location	INDIANA	Indianapolis	3
Frances's location	MISSOURI	Jefferson City	2

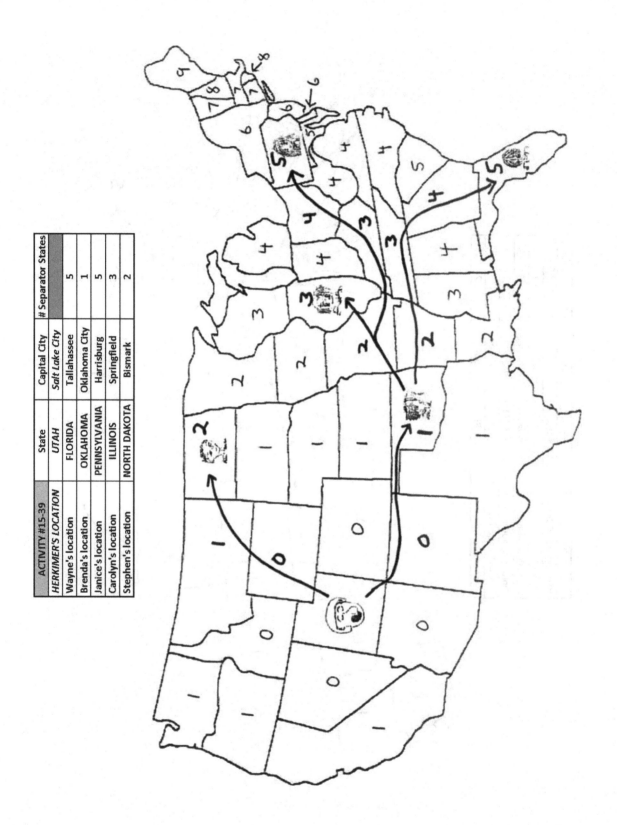

ACTIVITY #15-39			
HERKIMER'S LOCATION	State	Capital City	# Separator States
	UTAH	*Salt Lake City*	
Wayne's location	FLORIDA	Tallahassee	5
Brenda's location	OKLAHOMA	Oklahoma City	1
Janice's location	PENNSYLVANIA	Harrisburg	5
Carolyn's location	ILLINOIS	Springfield	3
Stephen's location	NORTH DAKOTA	Bismark	2

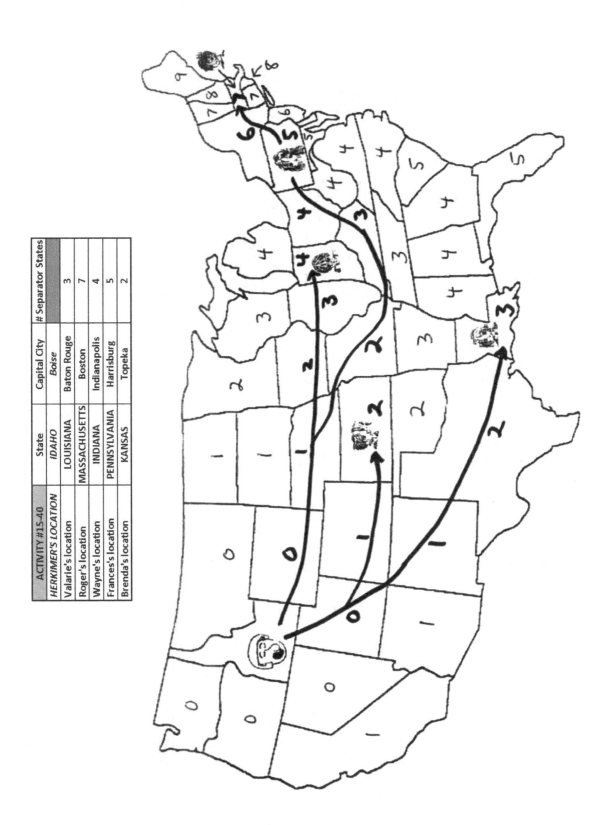

ACTIVITY #15-40	State	Capital City	# Separator States
HERKIMER'S LOCATION	*IDAHO*	*Boise*	
Valarie's location	LOUISIANA	Baton Rouge	3
Roger's location	MASSACHUSETTS	Boston	7
Wayne's location	INDIANA	Indianapolis	4
Frances's location	PENNSYLVANIA	Harrisburg	5
Brenda's location	KANSAS	Topeka	2

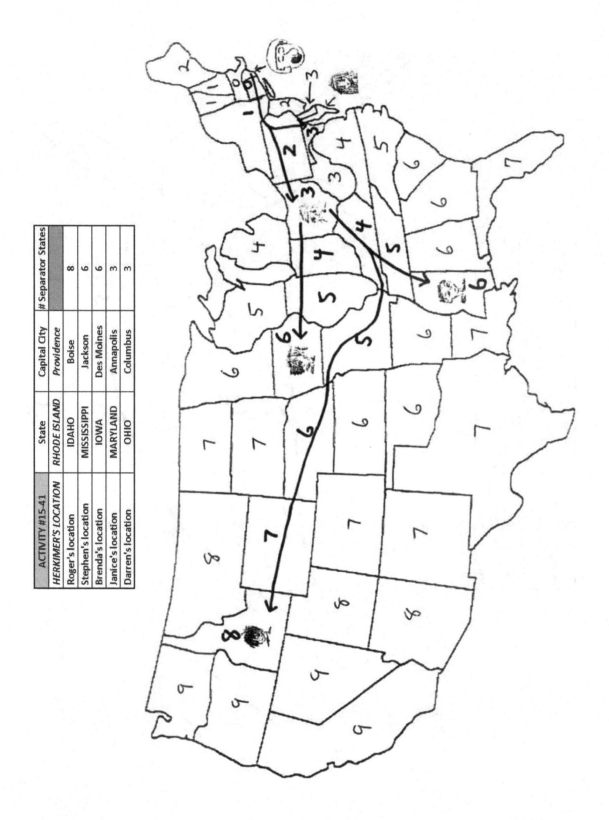

ACTIVITY #15-41	State	Capital City	# Separator States
HERKIMER'S LOCATION	RHODE ISLAND	Providence	
Roger's location	IDAHO	Boise	8
Stephen's location	MISSISSIPPI	Jackson	6
Brenda's location	IOWA	Des Moines	6
Janice's location	MARYLAND	Annapolis	3
Darren's location	OHIO	Columbus	3

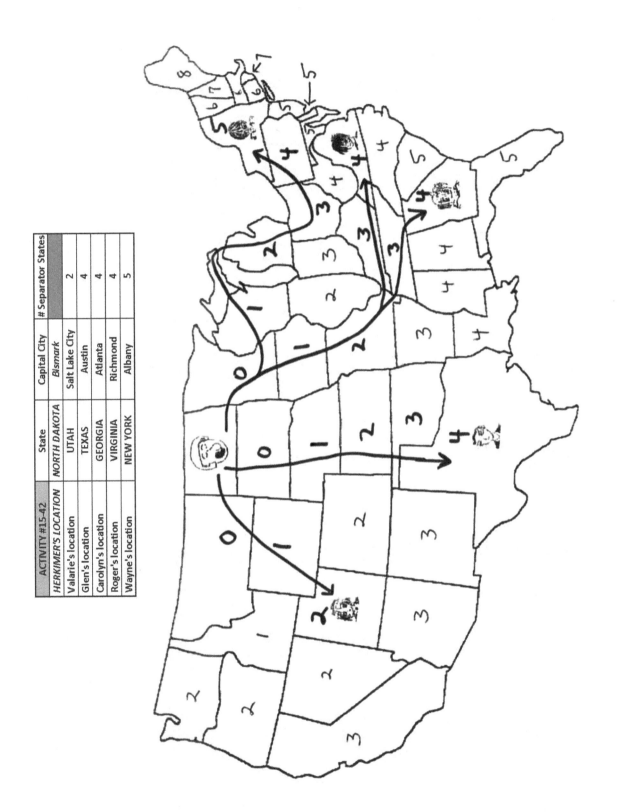

ACTIVITY #15-42	State	Capital City	# Separator States
HERKIMER'S LOCATION	NORTH DAKOTA	Bismark	2
Valarie's location	UTAH	Salt Lake City	4
Glen's location	TEXAS	Austin	4
Carolyn's location	GEORGIA	Atlanta	4
Roger's location	VIRGINIA	Richmond	4
Wayne's location	NEW YORK	Albany	5

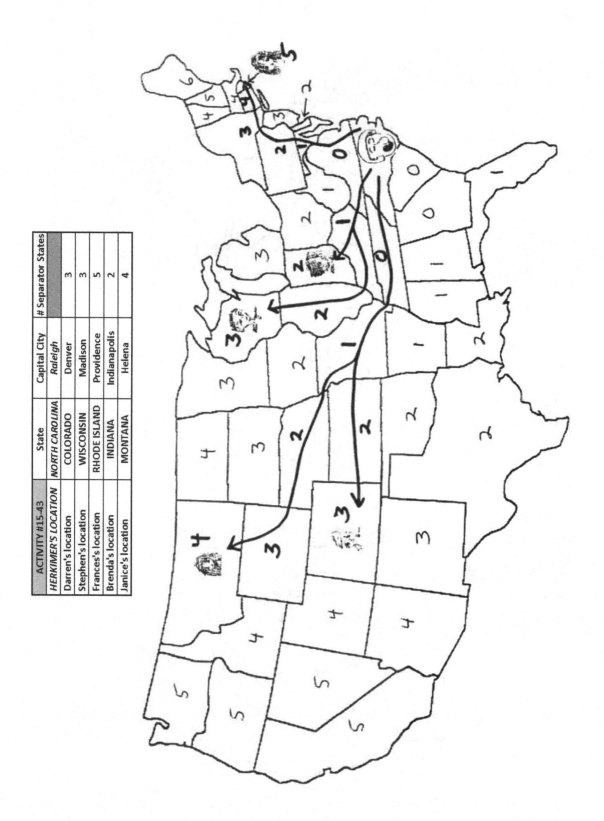

ACTIVITY #15-43	State	Capital City	# Separator States
HERKIMER'S LOCATION	*NORTH CAROLINA*	*Raleigh*	
Darren's location	COLORADO	Denver	3
Stephen's location	WISCONSIN	Madison	3
Frances's location	RHODE ISLAND	Providence	5
Brenda's location	INDIANA	Indianapolis	2
Janice's location	MONTANA	Helena	4

ACTIVITY #15-44			
HERKIMER'S LOCATION	State	Capital City	# Separator States
Glen's location	VIRGINIA	Richmond	
Stephen's location	NEW JERSEY	Trenton	2
Valarie's location	MONTANA	Helena	4
Darren's location	ARIZONA	Phoenix	4
Brenda's location	NEBRASKA	Lincoln	2
	TENNESSEE	Nashville	0

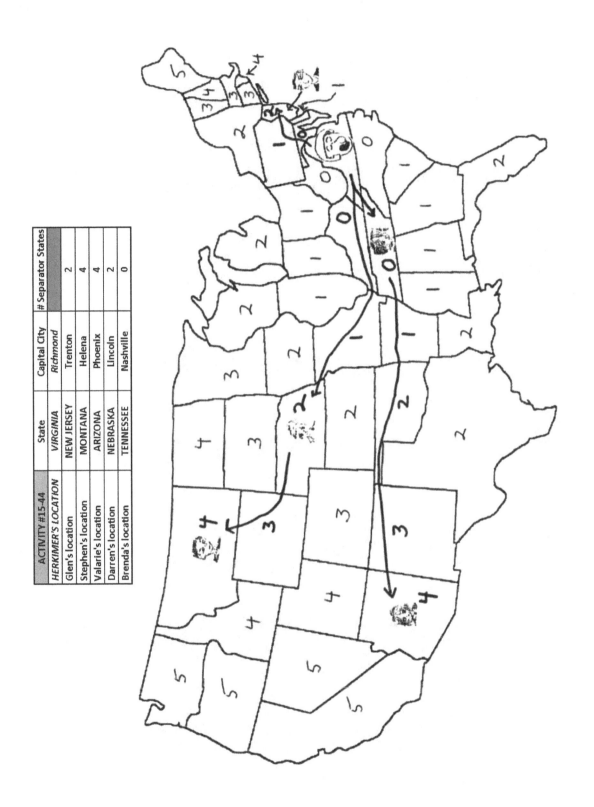

257

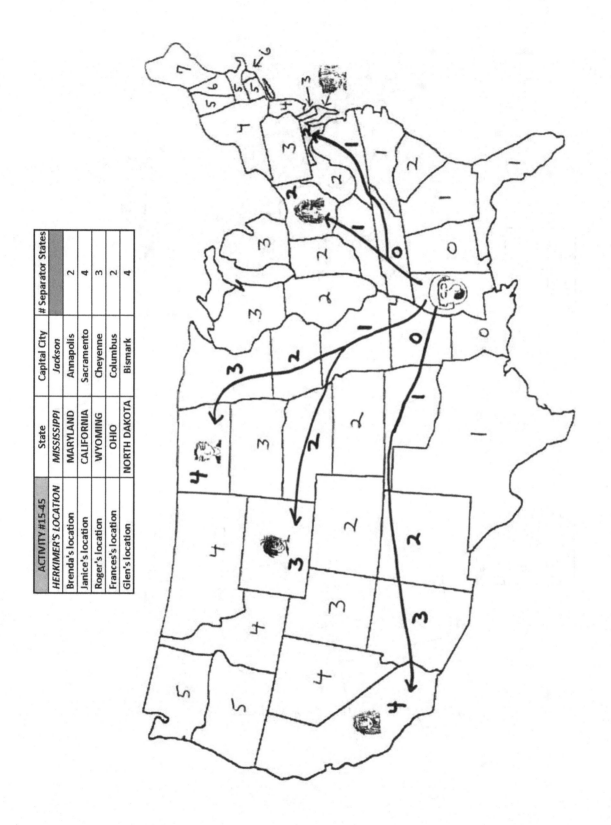

ACTIVITY #15-45	State	Capital City	# Separator States
HERKIMER'S LOCATION	*MISSISSIPPI*	*Jackson*	
Brenda's location	MARYLAND	Annapolis	2
Janice's location	CALIFORNIA	Sacramento	4
Roger's location	WYOMING	Cheyenne	3
Frances's location	OHIO	Columbus	2
Glen's location	NORTH DAKOTA	Bismark	4

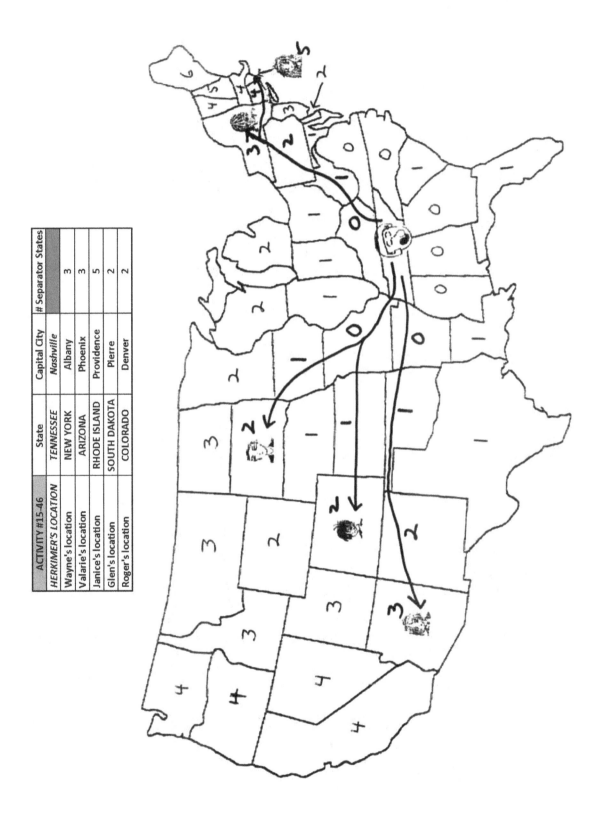

ACTIVITY #15-46	State	Capital City	# Separator States
HERKIMER'S LOCATION	*TENNESSEE*	*Nashville*	
Wayne's location	NEW YORK	Albany	3
Valarie's location	ARIZONA	Phoenix	3
Janice's location	RHODE ISLAND	Providence	5
Glen's location	SOUTH DAKOTA	Pierre	2
Roger's location	COLORADO	Denver	2

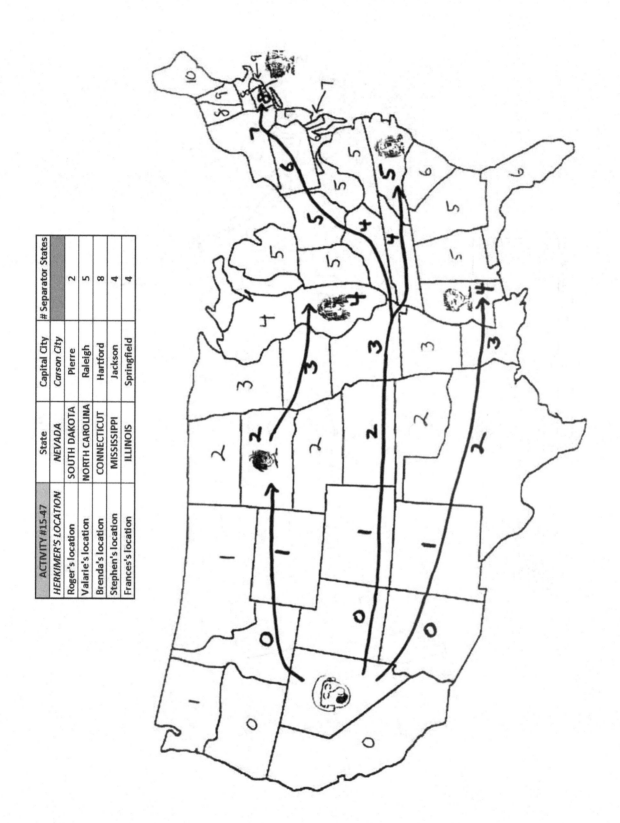

ACTIVITY #15-47			
HERKIMER'S LOCATION	State	Capital City	# Separator States
Roger's location	NEVADA	Carson City	2
Valarie's location	SOUTH DAKOTA	Pierre	5
Brenda's location	NORTH CAROLINA	Raleigh	8
Stephen's location	CONNECTICUT	Hartford	4
Frances's location	MISSISSIPPI	Jackson	4
Frances's location	ILLINOIS	Springfield	4

ACTIVITY #15-48	State	Capital City	# Separator States
HERKIMER'S LOCATION	*INDIANA*	*Indianapolis*	
Stephen's location	MINNESOTA	St. Paul	2
Janice's location	MARYLAND	Annapolis	2
Brenda's location	NEW MEXICO	Santa Fe	3
Glen's location	NEVADA	Carson City	5
Darren's location	FLORIDA	Tallahassee	3

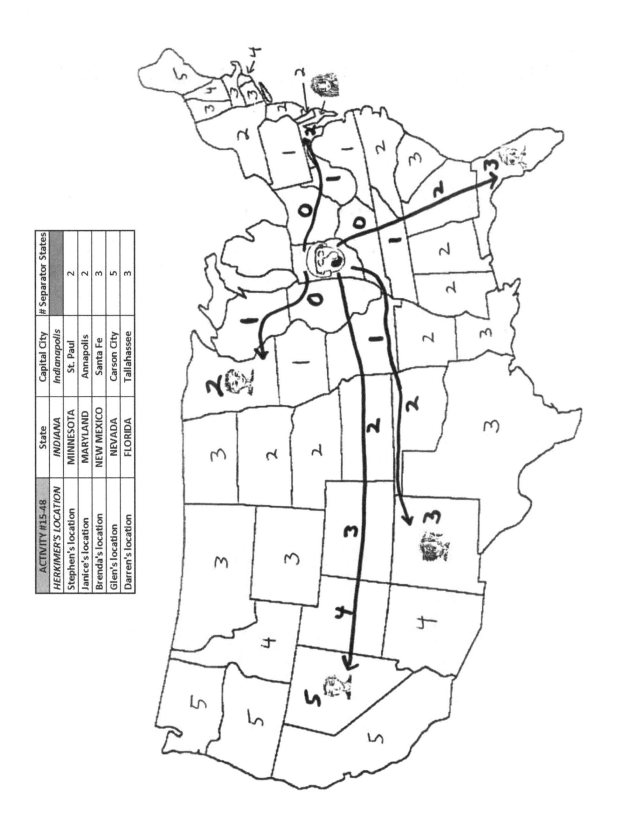

Lines from
THE BALLAD OF THE GREEN BERET

Put silver wings on my son's chest
Make him one of America's best
He'll be a man they'll test one day
Have him win the Green Beret.

The next page represents

U.S. ACTIVITY #16
STATE IDENTIFICATION CHALLENGE FROM SEPARATOR STATE HISTOGRAMS
SOLUTIONS

Herkimer sez:

Congratulations if you were able to correctly identify the state associated with each of the 48 displayed histograms.

Lines from
ANCHORS AWEIGH

Anchors Aweigh, my boys, Anchors Aweigh
Fairwell to college joys, we sail at
                    break of day-ay-ay-ay.
Through our last night on shore, drink
                    to the foam,
Until we meet once more, here's wishing
                    you a happy voyage home.

U.S. ACTIVITY #16 SOLUTIONS

Histogram Order	State
1	WASHINGTON
2	IOWA
3	KANSAS
4	CALIFORNIA
5	MISSOURI
6	PENNSYLVANIA
7	TENNESSEE
8	NEW HAMPSHIRE
9	MARYLAND
10	SOUTH DAKOTA
11	MISSISSIPPI
12	ILLINOIS
13	OREGON
14	KENTUCKY
15	COLORADO
16	GEORGIA
17	MINNESOTA
18	RHODE ISLAND
19	ALABAMA
20	NORTH CAROLINA
21	OKLAHOMA
22	NEBRASKA
23	OHIO
24	SOUTH CAROLINA
25	UTAH
26	NEW YORK
27	NEW MEXICO
28	WEST VIRGINIA
29	DELAWARE
30	NORTH DAKOTA
31	WISCONSIN
32	MICHIGAN
33	WYOMING
34	INDIANA
35	NEW JERSEY
36	ARKANSAS
37	VERMONT
38	MAINE
39	NEVADA
40	MASSACHUSETTS
41	LOUISIANA
42	FLORIDA
43	MONTANA
44	CONNECTICUT
45	ARIZONA
46	IDAHO
47	TEXAS
48	VIRGINIA
	ALASKA
	HAWAII

Lines from
THE STARS AND STRIPES FOREVER

Hurrah for the flag of the free!
May it wave as our standard forever,
The gem of the land and the sea,
The banner of the right.

Note the number of stars on the flag. When this was the flag of the USA, which two of the present 50 states were not states?

> *Unless a man undertakes more than he can possibly do, he will never do all that he can.*
>
> **(Henry Durmmond)**

The following pages represent

U.S. ACTIVITY #17
STATE TRIVIA QUIZ
SOLUTIONS

Herkimer sez:

The questions produced by the Pack required research and dedication for those who sought to answer them. You deserve a big pat on the back if you produced correct responses to each of the 100 questions

Lines from
YANKEE DOODLE

*Father and I went down to camp, along with
Captain Gooding:
And there we saw the men and boys, as think
as hasty pudding.
Yankee doodle, keep it up, Yankee doodle
dandy;
Mind the music and the step, and with the
girls be handy.*

U.S. ACTIVITY #17 solutions

1	*Which state is the #1 producer of peanuts, pecans, and peaches?*	Georgia
2	**Consider the letter x. If you add the number of state names containing the letter and the number of capital city names containing the letter, what is the total?**	3 (New Mexico, Texas, Phoenix)
3	*Which state capital city is on the Delaware River?*	Trenton
4	**How many state names contain the letter b?**	2 (Alabama, Nebraska)
5	**What are the only two states whose name begin with double consonants?**	Florida, Rhode Island
6	*In which major U.S. City do the Monongahela and Allegheny Rivers meet to form the Ohio River?*	Pittsburgh
7	*On which river is Washington, D.C. located?*	Potomac
8	*Which is the only state bordered by the rivers on both its east and west boundaries?*	Iowa (Mississippi River on the east, Missouri and Big Sioux Rivers on the west)
9	*Which east coast state has the shortest coastline?*	New Hampshire (about 14 miles)
10	*How many states have no counties?*	2 (Louisiana has *parishes* and Alaska has *divisions*).
11	**Which states have fewer representatives than senators in Congress?**	Alaska, Delaware, North Dakota, South Dakota, Vermont, Wyoming
12	*What is the only state to have different designs on the two sides of its state flag?*	Oregon
13	**Which 11-letter state name contains only 4 letters of the alphabet?**	Mississippi
14	**How many states were named after a U. S. President?**	1 (Washington)
15	*Which state capital city is named in honor of the third president of the U.S.?*	Jefferson City, Missouri
16	**How many states have more than 1,000 people per square mile?**	2 (New Jersey, Rhode Island)
17	**Which state name contains only 3 letters of the alphabet?**	Ohio
18	*Which state has a coastline that is longer than the length of all other state coastlines combined?*	Alaska (6,640 miles)
19	**Which four state names have the same first letter as their respective capital cities?**	Delaware (Dover), Hawaii (Honolulu), Indiana (Indianapolis), Oklahoma (Oklahoma City)
20	*Which of the contiguous 48 states has the northernmost land location?*	Minnesota (Angle Inlet)
21	**Which is the only state whose name begins with the letter A but does not end with the letter a?**	Arkansas
22	*Which state contains the oldest state university in the United States?*	North Carolina (University of North Carolina at Chapel Hill was first public university to admit students in 1795).
23	*Which is the only state whose flag is not rectangular?*	Ohio (flag is a pennant)
24	**How many states have a shoreline along at least one of the five Great Lakes?**	8 (Minnesota, Michigan, Wisconsin, Illinois, Indiana, Ohio, Pennsylvania, New York)

25	**Which state has the largest number of bordering states?**	Both Missouri and Tennessee have 8 bordering states.
26	**Which state is the only one whose name has just one syllable?**	Maine
27	*Which state was the first to give women the right to vote?*	Wyoming
28	*Which state capital city has the highest elevation?*	Santa Fe (7,000 feet)
29	**How many state names contain a specific letter at least three times?**	13 (Alabama, Alaska, Arkansas, Colorado, Connecticut, Illinois, Massachusetts, Mississippi, New Jersey, Pennsylvania, Tennessee, Virginia, West Virginia)
30	*Which state has no location that is more than 345 feet above sea level?*	Florida
31	**How many states were named in honor of a person?**	11 (Delaware, Georgia, Louisiana, Maryland, New York, North Carolina, Pennsylvania, South Carolina, Virginia, Washington, West Virginia) See state information table.
32	*In what state was the first intercollegiate football game played?*	New Jersey (Rutgers vs. Princeton in 1869).
33	*Which state contains the tallest building on the North American continent?*	Illinois (Sears Tower in Chicago)
34	*Which state has 2 non-connecting rivers with the same name?*	Florida has two non-connecting rivers, each called the Withlocoohee River.
35	*Which is the only state that borders 3 Canadian provinces?*	Montana
36	**How many state names contain the letter y?**	6 (Kentucky, Maryland, New Jersey, New York, Pennsylvania, Wyoming)
37	*"Home on the Range" is the official state song of which state?*	Kansas
38	**Which state has the greatest percentage of its border as coastline?**	Hawaii (100% of border is coastline)
39	**In terms of population, which is the smallest state capital city?**	Montpelier
40	*The praying mantis is the state insect of which state?*	Connecticut
41	*Which capital city originally had the word "Great" as part of its name?*	Salt Lake City was originally Great Salt Lake City. "Great" dropped in 1865.
42	**How many state names contain the letter f?**	2 (Florida, California)
43	*Which inland state has the most shoreline?*	Michigan
44	**How many states have less then 10 people per square mile?**	4 (North Dakota, Montana, Wyoming, Alaska)
45	*In which state was Elvis Presley born?*	Mississippi
46	**How many of the Great Lakes have only U. S. coastlines?**	1 (Lake Michigan)
47	*Which large U.S. City, not a state capital, is known as "the City of Roses?"*	Portland, Oregon
48	**The roadrunner is the official bird of which state?**	New Mexico
49	*Which are the northernmost, westernmost, easternmost and southernmost states?*	Alaska is northernmost, westernmost and easternmost; Hawaii is southernmost.

270

50	How many state names contain the letter k more than once?	1 (Kentucky)
51	Which letter is the most common first letter in state capital city names?	C and S. There are 6 capital city names beginning with C (Carson City, Charleston, Cheyenne, Columbia, Columbus, Concord) and 6 beginning with S (Sacramento, Salem, Salt Lake City, Sante Fe, Springfield, St. Paul)
52	*Which is the only state whose entire border has no straight line section?*	Hawaii
53	*Which state capital city is know as the Sailing Capital of the world?*	Annapolis
54	*Which four state capital cities are named after cities in England?*	Boston, Dover, Hartford, Richmond
55	*Which state contains the town of Dixon, the boyhood home of President Ronald Reagan?*	Illinois
56	*Which state has more mountain ranges than any other state?*	Nevada
57	How many names of state capital cities begin with the letter C?	6 (Carson City, Charleston, Cheyenne, Columbia, Columbus, Concord)
58	How many states share a border with Tennessee?	8 (Missouri, Arkansas, Mississippi, Alabama, Georgia, North Carolina, Virginia, Kentucky)
59	How many states share a border with California?	3 (Oregon, Nevada, Arizona)
60	*The name of which state capital means "sheltered harbor"?*	Honolulu
61	How many states share a border with Canada?	10 (Washington, Idaho, Montana, North Dakota, Minnesota, Michigan, New York, Vermont, New Hampshire, Maine)
62	Which is the only state whose name has no common letters with the name of its capital city?	South Dakota (Pierre)
63	Which four states share a common boundary?	Colorado, Utah, New Mexico, Arizona
64	Which state name is the only one starting with two vowels?	Iowa
65	(a) How many state names begin with the letter J? (b) How many state capital city names begin with the letter J?	(a) 0; (b) 3 (Jackson, Jefferson City, Juneau)
66	*Which state capital is the home of the National Cowboy Hall of Fame?*	Oklahoma City
67	How many states have borders that are just four straight sides?	Two (Colorado and Wyoming)
68	How many state have a direction in their names?	5; North Carolina, South Carolina, North Dakota, South Dakota, West Virginia
69	How many states share a border with South Carolina?	2 (North Carolina and Georgia)
70	*Which state raises more turkeys than any other state?*	California
71	How many state names contain only one of the vowels *a, e, i, o, u* ?	7(Alabama, Alaska, Arkansas, Kansas, Mississippi, New Jersey, Tennessee)
72	How many state names contain a specific letter 4 times?	4 (Alabama, Massachusetts, Mississippi, Tennessee)

73	How many states have the word "New" in their names?	4; New Hampshire, New Jersey, New Mexico, New York
74	How many state capital city names contain 3 words?	1 (Salt Lake City)
75	How many states share a border with Michigan?	3 (Wisconsin, Indiana, Ohio)
76	How many states entered the union before 1900?	45
77	Which state contains 75% of the land in the U.S. with an altitude exceeding 10,000 feet?	Colorado
78	Which state has more miles of river than any other state?	Nebraska (about 23,000 miles of river)
79	How many islands make up the state of Hawaii?	132 (8 major islands and 124 islets)
80	How many states share a border with Mexico?	4 (California, Arizona, New Mexico, Texas)
81	How many state capital cities have a population exceeding one million?	1 (Phoenix)
82	Which two states border Washington, D.C.?	Maryland and Virginia
83	Which state has a town called Hell?	Michigan
84	Which state has the largest lake entirely within its borders?	Utah (Great Salt Lake)
85	Which state has 75% of its land area covered by forests?	West Virginia
86	How many state names contain two words?	10 (New Hampshire, New Jersey, New Mexico, New York, North Carolina, North Dakota, Rhode Island, South Carolina, South Dakota, West Virginia)
87	What is the actual color of bluegrass in Kentucky, the Bluegrass State?	Green. The grass produces bluish purple buds that give a blue cast to the grass.
88	Which state has milk as its official beverage?	North Dakota
89	Which state shares a border with just one other state?	Maine
90	How many states have their lowest elevation point below sea level?	2 (California and Louisiana)
91	In a listing of the 50 state names, how many letters of the alphabet appear only once in the entire list?	2 (The letter J appears only in NEW JERSEY; the letter Z appears only in ARIZONA.)
92	In the list of 50 state names, which letter occurs most frequently?	The letter A. It occurs 61 times.
93	Which state has the most people per square mile?	New Jersey
94	In a listing of the 50 state names, which letter occurs the least number of times?	Q (It does not occur in any state name)
95	In the list of 50 state capital city names, how many times does the letter Q appear?	0
96	How many state capital city names contain the word "City"?	4 (Carson City, Jefferson City, Oklahoma City, Salt Lake City)
97	In which state is the Pro Football Hall of Fame located?	Ohio
98	In terms of land area, which are the three largest states?	(1) Alaska, (2) Texas, (3) California
99	Which state produces, by far, the most blueberries?	Maine
100	Which state has the property that one can get into any of its 6 bordering states by going directly south from somewhere in the state?	Arkansas

> *If you have an hour, will you not improve that hour, instead of idling it away?*
>
> **(Lord Chesterfield)**

Display #1
LETTER DISTRIBUTION IN STATE NAMES

Herkimer sez:

This table shows the distribution of letters in the names of each of the 50 states. It will be useful for those who do the 100 question trivia quiz in State Activity #17.

Lines from
GOD BLESS THE USA

I'm proud to be an American
Where at least I know I'm free,
And I won't forget the men who died
Who gave that right to me.

LETTER DISTRIBUTION IN STATE NAMES

		A	B	C	D	E	F	G	H	I	J	K	L	M	N	O	P	Q	R	S	T	U	V	W	X	Y	Z	TOTALS
1	ALABAMA	4	1										1	1														7
2	ALASKA	3										1	1							1								6
3	ARIZONA	2								1					1	1			1								1	7
4	ARKANSAS	3										1			1				1	2								8
5	CALIFORNIA	2		1			1			2			1		1	1			1									10
6	COLORADO	1		1	1								1			3			1									8
7	CONNECTICUT			3		1				1					2	1					2	1						11
8	DELAWARE	2			1	2							1						1					1				8
9	FLORIDA	1			1		1			1			1			1			1									7
10	GEORGIA	1				1		2		1						1			1									7
11	HAWAII	2							1	2														1				6
12	IDAHO	1			1				1	1						1												5
13	ILLINOIS									3			2		1	1			1									8
14	INDIANA	2			1					2					2													7
15	IOWA	1								1						1								1				4
16	KANSAS	2										1			1					2								6
17	KENTUCKY			1		1						2			1					1	1	1				1		8
18	LOUISIANA	2								2			1		1	1			1	1		1						9
19	MAINE	1			1					1				1	1													5
20	MARYLAND	2			1								1	1	1				1							1		8
21	MASSACHUSETTS	2		1		1			1					1						4	2	1						13
22	MICHIGAN	1		1				1	1	2				1	1													8
23	MINNESOTA	1				1				1				1	2	1				1	1							9
24	MISSISSIPPI									4				1			2			4								11
25	MISSOURI									2				1		1			1	2		1						8
26	MONTANA	2												1	2	1					1							7
27	NEBRASKA	2	1			1									1				1	1								8
28	NEVADA	2			1	1									1								1					6
29	NEW HAMPSHIRE	1				2			2	1				1	1		1		1	1				1				12
30	NEW JERSEY					3					1				1				1	1				1		1		9
31	NEW MEXICO			1		2				1				1	1	1								1	1			9
32	NEW YORK					1						1			1	1			1					1		1		7
33	NORTH CAROLINA	2		1					1	1			1		2	2			2		1							13
34	NORTH DAKOTA	2			1				1			1			1	2			1		2							11
35	OHIO								1	1						2												4
36	OKLAHOMA	2							1			1	1	1		2												8
37	OREGON				1	1									1	2			1									6
38	PENNSYLVANIA	2			1					1			1		3		1			1			1			1		12
39	RHODE ISLAND	1			2	1			1	1			1		1	1			1	1								11
40	SOUTH CAROLINA	2		1					1	1			1		1	2			1	1	1	1						13
41	SOUTH DAKOTA	2			1				1			1				2				1	2	1						11
42	TENNESSEE					4									2					2	1							9
43	TEXAS	1				1														1	1				1			5
44	UTAH	1							1												1	1						4
45	VERMONT					1								1	1	1			1		1		1					7
46	VIRGINIA	1					1		3						1				1				1					8
47	WASHINGTON	1						1	1	1					2	1				1	1			1				10
48	WEST VIRGINIA	1			1	1			3						1				1	1	1		1	1				12
49	WISCONSIN			1						2					2	1				2				1				9
50	WYOMING						1			1				1	1	1								1		1		7
	TOTALS ---->	61	2	12	11	28	2	8	15	44	1	10	15	14	43	36	4	0	22	32	19	8	5	11	2	6	1	412

Lines from
LET PEACE BEGIN WITH ME

Let there be peace on Earth,
And let it begin with me.
Let there be peace on Earth,
The peace that was meant to be.

> *First say to yourself what you would be; and then do what you have to do.*
>
> **(Epictetus)**

Display #2
STATE INFORMATION TABLE

Herkimer sez:

The following pages contain lots of very interesting information about each of the 50 states of the U.S.

A verse from "Taps"

Day is done
Gone the sun
From the Lakes
From the hills
From the sky.
All is well
Safely rest.
God is nigh.

STATE INFORMATION TABLE

ALABAMA

	Entered Union (Rank): December 4, 1819 (22)	Population (Rank): 4,710,000 (23)	Capital City: Montgomery	Nickname: Yellowhammer State
	State tree: Southern longleaf pine	State flower: Camellia	State bird: Yellowhammer	State motto: "We dare defend our rights."
	U.S. Representatives: 7	Electoral votes: 9	Land Area: 50,750 sq. miles	
	Origin of state name: Uncertain, but may have come from a river named "Alibamu" by European explorers after a local Indian tribe.			

ALASKA

	Entered Union (Rank): January 3, 1959 (49)	Population (Rank): 699,000 (47)	Capital City: Juneau	Nickname: The Last Frontier, Land of the Midnight Sun
	State tree: Sitka Spruce	State flower: Forget-me-not	State bird: Willow ptarmigan	State motto: "North to the Future."
	U.S. Representatives: 1	Electoral votes: 3	Land Area: 570,374 sq. miles	
	Origin of state name: From an Aleut word meaning "great land" or "that which the sea breaks against."			

ARIZONA

	Entered Union (Rank): February 4, 1912 (48)	Population (Rank): 6,596,000 (14)	Capital City: Phoenix	Nickname: Grand Canyon State
	State tree: Palo verde	State flower: Flower of saguaro cactus	State bird: Cactus wren	State motto: "God enriches."
	U.S. Representatives: 8	Electoral votes: 10	Land Area: 113,642 sq. miles	
	Origin of state name: Thought to be from Native American *Arizonac*, meaning "little spring."			

ARKANSAS

	Entered Union (Rank): June 15, 1836 (25)	Population (Rank): 2,890,000 (32)	Capital City: Little Rock	Nickname: The Natural State
	State tree: Pine	State flower: Apple blossom	State bird: Mockingbird	State motto: "The people rule."
	U.S. Representatives: 4	Electoral votes: 6	Land Area: 50,075 sq. miles	
	Origin of state name: From the Quapaw Indians.			

CALIFORNIA

	Entered Union (Rank): September 9, 1850 (31)	Population (Rank): 36,962,000 (1)	Capital City: Sacramento	Nickname: Golden State
	State tree: California redwood	State flower: Golden poppy	State bird: California valley quail	State motto: "I have found it."
	U.S. Representatives: 53	Electoral votes: 55	Land Area: 155,973 sq. miles	
	Origin of state name: From a book *Las Sergas de Esplandian*, by Garcia Ordonez de Montalvo, circa 1500.			

COLORADO

Entered Union (Rank): August 1, 1876 (38)	Population (Rank): 5,025,000 (22)	Capital City: Denver	Nickname: Centennial State
State tree: Colorado blue spruce	State flower: Rocky Mountain columbine	State bird: Lark bunting	State motto: "Nothing without providence."
U.S. Representatives: 7	Electoral votes: 9	Land Area: 103,730 sq. miles	
Origin of state name: From the Spanish, "ruddy" or "red."			

CONNECTICUT

Entered Union (Rank): January 9, 1788 (5)	Population (Rank): 3,519,000 (29)	Capital City: Hartford	Nickname: Nutmeg State
State tree: White Oak	State flower: Mountain laurel	State bird: American robin	State motto: "He who transplanted still sustains."
U.S. Representatives: 5	Electoral votes: 7	Land Area: 4,845 sq. miles	
Origin of state name: From a Quinnehtukqut Indian word meaning "beside the long tidal river."			

DELAWARE

Entered Union (Rank): December 7, 1787 (1)	Population (Rank): 885,122 (45)	Capital City: Dover	Nickname: First State, Diamond State
State tree: American holly	State flower: Peach blossom	State bird: Blue hen chicken	State motto: "Liberty and independence."
U.S. Representatives: 1	Electoral votes: 3	Land Area: 1,955 sq. miles	
Origin of state name: From the Delaware River and Bay, named for Sir Thomas West, Baron De La Warr.			

FLORIDA

Entered Union (Rank): March 3, 1845 (27)	Population (Rank): 18,538,000 (4)	Capital City: Tallahassee	Nickname: Sunshine Sate
State tree: Sabal palm	State flower: Orange blossom	State bird: Mockingbird	State motto: "In God we trust."
U.S. Representatives: 25	Electoral votes: 27	Land Area: 54,153 sq. miles	
Origin of state name: From the Spanish *Pascua Florida*, meaning "feast of flowers."			

GEORGIA

Entered Union (Rank): January 2, 1788 (4)	Population (Rank): 9,830,000 (9)	Capital City: Atlanta	Nickname: Peach State
State tree: Live oak	State flower: Cherokee rose	State bird: Brown thrasher	State motto: "Wisdom, justice and moderation."
U.S. Representatives: 13	Electoral votes: 15	Land Area: 57,919 sq. miles	
Origin of state name: In honor of George II of England.			

HAWAII

Entered Union (Rank): August 21, 1959 (50)	Population (Rank): 1,296,000 (42)	Capital City: Honolulu	Nickname: Aloha State
State tree: Kukui (Candlenut)	State flower: Yellow hibiscus	State bird: Nene (Hawaiian goose)	State motto: "The life of the land is perpetuated in righteousness."
U.S. Representatives: 2	Electoral votes: 4	Land Area: 6,423 sq. miles	
Origin of state name: Uncertain, but possibly from a Polynesian word meaning "ancestral home."			

IDAHO

		Entered Union (Rank): July 3, 1890 (43)	Population (Rank): 1,546,000 (39)	Capital City: Boise	Nickname: Gem State
		State tree: White pine	State flower: Syringa (lilac)	State bird: Mountain bluebird	State motto: "It is forever."
		U.S. Representatives: 2	Electoral votes: 4	Land Area: 82,751 sq. miles	
		Origin of state name: An invented name; the meaning is unknown.			

ILLINOIS

		Entered Union (Rank): December 3, 1818 (21)	Population (Rank): 12,911,000 (5)	Capital City: Springfield	Nickname: Prairie State
		State tree: White oak	State flower: Violet	State bird: Cardinal	State motto: "State sovereignty, national union."
		U.S. Representatives: 19	Electoral votes: 21	Land Area: 55,053 sq. miles	
		Origin of state name: Algonquian for "tribe of superior men."			

INDIANA

		Entered Union (Rank): December 11, 1816 (19)	Population (Rank): 6,424,000 (16)	Capital City: Indianapolis	Nickname: Hoosier State
		State tree: Tulip tree	State flower: Peony	State bird: Cardinal	State motto: "The crossroads of America."
		U.S. Representatives: 9	Electoral votes: 11	Land Area: 35,870 sq. miles	
		Origin of state name: Means "land of Indians."			

IOWA

		Entered Union (Rank): December 28, 1846 (29)	Population (Rank): 3,008,000 (30)	Capital City: Des Moines	Nickname: Hawkeye State
		State tree: Oak	State flower: Wild rose	State bird: Eastern goldfinch	State motto: "Our liberties we prize and our rights we will maintain."
		U.S. Representatives: 5	Electoral votes: 7	Land Area: 55,875 sq. miles	
		Origin of state name: From the Iowa River which was named after the Ioway Indian tribe.			

KANSAS

		Entered Union (Rank): January 29, 1861 (34)	Population (Rank): 2,819,000 (33)	Capital City: Topeka	Nickname: Sunflower State, Jayhawk State
		State tree: Cottonwood	State flower: Sunflower	State bird: Western meadowlark	State motto: "To the stars through difficulty."
		U.S. Representatives: 4	Electoral votes: 6	Land Area: 81,823 sq. miles	
		Origin of state name: From a Sioux word meaning "people of the south wind."			

KENTUCKY

Entered Union (Rank): June 1, 1792 (15)	Population (Rank): 4,315,000 (26)	Capital City: Frankfort	Nickname: Bluegrass State
State tree: Tulip poplar	State flower: Goldenrod	State bird: Kentucky cardinal	State motto: "United we stand, divided we fall."
U.S. Representatives: 6	Electoral votes: 8	Land Area: 39,732 sq. miles	
Origin of state name: From an Iroquoian word meaning "land of tomorrow."			

LOUISIANA

Entered Union (Rank): April 30, 1812 (18)	Population (Rank): 4,493,000 (25)	Capital City: Baton Rouge	Nickname: Pelican State
State tree: Bald cypress	State flower: Magnolia	State bird: Eastern brown pelican	State motto: "Union, justice and confidence."
U.S. Representatives: 7	Electoral votes: 9	Land Area: 43,566 sq. miles	
Origin of state name: Named to honor of Louis XIV of France.			

MAINE

Entered Union (Rank): March 15, 1820 (23)	Population (Rank): 1,319,000 (40)	Capital City: Augusta	Nickname: Pine Tree State
State tree: White pine tree	State flower: White pine cone and tassel	State bird: Chickadee	State motto: "I lead."
U.S. Representatives: 2	Electoral votes: 4	Land Area: 30,865 sq. miles	
Origin of state name: First used to distinguish the mainland from the offshore islands.			

MARYLAND

Entered Union (Rank): April 28, 1788 (7)	Population (Rank): 5,700,000 (19)	Capital City: Annapolis	Nickname: Free State, Old Line State
State tree: White oak	State flower: Black-eyed Susan	State bird: Baltimore oriole	State motto: "Manly deeds, womanly words."
U.S. Representatives: 8	Electoral votes: 10	Land Area: 9,775 sq. miles	
Origin of state name: In honor of Henrietta Maria, queen of Charles I of England.			

MASSACHUSETTS

Entered Union (Rank): February 6, 1788 (6)	Population (Rank): 6,594,000 (15)	Capital City: Boston	Nickname: Bay State, Old Colony State
State tree: American elm	State flower: Mayflower	State bird: Chickadee	State motto: "By the sword we seek peace, but peace only under liberty."
U.S. Representatives: 10	Electoral votes: 12	Land Area: 7,838 sq. miles	
Origin of state name: From Massachusett tribe of Native Americans, meaning "at or about the great hill."			

MICHIGAN

	Entered Union (Rank): January 26, 1837 (26)	Population (Rank): 9,970,000 (8)	Capital City: Lansing	Nickname: Wolverine State
	State tree: White pine	State flower: Apple blossom	State bird: Robin	State motto: "If you seek a pleasant peninsula, look around you."
	U.S. Representatives: 15	Electoral votes: 17	Land Area: 56,809 sq. miles	
	Origin of state name: From Indian word "Michigana" meaning "great or large lake."			

MINNESOTA

	Entered Union (Rank): May 11, 1858 (32)	Population (Rank): 5,267,000 (21)	Capital City: St. Paul	Nickname: North Star State, Gopher State, Land of 10,000 Lakes
	State tree: Red pine	State flower: Lady slipper	State bird: Common loon	State motto: "The North Star."
	U.S. Representatives: 8	Electoral votes: 10	Land Area: 79,617 sq. miles	
	Origin of state name: From a Dakota Indian word meaning "sky-tinted water."			

MISSISSIPPI

	Entered Union (Rank): December 10, 1817 (20)	Population (Rank): 2,952,000 (31)	Capital City: Jackson	Nickname: Magnolia State
	State tree: Magnolia	State flower: Flower of evergreen magnolia	State bird: Mockingbird	State motto: "By valor and arms."
	U.S. Representatives: 4	Electoral votes: 6	Land Area: 46,914 sq. miles	
	Origin of state name: From an Indian word meaning "Father of Waters."			

MISSOURI

	Entered Union (Rank): August 10, 1821 (24)	Population (Rank): 5,988,000 (18)	Capital City: Jefferson City	Nickname: Show-Me State
	State tree: Flowering dogwood	State flower: Hawthorn	State bird: Bluebird	State motto: "The welfare of the people shall be the supreme law."
	U.S. Representatives: 9	Electoral votes: 11	Land Area: 68,898 sq. miles	
	Origin of state name: Named after the Missouri Indian tribe. "Missouri" means "town of the large canoes."			

MONTANA

	Entered Union (Rank): November 8, 1889 (41)	Population (Rank): 975,000 (44)	Capital City: Helena	Nickname: Treasure State
	State tree: Ponderosa Pine	State flower: Bitterroot	State bird: Western meadowlark	State motto: "Gold and silver."
	U.S. Representatives: 1	Electoral votes: 3	Land Area: 145,556 sq. miles	
	Origin of state name: From a Spanish word meaning "mountainous."			

NEBRASKA

Entered Union (Rank): March 1, 1867 (37)	Population (Rank): 1,797,0000 (38)	Capital City: Lincoln	Nickname: Cornhusker State, Beef State
State tree: Cottonwood	State flower: Goldenrod	State bird: Western Meadowlark	State motto: "Equality before the law."
U.S. Representatives: 3	Electoral votes: 5	Land Area: 76,878 sq. miles	
Origin of state name: From an Oto Indian word meaning "flat water."			

NEVADA

Entered Union (Rank): October 31, 1864 (36)	Population (Rank): 2,644,000 (35)	Capital City: Carson City	Nickname: Sagebrush State, Silver State, Battle Born State
State tree: Single-leaf pinon and bristlecone pine	State flower: Sagebrush	State bird: Mountain bluebird	State motto: "All for our country."
U.S. Representatives: 3	Electoral votes: 5	Land Area: 109,806 sq. miles	
Origin of state name: From the Spanish meaning "snowcapped."			

NEW HAMPSHIRE

Entered Union (Rank): June 21, 1788 (9)	Population (Rank): 1,325,000 (41)	Capital City: Concord	Nickname: Granite State
State tree: White birch	State flower: Purple lilac	State bird: Purple finch	State motto: "Live free or die."
U.S. Representatives: 2	Electoral votes: 4	Land Area: 8,969 sq. miles	
Origin of state name: From the English county of Hampshire.			

NEW JERSEY

Entered Union (Rank): December 18, 1787 (3)	Population (Rank): 8,708,000 (11)	Capital City: Trenton	Nickname: Garden State
State tree: Red oak	State flower: Purple violet	State bird: Eastern goldfinch	State motto: "Liberty and prosperity."
U.S. Representatives: 13	Electoral votes: 15	Land Area: 7,419 sq. miles	
Origin of state name: From the Isle of Jersey in the English Channel.			

NEW MEXICO

Entered Union (Rank): January 6, 1912 (47)	Population (Rank): 2,010,000 (36)	Capital City: Santa Fe	Nickname: Land of Enchantment
State tree: Pinon	State flower: Yucca	State bird: Roadrunner	State motto: "It grows as it goes."
U.S. Representatives: 3	Electoral votes: 5	Land Area: 121,365 sq. miles	
Origin of state name: From Mexico, "place of Mexitli," an Aztec god or leader.			

NEW YORK

Entered Union (Rank): July 26, 1788 (11)	Population (Rank): 19,542,000 (3)	Capital City: Albany	Nickname: Empire State
State tree: Sugar maple	State flower: Rose	State bird: Bluebird	State motto: "Ever upward."
U.S. Representatives: 29	Electoral votes: 31	Land Area: 47,224 sq. miles	
Origin of state name: Named in honor of the Duke of York.			

NORTH CAROLINA

Entered Union (Rank): November 21, 1789 (12)	Population (Rank): 9,381,000 (10)	Capital City: Raleigh	Nickname: Tar Heel State
State tree: Pine	State flower: Dogwood	State bird: Cardinal	State motto: "To be rather than to seem."
U.S. Representatives: 13	Electoral votes: 15	Land Area: 48,718 sq. miles	
Origin of state name: In honor of Charlie I of England.			

NORTH DAKOTA

Entered Union (Rank): November 2, 1889 (39)	Population (Rank): 647,000 (48)	Capital City: Bismark	Nickname: Sioux State, Flickertail State, Peace Garden State, Rough Rider State
State tree: American elm	State flower: Wild prairie rose	State bird: Western meadowlark	State motto: "Liberty and union, now and forever: one and inseparable."
U.S. Representatives: 1	Electoral votes: 3	Land Area: 70,704 sq. miles	
Origin of state name: From the Sioux tribe, meaning "allies."			

OHIO

Entered Union (Rank): March 1, 1803 (17)	Population (Rank): 11,543,000 (7)	Capital City: Columbus	Nickname: Buckeye State
State tree: Buckeye	State flower: Scarlet carnation	State bird: Cardinal	State motto: "With God all things are possible."
U.S. Representatives: 18	Electoral votes: 20	Land Area: 40,953 sq. miles	
Origin of state name: From an Iroquoian word meaning "great river."			

OKLAHOMA

Entered Union (Rank): November 16, 1907 (46)	Population (Rank): 3,688,000 (28)	Capital City: Oklahoma City	Nickname: Sooner State
State tree: Redbud	State flower: Mistletoe	State bird: Scissor-tailed flycatcher	State motto: "Labor conquers all things."
U.S. Representatives: 5	Electoral votes: 7	Land Area: 68,679 sq. miles	
Origin of state name: From two Choctaw Indian words meaning "red people."			

OREGON

Entered Union (Rank): February 14, 1859 (33)	Population (Rank): 3,826,000 (27)	Capital City: Salem	Nickname: Beaver State
State tree: Douglas fir	State flower: Oregon grape	State bird: Western meadowlark	State motto: "She flies with her own wings."
U.S. Representatives: 5	Electoral votes: 7	Land Area: 96,003 sq. miles	
Origin of state name: Unknown, but it is thought that the name was taken from the writings of Maj. Robert Rogers, and English army officer.			

PENNSYLVANIA

	Entered Union (Rank): December 12, 1787 (2)	Population (Rank): 12,605,000 (6)	Capital City: Harrisburg	Nickname: Keystone State
	State tree: Hemlock	State flower: Mountain laurel	State bird: Ruffed grouse	State motto: "Virtue, liberty and independence."
	U.S. Representatives: 19	Electoral votes: 21	Land Area: 44,820 sq. miles	
	Origin of state name: In honor of Sir William Penn, father of state founder William Penn. It means "Penn's Woodland."			

RHODE ISLAND

	Entered Union (Rank): May 29, 1790 (13)	Population (Rank): 1,054,000 (43)	Capital City: Providence	Nickname: Ocean State
	State tree: Red Maple	State flower: Violet	State bird: Rhode Island red hen	State motto: "Hope."
	U.S. Representatives: 2	Electoral votes: 4	Land Area: 1,045 sq. miles	
	Origin of state name: From the Greek island of Rhodes.			

SOUTH CAROLINA

	Entered Union (Rank): May 23, 1788 (8)	Population (Rank): 4,562,000 (24)	Capital City: Columbia	Nickname: Palmetto State
	State tree: Palmetto	State flower: Yellow jessamine	State bird: Carolina wren	State motto: "While I breathe, I hope."
	U.S. Representatives: 6	Electoral votes: 8	Land Area: 30,111 sq. miles	
	Origin of state name: In honor of Charles I of England.			

SOUTH DAKOTA

	Entered Union (Rank): November 2, 1889 (40)	Population (Rank): 812,400 (46)	Capital City: Pierre	Nickname: Mount Rushmore State, Coyote State
	State tree: Black Hills spruce	State flower: American pasqueflower	State bird: Ring-necked pheasant	State motto: "Under God the people rule."
	U.S. Representatives: 1	Electoral votes: 3	Land Area: 75,898 sq. miles	
	Origin of state name: From the Sioux tribe, meaning "allies."			

TENNESSEE

	Entered Union (Rank): June 1, 1796 (16)	Population (Rank): 6,297,000 (17)	Capital City: Nashville	Nickname: Volunteer State
	State tree: Tulip poplar	State flower: Iris	State bird: Mockingbird	State motto: "Agriculture and commerce."
	U.S. Representatives: 9	Electoral votes: 11	Land Area: 41,220 sq. miles	
	Origin of state name: Meaning unknown but of Cherokee origin.			

TEXAS

	Entered Union (Rank): December 29, 1845 (28)	Population (Rank): 24,783,000 (2)	Capital City: Austin	Nickname: Lone Star State
	State tree: Pecan	State flower: Bluebonnet	State bird: Mockingbird	State motto: "Friendship."
	U.S. Representatives: 32	Electoral votes: 34	Land Area: 261,914 sq. miles	
	Origin of state name: From an Indian word meaning "friends."			

UTAH

	Entered Union (Rank): January 4, 1896 (45)	Population (Rank): 2,785,000 (34)	Capital City: Salt Lake City	Nickname: Beehive State
	State tree: Blue spruce	State flower: Sego lily	State bird: California gull	State motto: "Industry."
	U.S. Representatives: 3	Electoral votes: 5	Land Area: 82,168 sq. miles	
Origin of state name: From the Ute tribe, meaning "people of the mountains."					

VERMONT

	Entered Union (Rank): March 4, 1791 (14)	Population (Rank): 622,000 (49)	Capital City: Montpelier	Nickname: Green Mountain State
	State tree: Sugar maple	State flower: Red clover	State bird: Hermit thrush	State motto: "Vermont, freedom and unity."
	U.S. Representatives: 1	Electoral votes: 3	Land Area: 9,249 sq. miles	
Origin of state name: From the French *vert mont*, meaning "green mountain."					

VIRGINIA

	Entered Union (Rank): June 25, 1788 (10)	Population (Rank): 7,883,000 (12)	Capital City: Richmond	Nickname: Old Dominion, Mother of Presidents
	State tree: Dogwood	State flower: American dogwood	State bird: Cardinal	State motto: "Thus always to tyrants."
	U.S. Representatives: 11	Electoral votes: 13	Land Area: 39,598 sq. miles	
Origin of state name: In honor of Elizabeth I, "Virgin Queen" of England.					

WASHINGTON

	Entered Union (Rank): November 11, 1889 (42)	Population (Rank): 6,665,000 (13)	Capital City: Olympia	Nickname: Evergreen State
	State tree: Western hemlock	State flower: Coast rhododendron	State bird: Willow goldfinch	State motto: "By and by."
	U.S. Representatives: 9	Electoral votes: 11	Land Area: 66,582 sq. miles	
Origin of state name: In honor of George Washington.					

WEST VIRGINIA

	Entered Union (Rank): June 20, 1863 (35)	Population (Rank): 1,820,000 (37)	Capital City: Charleston	Nickname: Mountain State
	State tree: Sugar maple	State flower: Rhododendron	State bird: Cardinal	State motto: "Mountains are always free."
	U.S. Representatives: 3	Electoral votes: 5	Land Area: 24,087 sq. miles	
Origin of state name: In honor of Elizabeth I, "Virgin Queen" of England.					

WISCONSIN				
	Entered Union (Rank): May 29, 1848 (30)	Population (Rank): 5,655,000 (20)	Capital City: Madison	Nickname: Badger State
	State tree: Sugar maple	State flower: Wood violet	State bird: Robin	State motto: "Forward"
	U.S. Representatives: 8	Electoral votes: 10	Land Area: 54,314 sq. miles	
	Origin of state name: French corruption of an Indian word whose meaning is disputed.			

WYOMING				
	Entered Union (Rank): July 10, 1890 (44)	Population (Rank): 545,000 (50)	Capital City: Cheyenne	Nickname: Equality State
	State tree: Cottonwood	State flower: Indian paintbrush	State bird: Meadowlark	State motto: "Equal rights."
	U.S. Representatives: 1	Electoral votes: 3	Land Area: 97,105 sq. miles	
	Origin of state name: From a Delaware Indian word mean "mountains and valley alternating."			

United States of America

> *There are no speed limits*
> *on the road to excellence.*
>
> **(David Johnson)**

Display #3
SEPARATOR STATE SUMMARY

Herkimer sez:

The following table represents a one-page numerical summary of the 48 graphical displays in U. S. Activity #16.

SEPERATOR STATE SUMMARY

Number of separator states (0 indicates a bordering state)

	State	0	1	2	3	4	5	6	7	8	9	10	MAX	Sum Check
1	ALABAMA	4	7	10	9	7	7	2	1				10	47
2	ARIZONA	5	7	7	7	8	4	3	3	2	1		8	47
3	ARKANSAS	6	11	12	8	4	3	2	1				12	47
4	CALIFORNIA	3	5	6	6	6	8	4	3	3	2	1	8	47
5	COLORADO	7	9	10	8	4	3	3	2	1			10	47
6	CONNECTICUT	3	4	5	4	5	10	8	4	4			10	47
7	DELAWARE	3	4	8	10	9	5	4	4				10	47
8	FLORIDA	2	4	5	10	9	7	7	2	1			10	47
9	GEORGIA	5	5	11	9	7	7	2	1				11	47
10	IDAHO	6	7	6	6	9	4	3	3	2	1		9	47
11	ILLINOIS	5	11	13	8	7	2	1					13	47
12	INDIANA	4	7	14	12	5	5						14	47
13	IOWA	6	11	13	8	3	3	2	1				13	47
14	KANSAS	4	11	16	7	3	3	2	1				16	47
15	KENTUCKY	7	13	12	8	6	1						13	47
16	LOUISIANA	3	5	12	12	7	2	3	2	1			12	47
17	MAINE	1	2	3	2	4	4	5	18	8			18	47
18	MARYLAND	4	6	12	10	6	5	4					12	47
19	MASSACHUSETTS	5	3	4	4	5	10	8	4	4			10	47
20	MICHIGAN	3	6	10	13	10	5						13	47
21	MINNESOTA	4	6	10	14	6	4	2	1				14	47
22	MISSISSIPPI	4	8	11	9	7	5	2	1				11	47
23	MISSOURI	8	16	10	7	3	2	1					16	47
24	MONTANA	4	8	8	6	8	4	3	3	2	1		8	47
25	NEBRASKA	6	13	15	4	3	3	2	1				15	47
26	NEVADA	5	5	6	5	5	8	4	3	3	2	1	8	47
27	NEW HAMPSHIRE	3	3	2	4	4	5	10	8	4	4		10	47
28	NEW JERSEY	3	6	6	6	10	8	4	4				10	47
29	NEW MEXICO	5	9	9	10	5	3	3	2	1			10	47
30	NEW YORK	5	6	5	5	10	8	4	4				10	47
31	NORTH CAROLINA	4	8	11	9	8	6	1					11	47
32	NORTH DAKOTA	3	5	9	9	9	6	3	2	1			9	47
33	OHIO	5	9	13	11	5	4						13	47
34	OKLAHOMA	6	10	14	8	3	3	2	1				14	47
35	OREGON	4	4	5	6	6	9	4	3	3	2	1	9	47
36	PENNSYLVANIA	6	7	7	11	8	4	4					11	47
37	RHODE ISLAND	2	3	3	4	4	5	10	8	4	4		10	47
38	SOUTH CAROLINA	2	4	6	11	9	8	6	1				11	47
39	SOUTH DAKOTA	6	7	11	10	4	3	3	2	1			11	47
40	TENNESSEE	8	13	9	7	7	2	1					13	47
41	TEXAS	4	7	12	12	4	2	3	2	1			12	47
42	UTAH	6	9	6	5	8	4	3	3	2	1		9	47
43	VERMONT	3	5	4	4	5	10	8	4	4			10	47
44	VIRGINIA	5	11	11	8	7	5						11	47
45	WASHINGTON	2	5	6	6	6	9	4	3	3	2	1	9	47
46	WEST VIRGINIA	5	9	13	10	6	4						13	47
47	WISCONSIN	4	7	10	14	9	2	1					14	47
48	WYOMING	6	11	7	10	4	3	3	2	1			11	47

> *It's a funny thing about life; if you refuse to accept anything but the best, you very often get it.*
>
> (W. Somerset Maugham)

Display #4
SEPARATOR STATE TABLE

Herkimer sez:

The Stat Pack students produced the amazing table that follows this page. Here is an example of how to use it. If you go to CA (California) in the first row of the table and to DE (Delaware) in the first column of the table you will find the intersection of the row and column contains the number 7. In a nutshell, you can travel on land from California to Delaware by going through a minimum of 7 other states.

Niagra Falls, New York (1905)

STATE SEPARATOR TABLE

* Column totals

	AL	AZ	AR	CA	C0	CT	DE	FL	GA	ID	IL	IN	IA	KS	KY	LA	ME	MD	MA	MI	MN	MS	MO	MT	NE	NV	NH	NJ	NM	NY	NC	ND	OH	OK	OR	PA	RI	SC	SD	TN	TX	UT	VT	VA	WA	WV	WI	WY	TOTAL	MEAN	MAX	* CHECK
AL		4	1	5	3	5	3	0	0	4	2	2	2	2	1	1	7	2	5	3	3	0	1	4	2	5	6	4	3	4	1	4	2	2	5	3	6	1	3	0	2	4	5	1	5	2	3	3	136	2.89	7	136
AZ	4		2	0	0	7	6	5	4	1	3	4	2	1	3	2	9	5	7	4	3	3	2	2	1	0	8	6	0	6	4	3	4	1	1	5	8	5	2	3	1	0	7	4	2	4	3	1	158	3.36	9	158
AR	1	2		3	1	5	3	2	1	3	1	2	1	1	1	0	7	2	5	3	2	0	0	3	1	3	6	4	1	4	1	3	2	0	4	3	6	2	2	0	0	2	5	1	4	2	2	2	109	2.32	7	109
CA	5	0	3		1	8	7	6	5	1	4	5	3	2	4	3	10	6	8	5	4	4	3	2	2	0	9	7	1	7	5	3	5	2	0	6	9	6	3	4	2	1	8	5	1	5	4	2	196	4.17	10	196
CO	3	0	1	1		6	5	4	3	1	2	3	1	0	2	2	8	4	6	3	2	2	1	1	0	1	7	5	0	5	3	2	3	0	2	4	7	4	1	2	1	0	6	3	2	3	2	0	124	2.64	8	124
CT	5	7	5	8	6		2	6	5	7	4	3	5	5	3	6	2	2	0	3	5	5	4	7	5	8	1	1	6	0	4	6	2	5	8	1	0	5	6	4	6	7	1	3	8	2	4	6	204	4.34	8	204
DE	3	6	3	7	5	2		4	3	6	3	2	4	4	2	4	4	0	2	2	4	3	3	6	4	7	3	0	5	1	2	5	1	4	7	0	3	3	5	2	4	6	2	1	7	1	3	5	163	3.47	7	163
FL	0	5	2	6	4	6	4		0	5	3	3	3	3	2	2	8	3	6	4	4	1	2	5	3	6	7	5	4	5	1	5	3	3	6	4	7	1	4	1	3	5	6	2	6	3	4	4	179	3.81	8	179
GA	0	4	1	5	3	5	3	0		4	2	2	2	2	1	2	7	2	5	3	3	1	1	4	2	5	6	4	3	4	0	4	2	2	5	3	6	0	3	0	2	4	5	1	5	2	3	3	136	2.89	7	136
ID	4	1	3	1	1	7	6	5	4		3	4	2	2	3	3	9	5	7	4	2	4	2	0	1	0	8	6	1	6	4	1	4	2	0	5	8	5	1	3	2	0	7	4	0	4	3	0	157	3.34	9	157
IL	2	3	1	4	2	4	3	3	2	3		0	0	1	0	2	6	2	4	1	1	2	0	2	1	4	5	3	2	3	2	2	1	1	4	2	5	3	1	1	2	3	4	1	4	1	0	2	105	2.23	6	105
IN	2	4	2	5	3	3	2	3	2	4	0		1	2	0	3	5	2	3	0	2	2	1	3	2	5	4	2	3	2	2	3	0	2	5	1	4	3	2	1	3	4	3	1	5	1	1	3	116	2.47	5	116
IA	2	2	1	3	1	5	4	3	2	2	0	1		1	1	2	7	3	5	1	0	2	0	1	0	3	6	4	2	4	2	1	2	1	3	3	6	3	0	1	2	2	5	2	3	2	0	1	107	2.28	7	107
KS	2	1	1	2	0	5	4	3	2	2	1	2	1		1	2	7	3	5	3	2	2	0	2	0	2	6	4	1	4	2	2	2	0	3	3	6	3	1	1	1	1	5	2	3	2	2	1	110	2.34	7	110
KY	1	3	1	4	2	3	2	2	1	3	0	0	1	1		2	5	1	3	1	2	1	0	3	1	4	4	2	2	2	1	3	0	1	4	1	4	2	2	0	2	3	3	0	4	0	1	2	90	1.91	5	90
LA	1	2	0	3	2	6	4	2	2	3	2	3	2	2	2		8	3	6	4	3	0	1	4	2	3	7	5	1	5	2	4	3	1	4	4	7	3	3	1	0	2	6	2	4	3	3	3	143	3.04	8	143
ME	7	9	7	10	8	2	4	8	7	9	6	5	7	7	5	8		4	1	5	7	7	6	9	7	10	0	3	8	2	6	8	4	7	10	3	2	7	8	6	8	9	1	5	10	4	6	8	290	6.17	10	290
MD	2	5	2	6	4	2	0	3	2	5	2	2	3	3	1	3	4		2	2	4	2	2	5	3	6	3	1	4	1	1	5	1	3	6	0	3	2	4	1	3	5	2	0	6	0	3	4	133	2.83	6	133
MA	5	7	5	8	6	0	2	6	5	7	4	3	5	5	3	6	1	2		3	5	5	4	7	5	8	0	1	6	0	4	6	2	5	8	1	0	5	6	4	6	7	0	3	8	2	4	6	201	4.28	8	201
MI	3	4	3	5	3	3	2	4	3	4	1	0	1	3	1	4	5	2	3		1	3	2	3	2	5	4	2	4	2	3	2	0	3	5	1	4	4	2	2	4	4	3	2	5	1	0	3	130	2.77	5	130
MN	3	3	2	4	2	5	4	4	3	2	1	2	0	2	2	3	7	4	5	1		3	1	1	1	3	6	4	3	4	3	0	2	2	3	3	6	4	0	2	3	2	5	3	3	3	0	1	130	2.77	7	130
MS	0	3	0	4	2	5	3	1	1	4	2	2	2	2	1	0	7	2	5	3	3		1	4	2	4	6	4	2	4	1	4	2	1	5	3	6	2	3	0	1	3	5	1	5	2	3	3	129	2.74	7	129
MO	1	2	0	3	1	4	3	2	1	2	0	1	0	0	0	1	6	2	4	2	1	1		2	0	3	5	3	1	3	1	2	1	0	3	2	5	2	1	0	1	2	4	1	3	1	1	1	85	1.81	6	85
MT	4	2	3	2	1	7	6	5	4	0	2	3	1	2	3	4	9	5	7	3	1	4	2		1	1	8	6	2	6	4	0	4	2	1	5	8	5	0	3	3	1	7	4	1	4	2	0	158	3.36	9	158
NE	2	1	1	2	0	5	4	3	2	1	1	2	0	0	1	2	7	3	5	2	1	2	0	1		2	6	4	1	4	2	1	2	1	2	3	6	3	0	1	2	1	5	2	2	2	1	0	101	2.15	7	101
NV	5	0	3	0	1	8	7	6	5	0	4	5	3	2	4	3	10	6	8	5	3	4	3	1	2		9	7	1	7	5	2	5	2	0	6	9	6	2	4	2	0	8	5	1	5	4	1	189	4.02	10	189
NH	6	8	6	9	7	1	3	7	6	8	5	4	6	6	4	7	0	3	0	4	6	6	5	8	6	9		2	7	1	5	7	3	6	9	2	1	6	7	5	7	8	0	4	9	3	5	7	244	5.19	9	244
NJ	4	6	4	7	5	1	0	5	4	6	3	2	4	4	2	5	3	1	1	2	4	4	3	6	4	7	2		5	0	3	5	1	4	7	0	2	4	5	3	5	6	1	2	7	1	3	5	168	3.57	7	168
NM	3	0	1	1	0	6	5	4	3	1	2	3	2	1	2	1	8	4	6	4	3	2	1	2	1	1	7	5		5	3	3	3	0	2	4	7	4	2	2	0	0	6	3	2	3	3	1	132	2.81	8	132
NY	4	6	4	7	5	0	1	5	4	6	3	2	4	4	2	5	2	1	0	2	4	4	3	6	4	7	1	0	5		3	5	1	4	7	0	1	4	5	3	5	6	0	2	7	1	3	5	163	3.47	7	163
NC	1	4	1	5	3	4	2	1	0	4	2	2	2	2	1	2	6	1	4	3	3	1	1	4	2	5	5	3	3	3		4	2	2	5	2	5	0	3	0	2	4	4	0	5	1	3	3	125	2.66	6	125
ND	4	3	3	3	2	6	5	5	4	1	2	3	1	2	3	4	8	5	6	2	0	4	2	0	1	2	7	5	3	5	4		3	3	2	4	7	5	0	3	4	2	6	4	2	4	1	1	156	3.32	8	156
OH	2	4	2	5	3	2	1	3	2	4	1	0	2	2	0	3	4	1	2	0	2	2	1	4	2	5	3	1	3	1	2	3		2	5	0	3	3	3	1	3	4	2	1	5	0	1	3	108	2.30	5	108
OK	2	1	0	2	0	5	4	3	2	2	1	2	1	0	1	1	7	3	5	3	2	1	0	2	1	2	6	4	0	4	2	3	2		3	3	6	3	2	1	0	1	5	2	3	2	2	1	108	2.30	7	108
OR	5	1	4	0	2	8	7	6	5	0	4	5	3	3	4	4	10	6	8	5	3	5	3	1	2	0	9	7	2	7	5	2	5	3		6	9	6	2	4	3	1	8	5	0	5	4	1	198	4.21	10	198
PA	3	5	3	6	4	1	0	4	3	5	2	1	3	3	1	4	3	0	1	1	3	3	2	5	3	6	2	0	4	0	2	4	0	3	6		2	3	4	2	4	5	1	1	6	0	2	4	130	2.77	6	130
RI	6	8	6	9	7	0	3	7	6	8	5	4	6	6	4	7	2	3	0	4	6	6	5	8	6	9	1	2	7	1	5	7	3	6	9	2		6	7	5	7	8	1	4	9	3	5	7	246	5.23	9	246
SC	1	5	2	6	4	5	3	1	0	5	3	3	3	3	2	3	7	2	5	4	4	2	2	5	3	6	6	4	4	4	0	5	3	3	6	3	6		4	1	3	5	5	1	6	2	4	4	168	3.57	7	168
SD	3	2	2	3	1	6	5	4	3	1	1	2	0	1	2	3	8	4	6	2	0	3	1	0	0	2	7	5	2	5	3	0	3	2	2	4	7	4		2	3	1	6	3	2	3	1	0	130	2.77	8	130
TN	0	3	0	4	2	4	2	1	0	3	1	1	1	1	0	1	6	1	4	2	2	0	0	3	1	4	5	3	2	3	0	3	1	1	4	2	5	1	2		1	3	4	0	4	1	2	2	96	2.04	6	96
TX	2	1	0	2	1	6	4	3	2	2	2	3	2	1	2	0	8	3	6	4	3	1	1	3	2	2	7	5	0	5	2	4	3	0	3	4	7	3	3	1		1	6	2	3	3	3	2	133	2.83	8	133
UT	4	0	2	1	0	7	6	5	4	0	3	4	2	1	3	2	9	5	7	4	2	3	2	1	1	0	8	6	0	6	4	2	4	1	1	5	8	5	1	3	1		7	4	1	4	3	0	152	3.23	9	152
VT	5	7	5	8	6	1	2	6	5	7	4	3	5	5	3	6	1	2	0	3	5	5	4	7	5	8	0	1	6	0	4	6	2	5	8	1	1	5	6	4	6	7		3	8	2	4	6	203	4.32	8	203
VA	1	4	1	5	3	3	1	2	1	4	1	1	2	2	0	2	5	0	3	2	3	1	1	4	2	5	4	2	3	2	0	4	1	2	5	1	4	1	3	0	2	4	3		5	0	2	3	110	2.34	5	110
WA	5	2	4	1	2	8	7	6	5	0	4	5	3	3	4	4	10	6	8	5	3	5	3	1	2	1	9	7	2	7	5	2	5	3	0	6	9	6	2	4	3	1	8	5		5	4	1	201	4.28	10	201
WV	2	4	2	5	3	2	1	3	2	4	1	1	2	2	0	3	4	0	2	1	3	2	1	4	2	5	3	1	3	1	1	4	0	2	5	0	3	2	3	1	3	4	2	0	5		2	3	109	2.32	5	109
WI	3	3	2	4	2	4	3	4	3	3	0	1	0	2	1	3	6	3	4	0	0	3	1	2	1	4	5	3	3	3	3	1	1	2	4	2	5	4	1	2	3	3	4	2	4	2		2	121	2.57	6	121
WY	3	1	2	2	0	6	5	4	3	0	2	3	1	1	2	3	8	4	6	3	1	3	1	0	0	1	7	5	1	5	3	1	3	1	1	4	7	4	0	2	2	0	6	3	1	3	2		126	2.68	8	126

We never know how high we are until we are called to rise.

(Emily Dickinson)

Supplemental materials

Herkimer sez:

The final pages contain materials, including maps of the United States, that might be useful for the activities presented in this book.

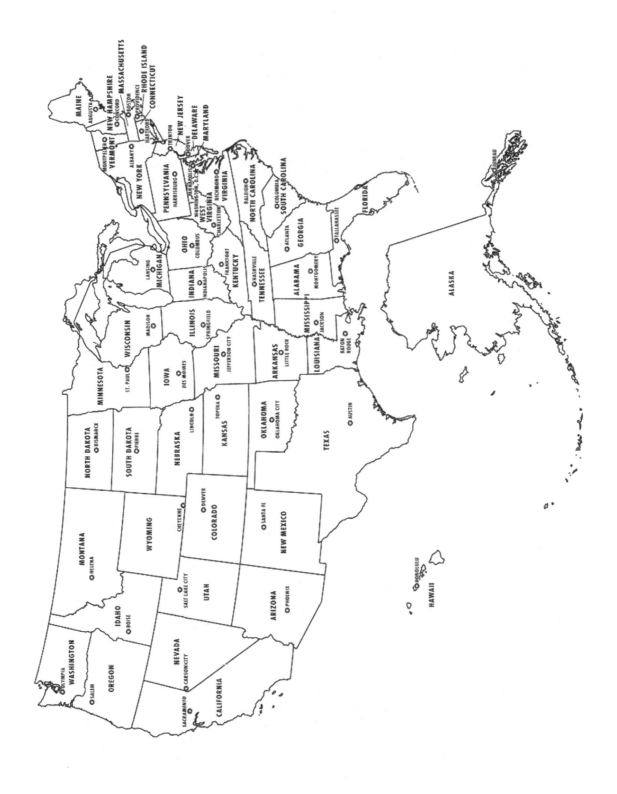

299

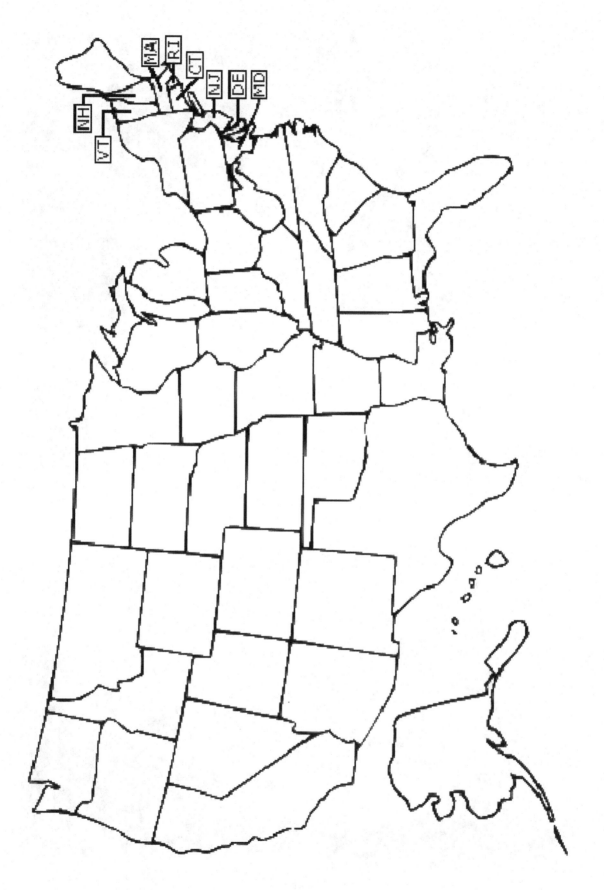

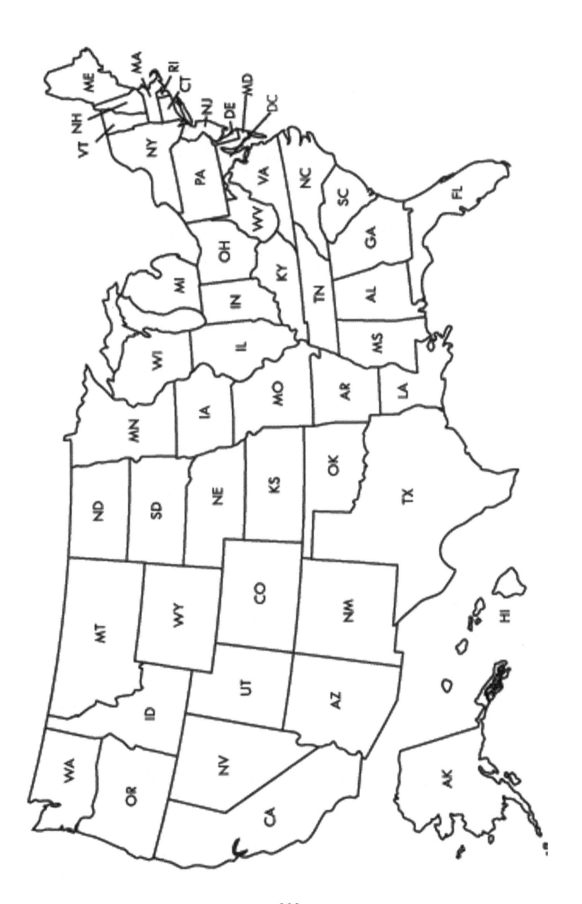

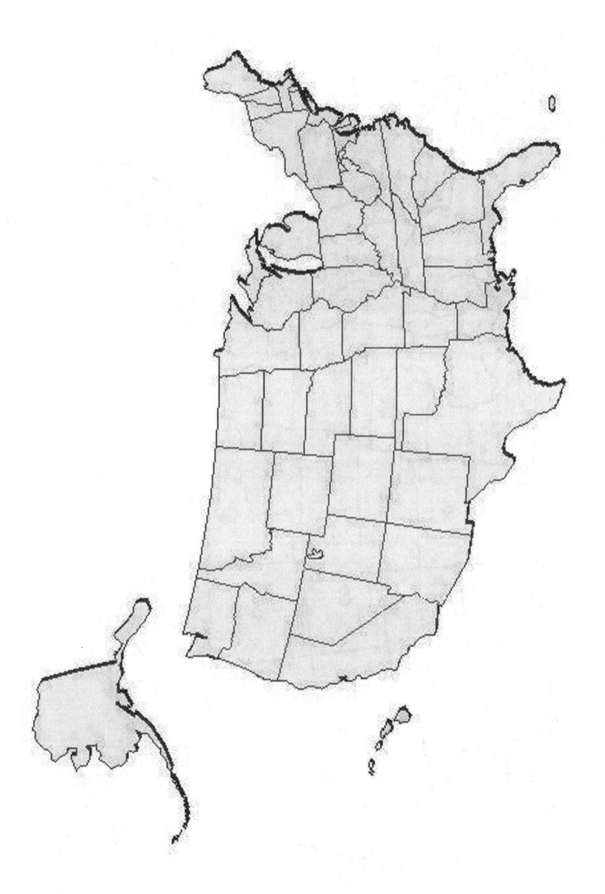

304

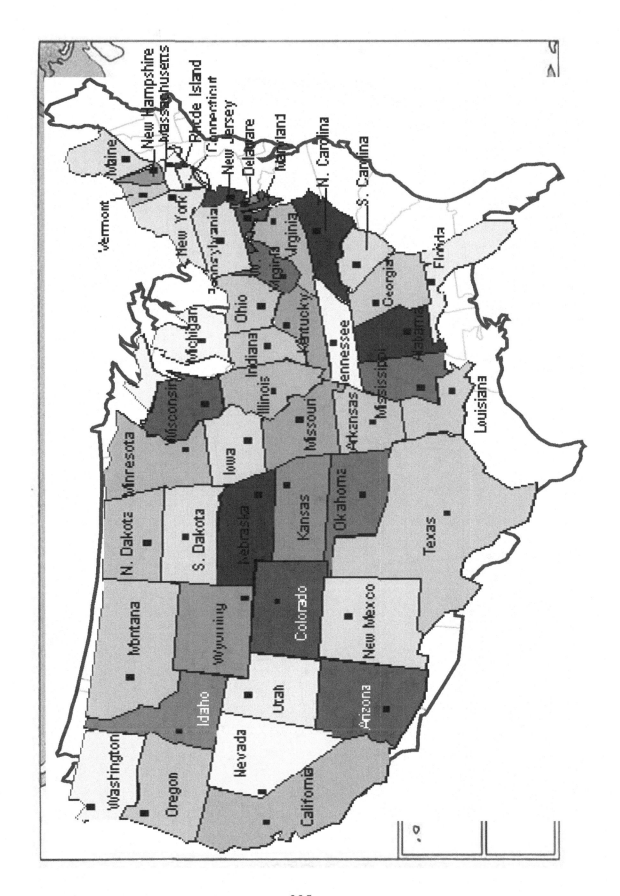

305

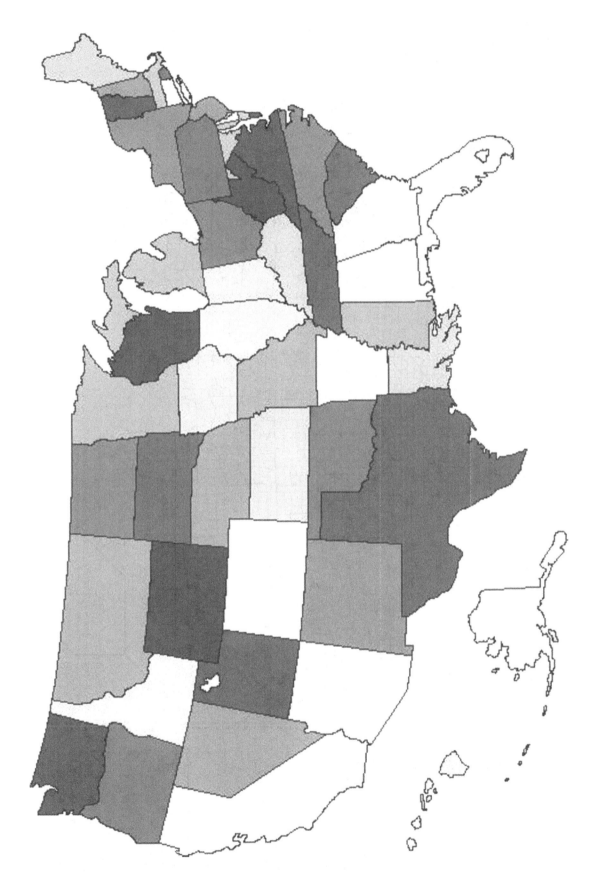

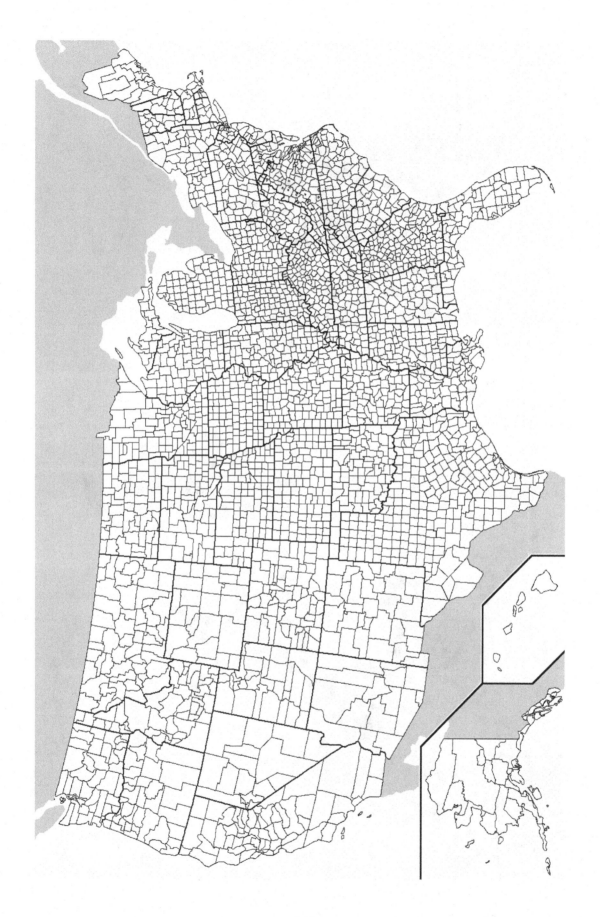

310

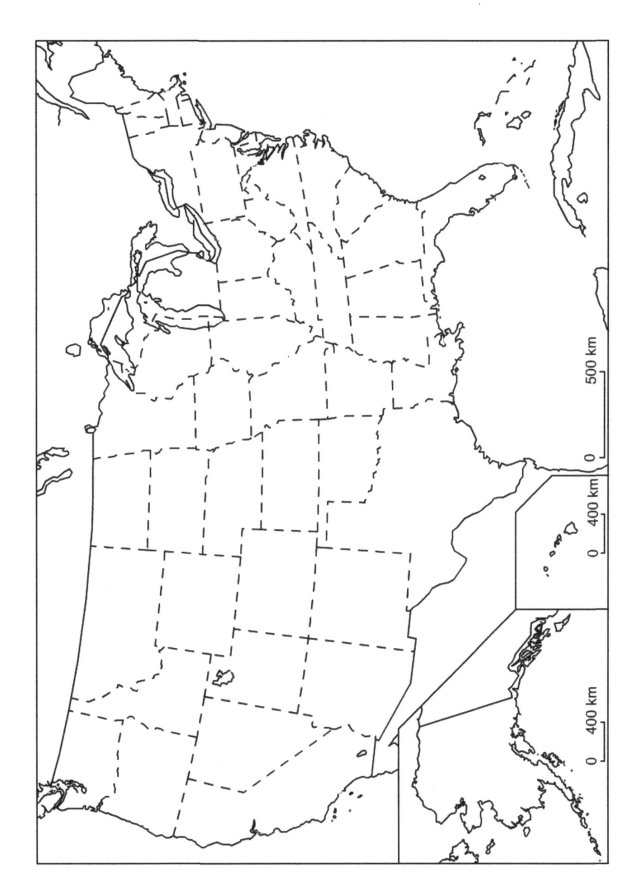

500 km

0

400 km

0

400 km

0

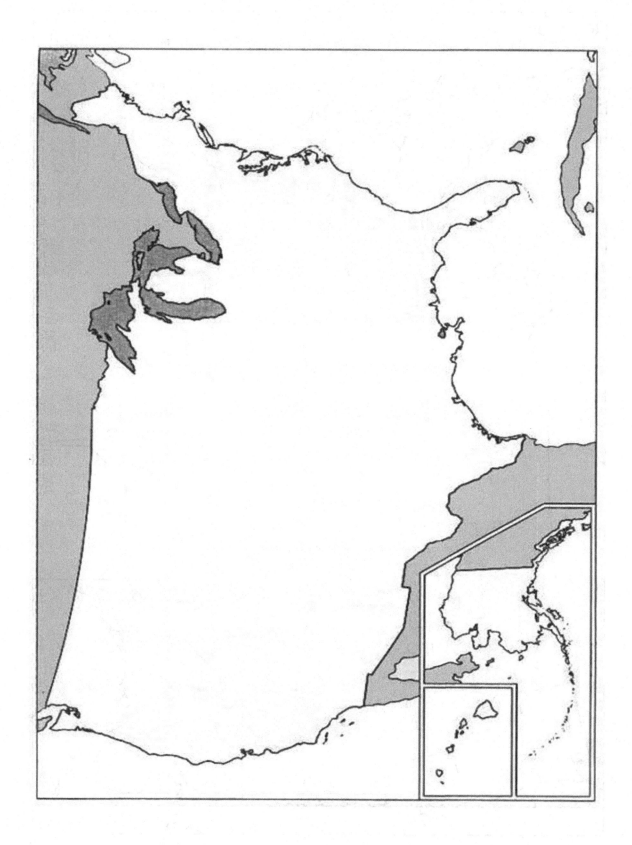

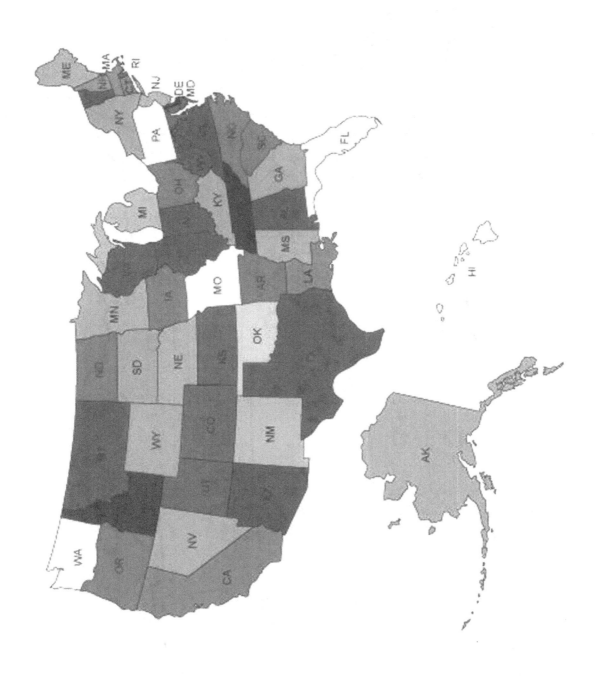

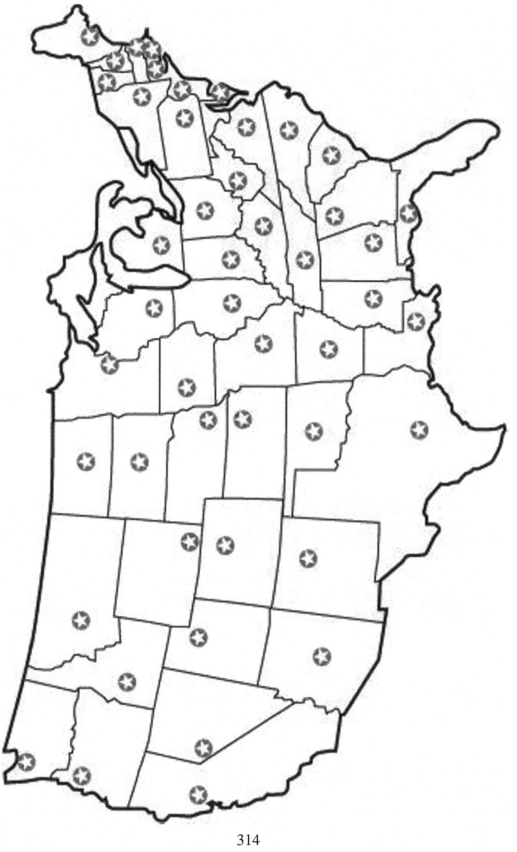

APPRECIATION PAGE

Herkimer and the Stat Pack express gratitude to the following sources for providing free patriotic clip art used in the pages of this book.

www.pdclipart.org
www.gospelgifs.com
www.ace-clipart.com
www.historyimages.com
www.brighthub.com
www.bing.com
www.freeusaandworldmaps.com
www.worldatlas.com

With Honor & Gratitude

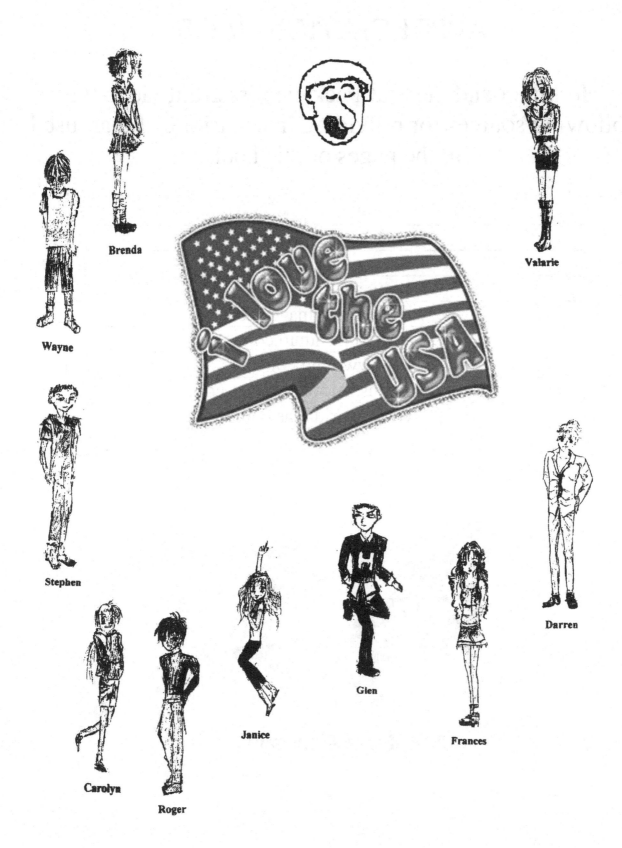

Brenda

Valarie

Wayne

Stephen

Carolyn

Roger

Janice

Glen

Frances

Darren